THIS VOLUME HAS BEEN PRESENTED BY

LOCAL CHURCH MINISTRIES
A COVENANTED MINISTRY OF THE

UNITED CHURCH OF CHRIST

THROUGH THE GENEROSITY OF THE

AMERICAN MISSIONARY ASSOCIATION'S

GREGORY BOOK FUND

their own
receive them not

their own
receive them not

*African American
Lesbians and Gays
in Black Churches*

HORACE L. GRIFFIN

THE
PILGRIM
PRESS
Cleveland

For my friend
Frederick Griffin Johnson
and all African American lesbians and gays
who have endured pain in black churches
because of their love relationships

The Pilgrim Press
700 Prospect Avenue
Cleveland, Ohio 44115-1100
thepilgrimpress.com

© 2006 by Horace L. Griffin

All rights reserved. Published 2006

Printed in the United States of America on acid-free paper

10 09 08 07 06   5 4 3 2

Library of Congress Cataloging-in-Publication Data
Griffin, Horace L., 1961-
    Their own receive them not : African American lesbians and gays in
Black churches / Horace L. Griffin.
        p.   cm.
    Includes bibliographical references and index.
    ISBN-13: 978-0-8298-1599-3 (alk. paper)
    1. Homosexuality – Religious aspects – Christianity. 2. African
Americans – Religion. 3. Gays – Religious life – United States.   I. Title.
BR115.H6G745 2006
277.3'08208664 – dc22

                                                              2006012491

ISBN-13: 978-0-8298-1599-3
ISBN-10: 0-8298-1599-6

Contents

Preface

THE BLACK CHURCH'S TEACHING that homosexuality is immoral has created a crisis for lesbian and gay Christians in black churches.[1] This book provides a historical overview and critical analysis of the black church and its current engagement with lesbian and gay Christians. It is an engagement I characterize as oppressive and duplicitous. For though black church leaders once refused to accept white church leaders' use of the Bible to justify oppressing them during the periods of slavery and segregation, presently many use the Bible in a similar fashion to justify oppressing lesbians and gays. African American lesbians and gays are generally born into black churches and as a consequence of this existence endure pain while their humanity, sexuality, and love relationships are denigrated. Such preaching and teaching create psychological and theological problems for lesbians and gays in black churches, and for their heterosexual friends, family members, and fellow congregants. As a counterpoint to these negative teachings, I offer new approaches to understanding scripture and homosexuality through pastoral theology and black Christian liberation theology.

As I wrote this book, I wondered what the reaction might be to a work that would break hundreds of years of silence about a topic that most African peoples, as well as others, would prefer not to "come out." Black author Delroy Constantine Simms notes that

---

1. Throughout this writing, I use the phrases "the black church" and "black churches" as a reference to churches affiliated with the seven historically black denominations or predominantly black congregations in white denominations. The "black church," as described by leading black church historians C. Eric Lincoln and Lawrence Mamiya, is an institution that organizes African Americans in their understanding of spirituality, morality, people, and issues of faith within faith communities. See *The Black Church in the African-American Experience* (Durham, NC: Duke University Press, 1990), 7–10.

homosexuality in black communities is our greatest taboo. While this may be true, I felt that it is time for a book that gives voice to a group frequently ignored, denied, dismissed, and rejected: African American gay and lesbian Christians.

My original book title, *Their Own Received Them Not: African American Lesbians and Gays in Black Churches*, connects two powerful forces in black Christian culture: the Bible and Jesus. "Their own received them not," a paraphrase from John's Gospel, recognizes that African American lesbians and gays have endured a history of misunderstanding, pain, sorrow, and rejection by their own people, not unlike Jesus' struggles with his fellow Jews.

In a newsletter article advertising this book, my former seminary faculty colleague Dr. Frank Yamada (faculty editor) inadvertently dropped the past tense of my title and sent it to the newsletter publisher as *Their Own Receive Them Not: African American Lesbians and Gays in Black Churches*. I prefer the changed title because it more accurately reflects many black church leaders' current opposition to a Christian view that same-sex sexual expression in loving relationships is a moral act and that lesbian and gay Christians deserve the same treatment as heterosexual Christians. The rage against same-sex marriage by a black heterosexual Christian majority is the most recent example of this rejection of lesbians and gays in black churches. So with the permission of Dr. Yamada, I chose to keep this title.[2]

When I found it especially difficult to continue writing this audacious work, I received encouragement from the words of the eminent scholar and former Morehouse College president, Benjamin Mays, "to never accept the world as it is handed to you"

---

2. I recognize that by using "own," I follow a common reference for black people. Although I understand historical reasons for this reference, I also know that African Americans are not a monolithic group. Thus, my use of the term has more to do with historical and cultural significance rather than an essentialist approach. I agree with Victor Anderson that there are limits to the "people" language. If there is overidentification with a natural blackness, all blacks suffer when some blacks exhibit vile behavior. See Victor Anderson, *Beyond Ontological Blackness: An Essay on African American Religious and Cultural Criticism* (New York: Continuum, 1995).

and "to leave the world a better place than [we] found it." I respond to Mays's charge by writing this book. This writing further engages a progressive Christian conversation about the black church and homosexuality. I hope others will follow and offer more progressive understandings of homosexuality and black religion, and broaden the focus to include Islam and needed discussions on bisexual and transgendered persons.

Throughout my career as a middle-class openly gay African American Christian pastoral theologian and seminary professor, I have been conscious that my scholarship and activism create tension. However, in that tension I have witnessed a needed and helpful dialogue on the black church and homosexuality. I have devoted my scholarly career to fostering the critical analysis of race and sexuality in the context of religion, assessing how they are parallel and how both are used as indicators of cultural morality.

In writing this book, I, like other African Americans who publicly critique black people and black culture, occasionally feared being labeled "Uncle Tom," "race traitor," or "sellout." While I realize that there are those who deserve such titles, I also recognize that such labeling can be a powerful weapon to silence any African American exposing the wrongdoing of other African Americans, such as black pastors denigrating women and gay men and keeping them in a subordinate place.

In her book *Speaking Truth to Power*, Anita Hill describes the pain of being attacked as a "race traitor" for providing testimony about her victimization by an African American, Clarence Thomas. In the wake of her testimony, it became clear that a majority of people cared more about the feelings and treatment of a black heterosexual man than a humiliated black woman. Thomas garnered sympathy from pained blacks and guilt-ridden whites in large part by invoking images of lynching, while many from the same groups vilified Hill. Black feminist Paula Giddings correctly points out that by going public, Hill committed what the black majority considers to be an unpardonable sin, "airing blacks' dirty laundry" before whites. The black majority's anger at Hill was not based on a feeling that she lied, but rather that she did not keep her mouth shut about Thomas's sexual violation against her. Rather than being allowed her rightful place as victim of Thomas's sexual misconduct, for many blacks, Hill became like a victimizing white person, adding to a black heterosexual man's pain and resurfacing old racist notions that black people are sexually perverse.[3]

While I understand Hill's dismay at being attacked, I have decided, nonetheless, not to remain silent about the unjust anti-gay practices within black church settings. If African Americans wish not to be challenged, reprimanded, or opposed publicly, then they must refrain from participating in the mistreatment of African American gays and others. For their part, lesbians, gays, and bisexuals must challenge black church homophobia, biphobia, and sexism and resist the notion that we are "sellouts," not committed to black causes and the black community, when we refuse to go along with black church and social exclusion against us simply because we are gay. The needed work against homophobia and sexism should never be preempted by the needed work against racism.

As I traveled throughout the country doing research on this book, I heard that other openly gay African Americans are also confronted with the maddening question, as black lesbian Barbara Smith puts it, of which do you put first, being black or being gay? (Black feminists and womanists dealt with a similar question decades ago regarding being black or being woman.) The common view (usually of black heterosexual men) is that black women and gay men should focus solely on issues related to race and racism. Although some African American women and gays share this view, black heterosexual men have the luxury of focusing solely on race because they are only marginalized by racism, escaping marginalization encountered by their sisters and gay brothers from sexism and homophobia. As lesbians and gay men, we must not retreat from addressing both issues, reminding African American heterosexuals and others to understand that when we engage in research and activities dedicated to improving the lives of African American

---

3. *Public Hearing, Private Pain: The Anita Hill–Clarence Thomas Hearings.* Produced and directed by *Frontline.* Narrated by Ofra Bikel, 1992. Videocassette.

gays and lesbians, we are doing the work of the black community. Indeed race is a primary oppression, but I believe oppression must be opposed whenever and wherever it occurs. Oppressions can and ought to be confronted simultaneously.

Frustrated and angry by black church ostracism, an increasing number of black lesbian and gay Christians do not view themselves or their relationships as inferior to heterosexuals and their relationships. Though I wrote with these proud lesbians and gays in mind, my greatest hope for this book is that it will reach the countless African American lesbians and gays who live every day with sexual shame and self-hatred, believing that their same-sex sexual attractions and love relationships are flawed, sinful, and immoral because of what they have learned from sermons and teachings of the church.

There will be those who will welcome this book with joy and celebration, relieved that finally black gay Christians whose experience has been diminished or ignored in black churches can now speak for themselves. Yet there will be others for whom this book will awaken dormant rage and hostility toward homosexuality. Some will decry this book as polemical, untrue, and a diabolical betrayal of the black church. In a society where African Americans have been the victims of racial oppression, it is difficult for many of the same people to be self-critical and view themselves as victimizers, treating others in ways that they deemed oppressive to themselves. Others will appreciate this book for being honest, brave, and liberating. But probably the most common response will be, "Why was this book written?" And by that, most will mean, "Why do you have to talk about it?"

At the very core of this question is resistance. At another level is bewilderment. In a world that talks about good things (and its heralding of heterosexuality as one of those good things), and is silent about failures, illnesses, and sexual maladies, many people cannot understand why homosexuality would be discussed. Since most African Americans still consider homosexuality shameful and are unwilling to consider that their silencing and moral denigration of gay people could be at all similar to the historical racist attacks by whites on black people's worth and moral legitimacy, they really are asking, why *would* you talk about people's sexual problems and the immorality of homosexuality? Standing in the two worlds of racial and sexual oppression and experiencing similar responses of hostility, prejudice, and discrimination directed at me because of my skin color and because of my sexual orientation, I felt the need to write a book that looked at this parallel and the hypocrisy of a people that claims liberation and equality while working to oppress lesbians and gays.

To this end, the book was written to save lives from lies and oppression. I have come to believe the words of the late African American lesbian writer Audre Lourde: "Our silences will not save us." Silence maintains the status quo of oppression. Lourde's words inspire me to give voice to African American lesbians and gays whose blackness is often ignored in majority European American lesbian and gay faith and social settings and whose gayness is often ignored in predominantly heterosexual African American churches and communities.

White gays' racism can be observed when they insist on ending homophobia while keeping their world white, resisting any contact with and equity for black people in their gentrified neighborhoods, Euro-centric gay churches, private dance clubs, and television programs, for example, *Queer as Folk* and *Will and Grace*. Black heterosexuals' homophobia and heterocentrism are apparent when they continue ignoring the voices, concerns, interests, and suffering of gay African Americans in their public forums, black publications (namely, *Ebony* and *Jet* magazines), black church organizations, community marches, and black college campuses.

These issues become even more complex as African Americans begin to challenge heterosexual supremacist structures that are entrenched in black churches. In my seminary days at Boston University and later as a graduate student at Vanderbilt University, I found myself frustrated by black heterosexual professors, clergy, and fellow seminarians who denied the victimization of black gays in black churches. Just as white oppressors avoided culpability in their mistreatment of black people, I heard black ministers either deny that black gays experience oppression or use the Bible to justify the inequality of black lesbians and gays. This behavior finally convinced me that the only way the world can know the truth about black church leaders' treatment of lesbians and gays is to put our story in writing.

I write as a son of the black church, born, nurtured, and "raised up" in the southern rural black Baptist church. Having been in black churches throughout my forty-five years, I know what it is like to be black and gay in historical black denominations and churches. And while I cannot speak for every gay African American in a black church, I share many experiences with other black gays in black churches. My hope is that this book will awaken our spirit to the dignity of every human, so that we will see ourselves in the other, recognize our common humanity, and celebrate our God-given gift of sexuality, whether it be with the same or opposite sex. I hope that in reading this book my heterosexual sisters and brothers will allow themselves to be self-critical about their participation in a system that has privileged them over lesbians and gays. In this respect, heterosexuals, especially African American heterosexuals, will better understand that historical and contemporary religious and social teachings have created a supremacist notion of their heterosexuality, one that dismisses the worth of lesbians and gays in families, communities, and churches. This is the challenge for African American Christians who read this book and take seriously the call of Christian faith and community, liberation, and the Gospel demands for justice and peace.

Most of all, I want to make public the often suppressed gay Christian narrative in black churches of victimization, ridicule, and rejection by a heterosexual majority. May this book embolden African American lesbians and gays, inside and outside of church communities, to confront the religious injustice imposed on them by African American clergy and laypeople and challenge them to understand homophobia and heterosexual supremacy as evil constructs akin to the racism and white supremacy that divide and destroy the human family of God.

This is an account about gay people hidden from heterosexuals. It presents gays as full human beings with frailties and short-comings like all humans — along with their gifts, talents, moral character, and love for God and the church. Here are their stories, their narratives of love and care, and witness. It is now time for a discussion that reassesses unfounded notions of lesbians and gays and invites them into black churches as equal members. I strongly believe that black people of faith, like other people of faith, are capable of having such a discussion. Considering that I have worked to make this writing useful for the academic and pastor and accessible to laypeople and others, I hope that this book will find its way into the pulpits and pews of black churches and the hands of those concerned about creating a better reality for African American lesbians and gays in black churches.[4]

---

4. Throughout this writing, I have used pseudonyms when appropriate to protect the lives, families, and livelihood of gays who have not been able to come out. My hope is that many reading this book will live to see the day when this is no longer necessary.

Acknowledgments

I AM ETERNALLY GRATEFUL to all my friends and colleagues who encouraged me to write this book, even when I was not sure that I wanted to take on such a task. It is through their abiding support that this vision has become a reality in these pages.

I thank my graduate professors, Drs. Volney Gay and Victor Anderson, for their encouragement and support during my graduate study and research on religion and homosexuality and early writings on the subject of the black church and homosexuality. Their questions inevitably left me thinking about many reasons that this topic is so important and complex. Moreover, I thank my colleagues, Drs. Ken Stone, Laurel Schneider, Sharon Welch, D. Mark Wilson, Renee Hill, and Andrew Isaacs, for helpful conversations, feedback, and editing of earlier versions of this book.

I realize that this book would not be a reality if it were not for Timothy Staveteig at Pilgrim, who let me know that there are courageous publishers in the universe who value new ways of thinking about black church issues and homosexuality. I am grateful to George Graham for convincing me that I could write this book and keep my job and sanity; so far, everything is intact. I am especially grateful to my editor, Ulrike Guthrie, for believing in this work, reading every page of the manuscript, and offering helpful critique and editorial assistance.

Many thanks to my student research assistant, the Reverend Michael Fincher, for spending many long hours in the library and on the computer and phone to provide clarity and excellent citation detail for this writing.

This writing is in part a product of the many lectures and discussions that took place in my classes and churches. Thus, I am grateful to the former students and seminarians for engaging this material in my "Human Sexuality," "Religion and Homosexuality," and "Sexuality and Pastoral Care classes"; thank you for helping me to think about religion and homosexuality in new ways. Also, many thanks to parishioners at St. Martin's Episcopal Church, Chicago, and my former parish, St. Edmund's, for showing me that the black church can be a community that accepts all people as one.

I owe special thanks to Dr. R. Williams and the Reverends Penny Campbell and Paul Tucker for helping me begin the journey of self-acceptance as a gay Christian two decades ago and pastors Alma Faith Crawford, Karen Hutt (Church of the Open Door, Chicago) and Carl Bean (the Unity Fellowship, Los Angeles), their clergy staff, and parishioners for welcoming me into their congregations and providing interviews that give voice and witness to this work.

I am very clear that this book would not have come together without the encouragement of friends, Beth Isaacs, James Wiard, Johari Jobir, Allen Wright, and Milton Wright; Drs. Ormond Smythe, Michael Mobley, Cheryl Anderson, and Juan Reed; and the organizational and institutional support of the African American Gay, Lesbian, Bisexual and Transgendered Roundtable, The Gay Men's Issues Group (American Academy of Religion), the University of Missouri–Columbia, and Seabury-Western Theological Seminary, and the General Theological Seminary of the Episcopal Church. When I grew weary from the lack of time that I could devote to this writing and frustrated that more had not been done on the subject, these voices and resources inspired me to finish the race. Most of all, I thank my friend, Lee Koonce, for sharing his home and allowing me the space to write creatively and passionately.

Introduction

They sang,
I will trust in the Lord till I die,
And they sang,
I'm gonna treat everybody right till I die. . . .

I T WAS IN MY HOME CHURCH, the Ebenezer Missionary Baptist Church, sitting on rough, hand-painted pews that moved to the rhythm and rock of soul-stirring worship, where I first heard the lyrics of this African American congregational song. Forty years later, I can still hear the resounding voices of that congregation, moaning the testimony of their religious faith, an unconditional vow that they would treat everybody right. This was my introduction to the black church, a place where my family members and neighbors gathered weekly to renew their faith, take refuge from racism, and find hope for the future.

Although I did not understand everything that went on in this place, I quickly learned that it was a safe haven from the racial turbulence of the 1960s. My rural hometown of Starke, Florida, existed as it had for decades, with segregated schools and public facilities. Later, I learned that sitting with my mother in the "colored" waiting room of the doctor's office and going to the back door of the dentist's office were traditions that carried social and religious value for a white majority that God favored them over the "weaker race" of black people.

While many southern white Christians believed that racial segregation and discrimination existed as part of God's natural order, I, along with other black Christians, believed a very different gospel. I listened attentively to the pastor as he told us about the need to stand together as God's children in the face of white people who

1

said terrible things about us. Subsequently, I would experience the truth of his statements as a student in white schools. I learned that racial hatred emerged not because we had imposed harm on whites, but because we were different.

I can remember my older sister telling my mother that one of the young white Christian women at her newly integrated high school argued that God intended for blacks to serve whites. Having undoubtedly learned this from her white Christian community, she referred to Genesis 9, commonly known as the Curse of Ham. In this story, Noah curses Ham's son, Canaan, and the Hamites, a traditionally accepted darker people, to serve his brothers, Shem and Japheth. Although it hurt me to know that people disliked me simply because of my skin color, Ebenezer Missionary Baptist Church stood as a refuge to which I could retreat in times of trouble.

I centered my life on Ebenezer and the rich nurture that it provided for me. Perhaps the most striking religious memory of my early childhood is the singing of the congregational song, "When the Saints Go Marchin' In," led by an older woman, Sister Mackie Mae Pittman, during the part of worship known in many black congregations as "testimony service." As she *sang* her testimony — that made clear her intentions to go to heaven with the other saints — the congregation shared her joy and entered a world far removed from their time and space. Influenced by her faith and fervor, I made a vow that I would also be a part of this special body of God's saints, and, in the language of the community, "accepted Jesus as my Savior and gave my life to the Lord."

In this regard, the black church has historically been and continues to be a wonderful institution of support, nurture, and uplift. Unfortunately, however, black church leaders and congregants have been resistant and even closed in treating gay and heterosexual congregants equally or, in many cases, offering simple compassion to the suffering of gay people. The black heterosexual majority is presently engaged in a biblical indictment that identifies gays as immoral.

Like other gays in the black church, I grew up with this tension. On the one hand, I experienced the rich nurture of black church worship and affirmation of my blackness, while on the other hand, I internalized shame and self-hatred because the black church taught other gays and me that same-sex sexual attraction is sin. As I grew into puberty and early adolescence, I experienced my same-sex sexual attraction as being as much a part of me as my brown skin or love for Ebenezer Church. Like other gays, I felt anxiety living in a world where heterosexuals generally felt something was wrong with gays. Growing up we heard our pastors preach against "unnatural" and sinful homosexuals who would spend eternity in hell. Their message resurrected the old racist notion that black people were cursed, immoral people without souls.

As black pastors continue to condemn gays to hell, many gay black Christians feel that heterosexual black Christians should learn from the racist moral failings of white ministers like Jerry Falwell, who in his early ministry used God and the Bible to oppose integration. Many white Christian ministers and congregants died fighting integration because of their Christian belief that racial integration violated biblical teachings and threatened the common good. While Falwell and other conservative Protestant ministers today admit that the Christian response to integration was flawed, most deny any parallel between their past racism and their present denouncements of homosexuality.

Understanding this history is important as we consider whether similar Christian opposition to the moral legitimacy and civil rights of lesbian and gay citizens can be justified. Like ghosts of the past, Falwell, Pat Robertson, and other contemporary church leaders haunt lesbian and gay people through negative stereotyping and dishonest claims that were used not so long ago against all African Americans.

Those leading the verbal attack on lesbian and gay lives often have high status within the nation's churches. They include many black heterosexual ministers and congregants across the country who join with their white counterparts to do to black lesbians and gays what was at one time done to them. And like white racist Christians, they do it in the name of God, the Bible, and the Christian tradition. Even amid the ever-growing number of openly gay and lesbian African Americans in black families and communities and the awareness of prominent and revered black gay and lesbian Christians like George Washington Carver, James Cleveland, and Barbara Jordan, African Americans continue to resist viewing homosexuality as anything but sin, a negative "lifestyle," and a white aberration, often dismissing its relevance to moral black people.[1] Rather than reflect upon the Christian witness of Carver, Cleveland, and Jordan and reassess their view of homosexuality, it is much easier for African American congregants to focus on the "sordid" lives of black nightclub gays, such as blues legend Bessie Smith and entertainers Gladys Bentley and Sylvester as validation for their view of homosexuality as sin.

As a gay African American pastoral theologian in the liberation tradition, I find this black church practice to be an ironic tragedy, antithetical to a black liberation theology and gospel of Jesus that offer justice for all people. Historically, black church leaders opposed oppressive actions against humans and played an active role to end slavery, mobilize African Americans in the political process, organize educational institutions, and provide places of worship, recreation, and training for black people. Many black church leaders protested social and religious injustice toward African Americans. As a result of the African American experience, black church leaders and members developed a theological perspective of justice and liberation taken from the Exodus story and the prophets of the Hebrew scriptures (for a nicely detailed study, see James Cone's *God of the Oppressed*).

Despite this historical perspective, most black ministers have failed in their application of this theology toward women and gay-identified men. Black heterosexual Christian men's objection to racial hierarchical practice, by and large, had to do with their resistance to being dominated by white men. In general, they did

---

1. James Sears, *Growing Up Black in the South: Race, Gender, and Journeys of the Spirit* (New York: Harrington Park Press, 1991), 6; Jessie Carney Smith, ed., *Notable Black American Men* (Detroit: Gale Publications, 1999), 340; and J. Jennings Moss, "Barbara Jordan: The Other Life," *Advocate* 702 (March 5, 1996): 38–45.

not object to, but rather supported, the domination of women and later gay men. Their use of scripture to support this domination is similar to that of conservative white Christians who converted, enslaved, and dominated black men. I agree with the assertion of my black gay friend Allen Wright, that the present black heterosexual majority emphasis on gay relationships as sinful is self-serving. He argues that African Americans pack black churches on Sunday to hear these anti-gay messages so that in their troubled lives, they can at least feel superior to gay people. Receiving accolades from President Bush and the white heterosexual majority for such a position, black heterosexuals are lifted from sharing a place of inferiority with a gay minority and adopt a "we are better than those people" attitude. This behavior has been observed in other groups and is being analyzed in theological and graduate schools.

Religious scholars are more involved in the discussion of homosexuality because they are being called upon to engage undergraduate, graduate, and seminary students, pastors, members of religious institutions, and political leaders in a sound and critical discussion. The twenty-first century will address lesbian and gay issues in unprecedented ways, including the legalization of same-sex marriage and the move toward full acceptance of lesbian and gay people. Although religious circles demonstrate significant resistance to reforming their attitudes about and practices toward lesbians and gays, some heterosexuals within these church communities are responding with more openness. In light of this progress, there is an increasing need for resources that critically engage this issue.

Although there is a burgeoning body of literature addressing homosexuality in predominantly Anglo-American denominations, there is little detailed scholarship to date that addresses homosexuality in African American congregations. This makes it difficult for pastors and professors to engage congregants and students in an honest dialogue on African American Christian responses to homosexuality. My colleagues express frustration at the dearth of scholarship on this very important topic. Given my research field, people contact me for resources — which often I cannot provide.

Typically, I refer them to chapters that mention homosexuality and black churches in larger works on African American homosexuality.

Whereas there is a diversity of African American religious views on some issues, such as women in ministry, social activism, evangelism, and interpretation of scripture, in the area of sexuality, and homosexuality in particular, black congregants do not show much variance. A significant number of black church leaders have responded to this issue in reactionary ways by strongly opposing gay marriage without a measured discussion of the larger issue of homosexuality. All black denominations hold the view that homosexuality is immoral. While a number of white mainline denominations hold a similar view, these communions have engaged the issue at their conventions for decades and show much greater variance. White denominations reflect the best of what Christian congregations can offer gay Christians and their committed relationships and children (the United Church of Christ provides ordination and marriage rites for openly lesbian and gay Christians) and the worst (the Southern Baptist Convention declares that "homosexuality is a manifestation of a depraved nature . . . and . . . an abomination in the eyes of God).["][2]

C. Eric Lincoln and Lawrence Mamiya point out in *The Black Church in the African American Experience* that black people became Christian during and after slavery by the more conservative/

---

2. In 1972, the United Church of Christ ordained the Reverend William Johnson, the first mainline denomination in Christendom to ordain an openly gay person. At its General Synod in the summer of 2005, the United Church of Christ became the first mainline Christian denomination to call for equal marriage rights for lesbians and gays. The Southern Baptist Convention (organized in 1845 due to its stance that African American slavery was moral and should be maintained) has passed a number of resolutions condemning homosexuality. In 1980, Resolution 25 states "our Convention deplore [*sic*] the proliferation of all homosexual practices, unnatural relations of any character, and sexual perversion whenever found in our society and reaffirm the traditional position of Southern Baptists that all such practices are sinned and are condemned by the Word of God." In June 2003, Resolution 4 was passed on same-sex marriage declaring that "legal and biblical marriage can only occur between one man and one woman." There was no mention of the polygynous marriages of Abraham and others in the Bible not ever condemned in scripture.

traditional strains of white Christianity such as the Baptist denomination. Currently, most black communions are Baptist, Methodist, and Pentecostal and generally support a Christian view of heterosexual supremacy, homosexuality as sinful, and gays as morally depraved. The few black heterosexual ministers that differ with this view tend to be in white liberal denominations, e.g., the United Church of Christ, the Episcopal Church, independent churches, and some liberal urban congregations in black denominations.

The purpose of this book is to provide a critical analysis of the black theological claim of justice and liberation, pointing out the failure of black church leaders and heterosexual Christians to exercise this principle as they encounter the lives of lesbian and gay Christians. This book points out many of the parallels between historical white Christian justifications for slavery and racial discrimination and present black Christian justifications for gay oppression (unjust exercise of power that denies gays equal treatment with heterosexuals). Such practices highlight the present dichotomy between, on the one hand, the historical black church as an agency opposed to religious practices of racial oppression and, on the other hand, the contemporary black church as an institution that enforces oppression of lesbians and gays through its teachings of homosexuality as immoral. Finally, this book examines the theological, social, and psychological problems that emerge from the view that "homosexuality is immoral" and offers new perspectives for assessing scripture and African American Christianity in the context of black liberation.

Chapter 1

Religious and Cultural Reflections on Race and Homosexuality

I've been here for 350 years but you've never seen me.
— James Baldwin

America's Historical Struggle with Difference

THROUGHOUT U.S. HISTORY there exists a similar religious and social derision toward those of African descent and those whose sexual attraction and expression are toward the same sex. Of course the two issues are different — one is about skin color and the other about sexual practice — and yet historical records document that religious and social responses directed toward both groups are indeed quite similar, and in some cases, identical.

Certainly, there are significant differences in the historical responses toward race and sexual orientation; this country never enslaved people based on sexual orientation, for example. By the same token, the U.S. military never discharged anyone from military service solely based on race. The most obvious differences are related to family. Black parents produce black children, whereas there is not as strong a link with sexual identity. Heterosexual parents can and do produce gay offspring and gay parents typically produce heterosexual offspring. In the shared racial makeup of blackness in a racist society, there has been understanding and support from black families, churches, and communities in the struggle against racism that is virtually unknown for black lesbians and gays in their battles against homophobia. And while "it is clear that in most other oppressions the church has given some support to the

9

oppressed, in this case the [black] church has been the leader in the oppression [for black gays]."[1] Therefore, it is true that the experiences of racial and sexual minorities are not the same; a more accurate statement of the parallel is that the negative attitudes and arguments against both groups have been similar and sometimes the same.

Such arguments have prevailed for hundreds of years in order to deny both groups social access and equal treatment with their counterparts. Both groups encountered: church discriminations; legal discriminations, including, but not limited to marriage and military service; social labels as sexual deviant and sex predator; religious and social perceptions as immoral; biblical passages supporting "God's curse" of them; the veiling of their histories; lies about who they are and what they do; and mockery, being laughed at, beatings, and death directed against them by members of the dominant group.

Since many of the negative views about blacks as subhuman are no longer held, or at least publicly expressed by European Americans, many present-day North Americans may not understand that virtually every derisive comment and discrimination against gays today was at one time experienced by all African Americans, gay and heterosexual, because of their race. One of the reasons that so many people remain uninformed about historical systemic racism is because of the unwillingness of white teachers, parents, and religious and political leaders to educate themselves and other whites in an honest way on matters of race.

A classic example of whitewashing history came from Republican president George W. Bush in July 2003. At a gathering in Monrovia, Liberia, Bush rightly condemned the horrors of slavery as "sinful," and correctly pointed out that whites and blacks died for its abolition. What followed in his speech, however, amounted to a romanticized selective account of this country's slave history. The president either remained uninformed about (a likely possibility) or

---

1. John Cobb, "Being Christian about Homosexuality," in *Homosexuality and the Christian Faith*, ed. Walter Wink (Minneapolis: Augsburg Fortress Press, 1999), 90.

simply ignored the complete historical record of U.S. slavery. While it is true that whites and blacks died for the abolition of slavery, few whites actively opposed slavery or perceived it as "sinful" during its first two hundred years; even fewer died for its abolition.

Often referring to the United States as a Christian nation, the president also failed to mention that slavery existed for centuries, in large part due to Christianity and white Christians who espoused slavery as a good and moral institution. Quakers, a tiny Christian body, along with other progressive white Christians and non-Christians, led protests against chattel slavery. Most Christians, however, argued that it should be maintained as part of God's will and "morality."[2]

When one understands that this history of slavery and the subsequent racial discrimination and segregation were cast as Christian moral values derived from the Bible (Gen. 9:25–27), one can also understand why so many people believe that homosexuality is immoral. Currently, most black and white church leaders, among others, use the Bible toward this end, refusing to acknowledge any similarity between the present anti-gay Christian responses and historical racist Christian responses. Since it is now generally agreed that white Christians assumed the wrong position on issues of slavery and segregation, admission from a heterosexual Christian majority that a parallel exists between Christian responses about slavery and homosexuality would also render the Christian majority wrong about homosexuality, a view that most are not willing to concede. However, given that the majority of Christians today would neither identify black people as "cursed" nor find it appropriate to uphold biblically sanctioned slavery as moral, a growing number of Christians and others recognize parallels and point out that it is also inappropriate for the Bible to be used in defining gay and lesbian people as immoral. They further recognize that such casting becomes the cornerstone for religious and social disdain and discrimination.

---

2. Hugh Thomas, *The Slave Trade* (New York: Simon and Schuster, 1997), 451.

Although legal discrimination and negative attitudes remain toward lesbian and gay Americans, it is difficult to convince a heterosexual majority, even a black heterosexual majority who experienced similar discrimination as do all gays, that discrimination against gay citizens is equally wrong. Conversely, those within black churches often understand the pain and suffering of gays in general and black lesbians and gays in particular that occur in black families, churches, and communities, as deserved for their "chosen depraved lifestyle." As a result of the different attitude and response, many politicians are comfortable recognizing race as a legitimate category to be included in nondiscrimination policies and hate crime legislation, but oppose adding sexual orientation, thus giving tacit approval for further discrimination against, and even death of any lesbian and gay person.

That African American heterosexuals frequently distance themselves from gays can be viewed as an attempt to gain respectability from the mainstream, to present themselves as normal Christian citizens over against immoral gays. Contemporary incidents, however, reflect that the best efforts of black heterosexuals to gain acceptance as respectable individuals in contrast to "perverse" gays often fail. Three incidents in the last decade and a half show how the two groups continue to be devalued.

In 1989, Milwaukee police failed to take seriously the calls they received from black women about a young neighborhood male bleeding from his rectum. Rather than investigating this disturbing situation, there is a recording of the two police officers laughing at their homophobic jokes regarding the case and dismissing its seriousness. We do not know whether it was because black women called or because a presumed "faggot" got what he deserved that the police did not take this case seriously; but we do know that if the police had done their job and protected the young man from immediate danger, they could have saved one victim from the savagery of homosexual psychopath Jeffrey Dahmer.

Almost ten years later in 1998, the exceptionally brutal hate crimes against African American James Byrd and a white gay student, Matthew Shepard, once again symbolize the similar hatred toward and violence against blacks and gays. The following year, a surprising number of U.S. citizens defended Atlanta Braves player John Rocker after he made racist and homophobic comments. This is another grim reminder of the parallel between racism and homophobia.

Despite the similar historical and contemporary responses toward racial and sexual minorities, African American heterosexuals often resist the parallel and rethinking of homosexuality. During the gays-in-the-military debate of the early 1990s, Colin Powell strongly repudiated this parallel in his position as chair of the U.S. Military Joint Chiefs of Staff. African American heterosexual Christians were some of the first to join Powell and the white heterosexual male military majority in making moral claims that gays should not be allowed to serve in the U.S. military.[3] African American columnists Gwenevere and Willie Richardson even went so far as to separate the issue from injustice and black people by entitling their article "Gays in the Military: Not a Black Cause." In this writing, they ignored the reality of black gays and lesbians. African Americans also ignored the fact that their behavior paralleled the moral reasoning and behavior of a white U.S. military that opposed integrating black people into its ranks, condemning them as morally inferior in the way that gays were being discussed.

Blacks, resisting any linkage, argue that unlike gays, they were born black. Skin color is an inherent visible marking that cannot be changed. Gays, they argue, are not in the position to use the "born that way" argument. While many gays and others consider one's sexual attraction to be an innate quality, some gays recognize that sexuality is much more complex. Some gays also argue that a "born that way" argument may do more harm than good. White lesbians Ann Pellegrini and Janet Jakobsen assert that "there are good historical reasons for objecting to the 'born that way' argument. . . . Grounding racial and sexual difference in nature has more often worked in the service of discrimination, rather

---

3. "Echoes of Prejudice Past," *Atlanta Constitution*, May 16, 1993, G8.

than against it."[4] They remind us "that slavery and racial segregation were defended on the grounds of nature in a similar manner
as we find homosexuality being opposed today."[5] Cultural and religious leaders maintained that due to the perceived natural moral
inferiority of blacks and gays, laws must exist to prevent the infil-
tration of these groups and the moral decay of society. Thus, it is
naive to think that a "born-this-way" argument will necessarily garner sympathy from society. A society that views homosexuality as
flawed will simply argue that gay people are born flawed and must
be treated as such. The more compelling argument is that discrimination and exclusion are never acceptable behaviors for treating
fellow human beings. When there is recognition of historical discrimination and contemporary parallels with that discrimination,
there can be movement toward justice for all.

African American Hostility to Homosexuality: Statement of the Problem

Even a cursory examination of our country's history reveals hundreds of years of religious and political actions sanctioning racism
and homophobia. In this country, Africans were bought and sold,
and inundated with rigid views about white supremacy and heterosexual normativity. Though most blacks would later challenge
claims about their "racial inferiority," religious dogmas about sexuality remained unchallenged. Religious and political institutions
dictated the limits of sexual practice. Patterns of religious messages,
social scripts, and family teaching enable individuals to understand
when they ought to have sex and how sex ought to be expressed.
These patterns construct sexual mores and lay the foundation for
sexual morality. Sexual morality, however, like morality in general,
has not remained a constant throughout this country's history.

---

4. Janet R. Jakobsen and Ann Pellegrini, *Love the Sin: Sexual Regulation and
the Limits of Religious Tolerance* (New York: New York University Press, 2003),
96.
5. Ibid.

Sexual morality exists as an evolving system based on the sexual experiences and moral reasoning of each generation.

At various times in U.S. history, adultery, premarital sex, and sex between whites and blacks were all considered crimes. Homosexuality and masturbation were considered both criminal and pathological. All cultures assert that sex laws define appropriate sexual conduct and maintain order for the common good. The common good concerns itself with members of the society devoted to the aims that offer the best possibility for happiness, knowledge, free will, the preservation of human life, and the power to choose for ultimate good.[6] Reason informs those of us living in the twenty-first century that, with the possible exception of adultery, the common good is not threatened by the above sexual practices.

Restricting sexual activities that do not threaten the common good is especially problematic in a country established on the principles of liberty, justice, and freedom. Throughout our country's history, religious edicts and laws fostering religious, racial, and social intolerance established a system in which many, and perhaps most, citizens were denied the right to be with those whom they loved. Laws prohibiting slaves, interracial couples, and most recently, lesbian and gay couples from marrying are all examples of a peculiar moral reasoning expressed at various periods that such arrangements violate God's intention for the races or humankind.

While many today find the argument against lesbian and gay couples and homosexuality in general obviously compelling and correct, few people today would argue that slavery is moral or that interracial relationships and marriages are immoral, positions that the majority of Christians supported within the last two centuries. These changes in attitude about slavery and interracial marriage rightfully lead some black Christians today to question the majority's convictions about the "immorality of homosexuality."

Within the past three decades, not only is the social and religious oppression of lesbians and gays being reassessed in the Western world, but questions are being raised in African and Asian

---

6. John Finnis, ed., *Natural Law* (New York: New York Press, 1991), xiii.

countries about the punishment and torture of women and men whose love relationships are with those of the same sex. Practically every mainline Christian denomination's annual convention in the United States addresses homosexuality, whether it be lesbian/gay ordination, same-sex marriage, or some other issue related to homosexuality. In some cases, there has been a reassessment of unfounded notions about lesbian and gay people and how they should serve the church. At its 2003 General Convention in Minneapolis, for example, the Episcopal Church USA emerged as the first mainline denomination in Christendom to consecrate an openly gay bishop, the Right Reverend V. Gene Robinson. This progressive action was remarkable for a religion generally opposed to lesbian and gay equality.

There are even white denominations not otherwise known to be especially liberal or progressive that have constructed responses toward gays that are more aligned with gospel principles than Pharisaic moralism. In assembly actions during the 1990s, the ELCA voted "to affirm that gay and lesbian people, as individuals created by God, are welcome to participate fully in the life of the congregations of the Evangelical Lutheran Church in America." And whereas the ELCA has a ways to go before it can claim this reality within the denomination, no black denomination has even constructed an inclusive statement of this nature for the millions of black gays serving and being served in black churches.[7]

Rather than engage in a dialogue of other Christian perspectives on homosexuality, such as the one taking place among Christians in the Episcopal Church, the historically black denominations are becoming more vocal in their opposition to homosexuality and the equal treatment of gay black Christians and other gays. A recent survey shows that only 40 percent of African American Protestants feel that lesbians and gays should be granted their civil rights. This

---

7. In 2005, my research assistant and I contacted the seven historically black denominations, requesting that they inform us if their denomination held a position that did not view homosexuality as immoral. The African Methodist Episcopal denomination provided the only response. This denomination did not give a position that differed with the aforementioned.

is down from a decade ago when a majority (65 percent) supported civil rights for lesbians and gays. The survey noted that as other groups are becoming more accepting of lesbian and gay people, African American heterosexuals are becoming less accepting and more hostile toward lesbians and gays, including African American lesbians and gays. (Asian American and Latino groups, for example, are not demonstrating and circulating petitions against marriage for lesbians and gays as is the case with African American groups.)[8]

What accounts for such black hostility related to homosexuality? How has the history of racism in the United States affected blacks' understanding of their sexuality and homosexuality? Did their Christian conversion and indoctrination during slavery instill or exacerbate sex-negative and antihomosexual views? Black Christians' understanding of homosexuality as immoral often makes it hard for them to see the discrimination against gays as unjust, even when the victims are their own people, African American lesbians and gays. While I find there is too much focus on which group is more homophobic, white or black heterosexuals (with the enormous degree of injustice and assault on gays in general, praise is not warranted for either group), it is worth noting why African Americans display greater difficulty in viewing gays as deserving full equality with heterosexuals. The high percentage of African Americans affiliated with conservative Baptist, Methodist, and Pentecostal denominations, typically machoistic and hetero-supremacist, explains why many African American heterosexuals are more opposed toward gays than many whites or other groups. While white heterosexual Christians in conservative Protestant denominations are just as resistant and sometimes more averse to gay equality, whites tend to be more varied on this issue than blacks, with a higher percentage of white Christians than black Christians viewing homosexuality as moral.

This more progressive moral response can be observed in nondiscrimination policies, e.g., equal marriage in the United Church of

---

8. *Christianity Today* 48, no. 12 (December 2004): 20.

Christ; and in theological statements, e.g., open and affirming congregations, gay-lesbian support groups, and antihomophobia workshops, teaching, and training. Despite changes occurring within white churches, African American pastors in black denominations are generally silent at best when it comes to gay/lesbian ordination, same-sex marriage, and affirming lesbian and gay Christians. This difference can also be observed in a number of white seminaries, educational institutions, and places of employment throughout the country led by religious leaders, mayors, and corporate executives advocating for lesbian and gay equality.[9] The lack of similar progress in black seminaries and institutions challenges the claim by some blacks that black heterosexuals are no more and perhaps even less homophobic than their white counterparts.[10]

That black heterosexuals are more homophobic, especially in terms of morality, cannot simply be chalked up to white racism. In light of historical racism and the indoctrination of rigid gender and sexual attitudes through the Christian church, African Americans generally possess a large degree of sexual shame and

---

9. The former white mayor of San Francisco, George Moscone, is still the only heterosexual on record who paid the ultimate price of death for his support of civil rights for lesbians and gays. No black heterosexual has been killed for standing with lesbians and gays against gay oppression. In 1978, Moscone was assassinated by board member Dan White after appointing Harvey Milk, the first openly gay politician in the country, as a member of San Francisco's Board of Supervisors. Dan White also assassinated Milk on the same day.

10. The *Princeton Review* (a study of student reports about their own colleges) has noted the unsupportive climate experienced at a disproportionate number of historically black colleges and universities. Morehouse College, the only all-black male college, stood out as especially homophobic. In the *Princeton Review*'s 1996 study, Morehouse was cited as the second most homophobic college in the country. During this period, campus incidents were so hostile that the local and national press covered the cases. The most hostile was an anti-gay beating in the fall of 2002. Aaron Price, the son of a Chicago minister, brutally beat fellow Morehouse student Gregory Love with a baseball bat because Love looked at him in the shower. Love said that he could not see clearly without his glasses and thought that Price was his roommate. Love suffered major trauma to the head. After a Georgia trial, Price was sentenced to ten years in prison. As a consequence of the presence of national gay and black gay organizations, the Morehouse administration reluctantly discussed the case. After the organizations left, Morehouse did not respond.

limited understandings of sexual morality.[11] When black ministers and church leaders speak on issues of sexuality, they almost always present a restricted vision of sexual morality as possible only within the confines of heterosexual marriage. This stunted approach to sexuality prevents African Americans from progressing toward a healthier and fuller sexuality, both in attitude and practice.[12]

While it would indeed be wrong to present black heterosexuals as more homophobic than whites if they are not, it would also be dishonest to present black people as better on the issue of homosexuality than they really are. For whites to present the truth is not racist; for blacks to do so is not betrayal. Covering up black homophobia serves no good purpose and will ultimately hinder black heterosexuals from confronting the many ways in which they *are* homophobic and participate in a system that promotes homophobic attitudes and practices. The challenge for black gay Christians is to come out and oppose the denigration and exclusion imposed by heterosupremacists.[13] And we must do so with the same comfort level that we display when opposing racist actions of white lesbians, gays, and heterosexuals.

---

11. Christianity does not represent the religion of all African Americans. A significant number of African Americans are Muslim and, to a lesser degree, members of other religions. While I find that scholarly religious work needs to be done on African American Islam and homosexuality, this is not the aim of this writing.

12. Robert M. Franklin, *Another Day's Journey: Black Churches Confronting the American Crisis* (Minneapolis: Fortress Press, 1997).

13. I use the term "homophobia" in much the same way that it is generally used in contemporary popular culture. It is not to be understood in a strict clinical sense that denotes simply a fear, but it has a broader meaning to include discomfort, disgust, and, in some cases where black heterosexuals have beaten and killed homosexuals, hatred. I have coined the term "heterosexual supremacy" to refer to other cases of inequality toward lesbian and gay people. I define heterosexual supremacy as any practice that values individuals solely on the basis of their sexual attraction toward the opposite sex and offers them and their relationships merit on that basis over and against homosexuals and their relationships. As white supremacy is defined as valuing whiteness over and against blackness, I define heterosexual supremacy as its sexual equivalent. Other related terms include heterosexism (see the definition in Audre Lourde's *Sister Outsider*) and Adrienne Rich's term, compulsory heterosexuality.

History will record the failure of African American heterosexuals as a group to be in solidarity with lesbians and gays. Heterosexuals typically do not stand with gays as they are being denied their civil rights, suffer under unjust public policy and government legislation, and experience religious and social oppression, family and community ostracism, hostile attacks and death. Like white preachers who remained silent while black people were being lynched, most black ministers remain silent about the ongoing beatings of all gays, including black gays Arthur Warren in West Virginia and Hattie Mae Cohen in Oregon. A few African Americans will be remembered as having had moral courage, but like other groups that stood silent during the most difficult days of the other's oppression, most African Americans will take a shameful place in history alongside all who participated in gay oppression, even if only by their silence.

Historical Racism and Homophobia

If one is trying to understand what accounts for this particular African American homophobia, one must look at more than the rigid sexual teachings of the Christian church. In addition to the sex-negative attitudes of the Puritans and the pristine heterosexuality of the Victorian era that whites and others in this culture carry with them, African Americans are also scarred by the history of racism that sexually demonized them. As in every other area of black life, racism is the culprit, this time causing difficulty for black people to move from sexual shame and become more open in their sexual attitudes and practice. African Americans have spent their years of freedom seeking to gain respectability by the mainstream as sexually moral beings and overcome the historical labeling as a sexually perverse people. In an effort to receive acceptance from a homophobic society, blacks strongly condemn and deny homosexuality within black communities and churches. While black church leaders and congregants tolerate a gay presence in choirs, congregations, and even the pulpit as long as gays cooperate and stay "in their closeted place," gays quickly experience the limits of this tolerance if they request the same recognition as their heterosexual counterparts.

Those arguing that gays are not oppressed in black churches because they have never had to sit in the back of the church or use segregated facilities, as one student told me, miss the point and fail to understand oppression. Oppression is any cruel and unjust use of power that restricts individuals solely on the basis of a pejorative understanding of their group. In the majority of black churches, even those churches that allow some tolerance for perceived lesbian and gay congregants, gays experience oppression. Gays in these churches do not receive affirmation of their love relationships, are subjected to biblical pronouncements on themselves as sinful, and are prohibited from the marriage rites and ordination (if they are out) that are extended to their fellow heterosexual parishioners.

I like Iris Marion Young's analysis of the relationship between racial and sexual oppression and find her book *Justice and the Politics of Difference* very helpful for this discussion. If African American pastors and seminary professors want others to take the issue of religious and social justice seriously, they will have to consider that justice extends beyond the confines of race and refers "not only to [equal] distribution, but also to the institutional conditions necessary for the development and exercise of individual capacities and collective communication and cooperation. Under this conception of justice, injustice refers primarily to two forms of disabling constraints, oppression and domination."[14]

Young acknowledges the problem in understanding oppression when African American heterosexuals or other historically oppressed groups only consider their "oppression [as] a unified and distinct structure or system.... This way of conceiving oppression fails to accommodate the similarities and overlaps in the oppressions of different groups."[15] As African American feminists and womanists pointed out decades ago, the simple race focus and insensitivity to the other ways black people suffer — for instance, the

---

14. Iris Marion Young, *Justice and the Politics of Difference* (Princeton, NJ: Princeton University Press, 1990), 39.

15. Ibid., 64.

discrimination experienced by women and gay men — "falsely represents the situation of all group members as the same."[16] Though oppression may manifest itself in different ways, women, gays, people of darker color, and Jews all experience types of social and religious oppression. Young understands that African American heterosexuals' often hostile resistance to recognize oppression of black, white, and other gays stems from a narrow view of oppression and the failure to consider that "all oppressed people suffer some inhibition of their ability to develop and exercise their capacities and express their needs, thoughts and feelings."[17]

Religion is commonly used within cultures to justify oppression. Often Bible stories are used to construct theological perspectives that define minority groups out of God's favor and deserving of a subordinate status and unequal treatment with the dominant group. By and large, Christians in the United States used Bible stories to define all African Americans as a cursed immoral people, relegated to slavery, segregation, and unequal treatment with whites and, in a similar manner, used another set of biblical stories to define homosexuals as a cursed immoral people undeserving of equal treatment with heterosexuals. The following are two of the most commonly referenced Bible stories used as justification of racism and homophobia.

Christian Constructions of Racism and Homophobia

In the late seventeenth and early eighteenth centuries, white Christian theologians, ministers, and missionaries appealed to the "Curse of Ham" as biblical support for the slave status of Africans. This theological perspective coincided with the social construction of race as a category. Since the Judeo-Christian scriptural tradition identified slaves as part of God's divine order, Christians generally accepted slavery as an institution morally sanctioned by the

---

16. Ibid.
17. Ibid., 40.

Almighty. Within scripture there are many examples of God's righteous people as slave owners: Abraham, the patriarch in both Jewish and Christian traditions, owned a slave and mistress, Hagar (Gen. 16:2); and the story of Job characterizes him as a righteous man of God with his slaves (Job 1:16). No scriptural passage condemns the long-standing practice, and most New Testament scholars point out that Paul not only recognizes the institution as legitimate, but also supports the institution. Thus, the practice of enslaving humans and trading them as goods survived until modernity as a value of the common good.

European Americans looked to their religion as they assigned meaning to the concept of race and the perceived superiority and inferiority of whites and blacks, respectively. Eighteenth-century white Christians turned to the Bible and read Genesis 9:18–27, the "Curse of Ham," as God's punishment for black sin and intention for the races: "Cursed be Canaan; the lowest of slaves shall he be to his brothers." In this theological construction of race, God placed those of European descent as a master class over a slave class of Africans, "and let Canaan be his slave."

African American biblical professor Cain Hope Felder is one scholar who has pointed out that the Bible does not identify populations, and thus slaves, in terms of race. His discussion of the popular use of the Genesis passage to support slavery of blacks tells us more about how it functioned in white Christian communities and cultures than about its literal meaning. It is what white religious leaders "used to denigrate black people."[18] The famous passage is a story about Noah's anger toward his youngest son, Ham, for looking at his nakedness, a disrespectful act within the culture. When Noah discovers what Ham has done, he curses Ham's son, Canaan, for Ham's misdeed.

> The sons of Noah who went out of the ark were Shem, Ham and Japheth. Ham was the father of Canaan. These three were the sons of Noah; and from these the whole earth was peopled.

18. Cain Hope Felder, *Troubling Biblical Waters: Race, Class, and Family* (Maryknoll, NY: Orbis Books, 1989), 38.

Noah, a man of the soil, was the first to plant a vineyard. He drank some of the wine and became drunk, and he lay uncovered in his tent. And Ham, the father of Canaan, saw the nakedness of his father, and told his two brothers outside. Then Shem and Japheth took a garment, laid it on both their shoulders and walked backward and covered the nakedness of their father; their faces were turned away and they did not see their father's nakedness. When Noah awoke from his sleep and knew what his youngest son had done to him, he said, "Cursed be Canaan; lowest of slaves shall he be to his brothers." He also said, "Blessed by the Lord my God be Shem; and let Canaan be his slave. May God make space for Japheth, and let him live in the tents of Shem; and let Canaan be his slave." (Gen. 9:18–27)

This text is problematic in that it neither explains nor provides crucial detail. Since Ham is guilty for having looked at his father's nudity, it is curious as to why Noah cursed the innocent grandson, Canaan, instead of the guilty son, Ham. In addition, Canaan is mentioned as being a slave to his brothers. It is not Canaan's brothers who are identified in the text as masters; rather, Canaan's uncles, Shem and Japheth, the brothers of Ham, are accorded this privileged status. Finally, did the Canaanites or Hamites have darker skin than the descendants of Shem and Japheth? The passage does not indicate that the Hamites (Ham's descendants) or Canaanites (Canaan's descendants) would be different in any physical manner.

The popularized "Curse of Ham" is a good example of how the accuracy of a story is less important than the meaning assigned to it by subsequent Christian leaders and followers. While the Bible clearly sanctioned slavery in all its forms, black people are not singled out to be slaves. When the dominant group draws conclusions about any despised group beforehand, like black people or gay people, including black gays, the scripture can appear to be clear in its identification and condemnation of that group as cursed or immoral, even when it is not clear. The Genesis story of Sodom and Gomorrah functions in a similar manner for Christians opposed to gays. It, like the "Curse of Ham" story, is unclear but has been interpreted to depict gays as morally depraved predators cursed by God.

Sodom and Gomorrah Revisited

Even churchgoers who cannot find Genesis 19:1–29 in the Bible are vaguely familiar with the story of Sodom and Gomorrah and have typically concluded, with little or no investigation, that the story is about God's destruction of two cities because of the wickedness of homosexuality. But the real lesson of the story is that God abhors sexual violence, not homosexuality. The passage reads:

> The two angels came to Sodom in the evening, and Lot was sitting in the gateway of Sodom. When Lot saw them, he rose to meet them, and bowed down with his face to the ground. He said, "Please, my lords, turn aside to your servant's house and spend the night, and wash your feet; then you can rise early and go on your way." They said, "No; we will spend the night in the square." But he urged them strongly; so they turned aside to him and entered his house; and he made them a feast, and baked unleavened bread, and they ate. But before they lay down, the men of the city, the men of Sodom, both young and old, all the people to the last man, surrounded the house; and they called to Lot, "Where are the men who came to you tonight? Bring them out to us, so that we may know them." Lot went out of the door to the men, shut the door after him, and said, "I beg you, my brothers, do not act so wickedly. Look, I have two daughters who have not known a man; let me bring them out to you, and do to them as you please; only do nothing to these men, for they have come under the shelter of my roof." But they replied, "Stand back!" And they said, "This fellow came here as an alien, and he would play the judge! Now we will deal worse with you than with them." Then they pressed hard against the man Lot, and came near the door to

break it down. But the men inside reached out their hands and brought Lot into the house with them, and shut the door. And they struck with blindness the men who were at the door of the house, both small and great, so that they were unable to find the door.

Then the men said to Lot, "Have you anyone else here? Sons-in-law, sons, daughters, or anyone you have in the city — bring them out of this place. For we are about to destroy this place, because the outcry against its people has become great before the LORD, and the LORD has sent us to destroy it." So Lot went out and said to his sons-in-law, who were to marry his daughters, "Up, get out of this place; for the LORD is about to destroy the city." But he seemed to his sons-in-law to be jesting.

When morning dawned, the angels urged Lot, saying, "Get up, take your wife and two daughters who are here, or else you will be consumed in the punishment of the city." But he lingered; so the men seized him and his wife and his two daughters by the hand, the LORD being merciful to him, and they brought him out and left him outside the city. When they had brought them outside, they said, "Flee for your life; do not look back or stop anywhere in the Plain; flee to the hills, or else you will be consumed." And Lot said to them, "Oh, no, my lords; your servant has found favor with you, and you have shown me great kindness in saving my life; but I cannot flee to the hills, for fear the disaster will overtake me and I die. Look, that city is near enough to flee to, and is a little one. Let me escape there — is it not a little one? — and my life will be saved!" He said to him, "Very well, I grant you this favor too, and will not overthrow the city of which you have spoken. Hurry, escape there, for I can do nothing until you arrive there." Therefore the city was called Zoar. . . .

Then the LORD rained on Sodom and Gomorrah sulfur and fire from the LORD out of heaven; and he overthrew those cities, and all the Plain, and all the inhabitants of the cities, and what grew on the ground. But Lot's wife, behind him, looked back, and she became a pillar of salt. Abraham went early in the morning to the place where he had stood before the LORD; and he looked down toward Sodom and Gomorrah and toward all the land of the Plain and saw the smoke of the land going up like the smoke of a furnace. So it was that, when God destroyed the cities of the Plain, God remembered Abraham, and sent Lot out of the midst of the overthrow, when he overthrew the cities in which Lot had settled.

As biblical scholars assert, a common way for males to humiliate others was to rape or impose sexual violence on them. Ken Stone and others point out that much of the humiliation is derived from placing the man being raped in the culturally imposed subordinate position of a woman.[19] The wickedness in the story of Sodom and Gomorrah is the attempted rape of the angels by the mob, which has to do with humiliation and violence by male perpetrators. This story is about the mob's threats on the male angels, which are an affront to Lot and his family's hospitality. The violent threat of gang rape is what breaks God's patience in the unfolding of this story. Indeed, we all would expect God to condemn such an act, whether it involved those of the same or opposite sex. Since this passage does not involve loving sexual expressions between men, we can only conclude that God condemns rape; we cannot draw any broader conclusion about God's attitude toward all homosexual contact.

The presence of this biblical story and the absence of a biblical passage depicting a positive sexual relationship between members of the same sex contribute to the unfortunate notion that homosexuality in and of itself is problematic and immoral. The prominence of this story is such that in the English language the name Sodom has evolved into the term "sodomy," or anal intercourse, typically depicted as perverse and violent. Rather than the perception of intercourse as lovemaking, what has become fixed in people's minds is a shameful act of anal intercourse. This homophobic reading further hardens extreme black heterosexual

19. Ken Stone, *Sex, Honor, and Power in the Deuteronomistic History* (Sheffield, England: Sheffield Academic Press, 1996), 76.

supremacist ministers like Gregory Daniels agreeing to ride with
the Ku Klux Klan if it opposes gay marriage and Rev. James Sykes
stating that he would join this terrorist force "if [he] knew that
was the only reason they were there."[20] Even more extreme is
their white supporter Rev. Fred Phelps, the leader of the infamous
GodHatesFags.com campaign.

The above are just two scripture passages that have contributed
to a certain cultural and Christian thinking about slavery and
racism and homophobia. Both texts functioned historically to impose a negative view of the despised group and justify cultural
oppression. Since the Bible typically functions as a supportive text
for an already accepted view of gays, it is often difficult for black
Christians and others to separate the cultural biases, assumptions,
and conclusions that are brought to the text. Outside of a few college
and seminary classrooms, those within our contemporary society
usually avoid discussing how a majority of U.S. citizens, including
Christians, could believe slavery to be moral when it is currently
strongly condemned as immoral. Many would rather avoid the topic
altogether, but when pushed for a response, dismiss this major historical institution by usually stating one of two things: slavery in
the Bible was different, or slave masters and other slavery proponents knew they were wrong. Proslavery Christians, however, like
most Christians today regarding popular cultural issues, argued
that God's word, the Bible, clearly dictated how they should live.

A leading minister with the Christian view of maintaining
slavery was the Reverend Thornton Stringfellow. A white Baptist
minister from Culpepper County, Virginia, in the 1800s Stringfellow became a moral leader for conservative Christians on the
issue of slavery. In his widely read *Scriptural and Statistical Views
in Favor of Slavery*, Stringfellow affirms that "Jesus Christ has not
abolished slavery by prohibitory command and . . . he has introduced no new moral principle which can work its destruction. . . . It

---

20. Keith Boykin, *One More River to Cross* (New York: Anchor Books/Doubleday, 1996), 127.

is a fundamental principle of the Mosaic law, under which slavery was introduced by Jehovah himself and...where the apostles planted churches, hereditary slavery existed, as it did among Jews, and as it does now among us."[21] The strongest supporters of this theological view were Baptist and Methodist church leaders and congregants. In 1844 and 1845, theological disagreements over slavery resulted in a division in the Methodist and Baptist denominations, respectively; the two denominations divided into the Methodist Church North and the Methodist Church South, and the American Baptist Convention and the Southern Baptist Convention.[22]

To be sure, contemporary biblical scholars like Cain Hope Felder are correct to point out that biblical slavery differed in that it was not race-based. Still, there is no evidence to support the claim made by many African American Christians, among others, that slavery in the ancient Near East and the early church era was any less cruel than the worst forms of slavery in the United States. That claim is often made as an attempt to legitimate slavery in the Bible while condemning the evil slavery in the United States.

According to historical documents and the description of New Testament slavery, there is a similar treatment of slaves in the Bible and the United States; some ancient and European American slave masters treated their slaves with civility, while others exercised cruelty. Paul, for example, refused to condemn slavery or cruel slave masters, even during the first century, when Roman law referred to slaves as things and not as humans, and allowed slave owners "to bind, torture, or kill the slaves." In Romans 13, he conversely wrote that Christians must "submit to all the laws imposed by the governing rulers because they were appointed by

---

21. Thornton Stringfellow, *Scriptural and Statistical Views in Favor of Slavery* (Freeport, NY: Books for Libraries Press, 1972; reprint of the 1856 edition first published in 1841 under the title *A Brief Examination of Scripture Testimony on the Institution of Slavery*), 94–95.

22. Albert J. Raboteau, *Slave Religion: The Invisible Institution in the Antebellum South* (New York: Oxford University Press, 1978), 160.

God."[23] Since Paul's biblical injunction here precludes the possibility for Christians to oppose slavery laws existing during his time or in the future, this text has been especially problematic for Christian opponents of slavery. The writing in 1 Peter 2:18, "slaves, accept the authority of your masters with all deference, not only those who are kind and gentle but also those who are harsh," appears to provide further evidence that biblical slavery was also a cruel fate for certain people. Despite this cruelty, there is no condemnation of slavery by God or the biblical writers.

Similarly, in U.S. slavery, some masters treated their slaves as distant family members, as was the case in much of New England slavery,[24] while others, especially in the South, were harsh and severe. Considering this use of scripture to support what the church and culture now understand as immoral, African American Christians ought to be suspicious of the antihomosexual use of scripture that defines all gays as immoral and calls for their oppression.

Constructions of Homophobia and Heterosexual Supremacy

Sex-negative teachings of the European Christian social order identified homosexuality as immoral, but other cultures demonstrate varying degrees of acceptance and opposition. While it is true that many cultures, like ancient Jewish culture, instituted proscriptions against homosexual expression due to their fears that nonprocreative sex would significantly lessen or end a population, other cultures tempered their responses, with some cultures appreciating the beauty or sacredness of same-sex sexual expression.[25]

23. Dale B. Martin, *Slavery as Salvation: The Metaphor of Slavery in Pauline Christianity* (New Haven, CT: Yale University Press, 1990), 13.

24. See William Piersen, *Black Yankees: The Development of an Afro-American Subculture in Eighteenth-Century New England* (Amherst: University of Massachusetts Press, 1988), and Janet Duitsman Cornelius, *"When I Can Read My Title Clear": Literacy, Slavery, and Religion in the Antebellum South* (Columbia: University of South Carolina Press, 1991).

25. Walter Williams, *The Spirit and the Flesh: Sexual Diversity in American Indian Culture* (Boston: Beacon Press, 1986), 133.

Early Christian culture, conversely, adopted antihomosexual views of the Pauline writings. Antisexual teachings of the early church led to heightened cultural and church persecutions of homosexual expressions during the low Middle Ages. Gay historian John Boswell notes that whereas for centuries men had viewed homosexuality as a sexual sin, the special disdain for men having sex with other men was a problem created in the Middle Ages when homosexual expression was compared to murder and "as one of two sins that 'cry out to heaven for vengeance.'"[26]

In the now infamous 1986 *Bowers v. Hardwick* case, which upheld Georgia's sodomy law, then Chief Justice Warren Burger argued that homosexuality was immoral because "homosexual conduct has been subject to state intervention throughout the history of Western Civilization . . . and that to protect homosexual acts would be to cast aside millennia of moral teaching."[27] The Supreme Court majority gave assent and in essence sanction to Georgia's law, which stated lesbians and gays do not have the right to private sexual expressions in their own home. This law allowed states with such laws to invade homes and charge and imprison all consenting adults involved in any nonheterosexual sexual expression. (This occurred in a 1999 Texas case involving John Lawrence, a white gay man, and his black partner, Tyrone Garner, who were charged and arrested under the Texas Homosexual Acts law. This case eventually ended up at the Supreme Court, and in 2003, the Supreme Court reversed the 1986 ruling that such laws were constitutional, ending centuries of legal persecution of gay sexual expression.)

In Burger's mind, however, "to protect homosexual acts would be *to cast aside millennia of moral teaching.*" His reasoning is largely grounded in the view that a law ought to be granted legitimacy based on its longevity. Such an argument ignores other practices

---

26. John Boswell, *Christianity, Social Tolerance, and Homosexuality: Gay People in Western Europe from the Beginning of the Christian Era to the Fourteenth Century* (Chicago: University of Chicago Press, 1980), 277.

27. Richard Mohr, *Gays/Justice: A Study of Ethics, Society, and Law* (New York: Columbia University Press, 1988), 78.

such as slavery and the subjugation of women which lasted millennia and received sanction by the major religions of the world but today are considered morally wrong. Any argument based solely on the grounds of longevity and popularity is insufficient. Burger is correct in only one respect: homosexuality has been condemned for millennia. What Burger does not consider is the ways in which homosexuality also found acceptance.[28]

Since the beginning of time cultures around the world have recognized the desire for humans to engage in sexual activity with those of the same sex. Ancient texts reveal a variety of responses, from affirmation and celebration in many Eastern and Native American cultures, to indifference, severe condemnation, and death in many Middle Eastern and Western cultures.[29]

Often uninformed about such homosexual expression in human history, Africans and African Americans are too dismissive of homosexual expression among indigenous African peoples while overgeneralizing its presence among and acceptance by European and European Americans.[30] Africans are like the rest of humanity in expressing themselves sexually with both the same and opposite sex. And except for a few ancient European cultures, such as the Greek, most Europeans did not view homosexuality favorably. Even in ancient Rome and Greece, only a particular form of male homosexuality was accepted, namely, intergenerational sex of the educated class.[31]

---

28. See Arlene Swidler, ed. *Homosexuality and World Religions* (Valley Forge, PA: Trinity Press International, 1993).

29. Robert Staples, *Black Masculinity: The Black Male's Role in American Society* (San Francisco: Black Scholar Press, 1982), 87; Robert Baum, "The Traditional Religions of the Americas and Africa," in *Homosexuality and World Religions*, ed. Arlene Swidler (Valley Forge, PA: Trinity Press International, 1993), 15; and Williams, *Spirit and the Flesh*, 133.

30. Stephen O. Murray and Will Roscoe, ed., *Boy Wives and Female Husbands: Studies of African Homosexualities* (New York: St. Martin's Press, 1998), 1, 200.

31. David M. Halperin, "Sex before Sexuality: Pederasty, Politics, and Power in Classical Athens," in *Hidden from History: Reclaiming the Gay and Lesbian Past*, ed. Martin Bauml Duberman et al. (New York: Meridian, 1989).

Medieval Attitudes

In the first centuries of the Christian church, the church fathers condemned homosexuality more explicitly. Augustine struggled with sexual passion and negative responses to sexual expression between those of the opposite sex, but he displayed a special disdain for male homoeroticism and homosexuality. He felt that men lived in constant danger of being overpowered by powerful sexual feelings. Given his fear, it is no surprise that in his rules he opposed small male groupings by writing that "no fewer than two or three monks shall go to public baths . . . nor should he who must go somewhere on business go with the companion he chooses, but he ought to go with whom the superior appoints."[32] He further stated without explanation that homosexual practices are transgressions of the command to love God and one's neighbors and declares that those shameful acts against nature, such as were committed in Sodom, ought to be detested and punished.[33] Like so many Christian attitudes that have remained for centuries, many contemporary African American Christians, as well as Christians in general, still feel bound by Augustine's words.

During the Middle Ages, the Catholic monk Thomas Aquinas wrote on the "lusts of the flesh" in his *Summa Theologica*, defining homosexuality as a manifestation of excessive lust or concupiscence. Aquinas's antipathy toward the already-despised homosexuality led him to coin the phrase "the unmentionable vice," largely contributing to the present view that homosexuality is the worst of all "sins."

Homosexuality in the New World

When European explorers and missionaries entered the New World, they found that the condemnation of homosexuality was not a

---

32. M. Clark, *Augustine of Hippo* (New York: Paulist Press, 1984), 16.

33. Derrick Bailey, *Homosexuality and the Western Christian Tradition* (New York: Longmans Green, 1955), 82.

universal practice. As historian Robert Baum states, "In many Native American communities, [homosexuals] were regarded as sacred people, chosen by gods and given special powers that could benefit the community."[34] Unlike the popular view espoused by many Christian church leaders today that "homosexuals destroy the family and the community," these religious communities looked at the benefits that they could receive from homosexuals in their families and community.

Puritan settlers of the New World, however, imposed the theological response of their medieval ancestors. New England colonies adopted antihomosexual teachings and emphasized homosexuality as a "monstrosity." In Frances Higgeson's 1629 writing, for example, he referred "in his journal, to '5 beastly Sodomitical boys' who committed the 'wickedness not to be named.'"[35]

Such teachings were reinforced by early Puritan Christian ministers, like the pro-slavery minister Cotton Mather, who preached sermons concerning the evils of homosexuality. In an effort to emphasize the value of work and the evil of "sloth," Mather equated idleness with the sexual "sins of Sodom." If Mather's sermon left anyone questioning what was the "sin of Sodom," Rev. Samuel Danforth removed all doubt in his 1674 published sermon, "Cry of Sodom." Danforth instilled fear among New Englanders by warning that if they did not kill those who had sex with the same sex, they "would bring God's vengeance on everyone." He defined "sodomy" as "filthiness" "committed by males with males and females with females" and linked it with "idleness, the violation of the marriage ordinance and family life, the disobedience of children to parents, and servants to masters."[36] The categorization of homosexuality as antifamily by Mather and Danforth in sermons praising the Puritans' "high valuation of family and socially useful work" is a reminder of the inappropriate references about

---

34. Baum, "The Traditional Religions of the Americas and Africa," 15.
35. Jonathan Katz, *Gay American History: Lesbians and Gay Men in the U.S.A.: A Documentary History*, rev. ed. (New York: Meridian, 1992), 40.
36. Ibid.

gay people still being used by the Christian Coalition, the Christian right, and much of the black church in their "family values" rhetoric.[37]

As a consequence of this Christian teaching, all of the New World colonies established sex laws condemning homosexuality as a crime punishable by death. During this same seventeenth century, John Winthrop, the first governor of the New England colonies, strongly advocated the death of anyone who engaged in sex with the same sex and contributed to the "monster" image that would eventually become associated with homosexuals in the late nineteenth and twentieth centuries. In his journal concerning the punishment for William Plaine, a married man who had been sexually involved with two men back in England, Winthrop advocates Plaine's death, writing that "indeed it was a dreadful crime, and he is a monster in human shape . . . , and it tended to the frustrating of the ordinance of marriage and the hindering the generation of mankind."[38] The fact that Plaine had helped in the settling of Guilford, Connecticut, did nothing to persuade Winthrop of his goodness. For these seventeenth-century leaders, Plaine's two private sexual affairs with men automatically made him a bad person, worthy of his death in 1646. As gay historian Jonathan Katz asserts, Winthrop perceived Plaine's actions as wicked because of his participation in what were deemed antimarriage and antiprocreative activities that violated the common good.

Finally, in the same year, the state-imposed death of a black man highlights the society's disdain toward homosexuality, especially when committed by blacks. In addition to being one of the first men put to death for having sex with a man, in 1646, Jan Creoli carried the double burden of also being a black man — the first African in America killed because of homosexual activity. His death "record stated: this crime being condemned of God . . . as an abomination, the prisoner is sentenced to death and then burnt to

---

37. Ibid., 42.
38. Ibid., 91.

ashes. . . . "[39] During this period, whites involved in same-sex sexual experiences (sodomy) were also sentenced to death. These laws would soon undergo reform. Ironically, despite their progressive attitudes against racial slavery, Pennsylvania Quaker lawmakers kept the death penalty for sodomy firmly in place for blacks while outlawing it for whites.

The late seventeenth century witnessed an increase in sodomy laws, going so far as to include masturbation among the acts punishable by death. In the eighteenth century, some death laws for homosexuals were replaced by cruel punishments. While Thomas Jefferson agreed with practically everyone of his day that homosexuality was immoral, he opposed putting to death those guilty under Virginia's sodomy law and recommended the less severe, though nonetheless cruel, punishment of castration. In 1777, this law stated that a male guilty of rape, polygamy, or sodomy would be castrated, while a female guilty of the same crime should be punished by "cutting thro' the cartilage of her nose a hole of one half inch diameter at the least."[40]

The Post-Enlightenment Construction of Homosexuality

Homosexuality continued to be a social and religious issue throughout the nineteenth century, but due to the death penalty for some homosexual liaisons and the clandestine nature in which people were forced to express same-sex desire, it is impossible to determine the prevalence of same-sex desire. The invisibility of those who had same-sex desire often meant that the problematic abuse cases, like that of author and child welfare advocate Horatio Algers, represented all of them. In the mid-nineteenth century, Algers, also a Unitarian pastor in Brewster, Massachusetts, was fired by the church committee for engaging in sex with boys and charged "with gross immorality and a most heinous crime, a crime of no less

---

39. Ibid., 90.
40. Ibid., 24.

magnitude than the abominable and revolting crime of unnatural familiarity with boys. . . . "[41]

Homosexuality, like race, is an invention and construction of the post-Enlightenment. As the eighteenth century created different "species" by racial classification, in the late nineteenth century social scientific classification created a sexual categorization in which lines were drawn between those with primary opposite sex sexual desire and those with primary sexual desire for the same sex. This sexual construction laid the foundation for the making of a homosexual class. The term "homosexual" emerged as a separate identity in the late nineteenth century, albeit a maladaptive one, as opposed to the earlier notion that same-sex desires stemmed from wicked passions of oversexed individuals.[42]

Homosexual behavior became associated with certain individuals, the third sex or inverts, who failed at "normal" development toward the opposite sex, and as a result of their abnormality exhibited a number of behaviors harmful to the society. Heterosexual prejudice toward this group created fears within the society as individuals absorbed antihomosexual lectures, writings, speeches, films, and most notably sermons. David Halperin notes that these

---

41. Ibid., 33.
42. Roger Biery provides helpful background for homosexual terms. The term "homosexual was first used in 1869 by Hungarian journalist Dr. Karoly M. Kertbeny. . . . Heterosexual did not exist until a few decades later" (Roger E. Biery, *Understanding Homosexuality: The Pride and the Prejudice* [Austin, Tex.: Edward-William, 1990], 4). The terms "homosexual" and "homosexuality" reveal "that there are actually two meanings at issue here. The first word would be more appropriately called homoaffectional. It refers to an emotional and erotic attraction to persons of the same gender. . . . The emotion is love; the eroticism is sexual arousal. Neither constitutes behavior. The second meaning . . . , homosexual, . . . refers to . . . same sex sexual activity — the behavior — which can be purely sexual without the presence of emotional or erotic attraction to persons of the same sex, i.e., the average prisoner." In contrast, a person who is "homosexual (possessing an emotional and erotic attraction to persons of the same gender) might not engage in same-sex sexual activity. This is because sexual orientation consists in feelings, not in behavior." Thus a more accurate way of understanding homosexuality, heterosexuality, and the combination of bisexuality is to view them as constructs of a "sexual-affectional orientation" (4).

teachings about the homosexual as a separate degenerate class contributed to the fear of the homosexual that heterosexuals, black and otherwise, have yet to overcome.

In a number of ways, from its inception, psychology attempted to "cure" the homosexual.[43] Like whiteness, heterosexuality was identified as supreme, as natural, in contrast to the arrested development of homosexuality. As a consequence, once homosexuals were discovered, they endured all sorts of torture and punishment, and occasionally paid the ultimate price for their erotic desires. For example, as an alternative to killing women who had sex with women in the seventeenth century, various treatments were used, including surgical removal of the ovaries and the clitoris. The fact that this "cure" was also used with women suffering from "erotomania" reflected the belief that women who had sex with women, and men who had sex with men, like black people in general, possessed uncontrollable sexual desires. Comparable religious labels for these different groups included lasciviousness, lust, and sexual immorality.

As some eighteenth-century leaders had chosen to deal with the problem of homosexuality by requiring that male homosexuals be castrated instead of killed, late nineteenth- and early twentieth-century leaders turned to medical professionals for solutions, which ranged from hypnosis and drug and shock therapy to lobotomies, which were performed as late as 1951.[44]

---

43. The term "straight" for heterosexuals unavoidably plays a similar function in a heteronormative society as the term "white" plays in a racist society. Both terms reinforce cultural thinking that one group is superior to the other aberrant group. Just as "white" signifies all that is good, "straight" signifies the correct way to be — normative, straight, well-adjusted, good, as opposed to crooked, bent, incorrect, bad. It becomes difficult to think about the "not-straight" group as equal in a culture that reinforces the value of heterosexuality — straight — with other positive references: straight as the good or right way to be. When someone comes off alcohol or drugs she/he is considered "straight." In this respect, an unhidden social message is that someone should come off homosexuality and become "straight."

44. Katz, *Gay American History,* 129.

As in the case of early leaders turning to Hebrew scriptures for homosexual punishment, this history of violent oppression influenced U.S. culture. It is not by accident, however, that male homosexual activity, and not female homosexual activity, was often written about in sacred texts. Since a large part of our religious understanding of homosexuality is a result of the Judeo-Christian tradition, understanding the Hebrew and Christian writers' emphasis on male sexuality and homosexuality assists us in understanding contemporary cultural and religious responses and African American church and cultural responses about gender as well as sexuality.

Ancient Hebrew culture, like other ancient cultures, emphasized procreation as a significant practice for survival. Indeed, many of the biblical passages on sexual matters, gender, and procreation appear to have been shaped by the need to have as many children as possible so that a few might survive the harsh environment.[45] In the orders of creation, God (Yahweh) calls for man and woman "to be fruitful and multiply." Fundamental to this sexual moral code was that all marital sex practices lead toward a reproductive end. Biblical scholars and theologians like James Nelson assert that this ethic is related to that time period's concern about extinction, given the constant loss of life in families and communities under siege from famine, disease, and wars.[46]

Not surprisingly, such concerns affected people's attitude toward homosexuality. Since there was no understanding of a male homosexual as such, male homosexual acts (which they perceived as a possibility for any man) seem to have been prohibited by Levitical law in part because reproduction could not occur, and because "the pre-scientific Hebrew mind, particularly the pre-scientific male mind, assumed that the man's semen contained the whole of nascent life. With no knowledge of egg and ovulation, it was assumed that the woman provided only the incubating space. Hence

---

45. C. Meyers, *Discovering Eve: Ancient Israelite Women in Context* (New York: Oxford University Press, 1988).

46. James Nelson, *Embodiment* (Minneapolis: Augsburg, 1978), 182.

the deliberate non-procreative spilling of semen was equivalent to the deliberate destruction of human life."[47]

A Gradual Progression of
Understanding Homosexuality

While the Algers case, like the "gross indecency" case of Oscar Wilde and similar cases, elicited religious and social disapproval, the burgeoning of scientific and psychological discoveries of the late nineteenth and early twentieth centuries witnessed some movement in the culture from viewing homosexuality as a societal wickedness to a malady existing in certain individuals. For religious communities, there was little change toward anyone not deemed heterosexual. Although a majority of persons who had same-sex desires understood their desires as sick and perverse, as the church and society defined them, critical studies by sexologist Havelock Ellis and others questioned traditionally held beliefs about sexual attraction and thus began a cultural shift in understanding human sexuality. Sigmund Freud and others contributed to this discussion by arguing that sexuality is fluid, a result of many biological, psychological, and sociological factors.

Around the same time, Dr. Magnus Hirschfield, a homosexual physician, sexologist, and founder of the first homosexual emancipation organization in Germany, argued that since homosexuality was an inborn sexual variation and unchangeable, its criminalization was unjustified. Even some homosexuals who may have thought of themselves as inferior to heterosexuals, in the same way as some blacks understood themselves to be inferior to whites, opposed the mistreatment and persecution that they faced by a heterosexual majority. In 1924, the Society for Human Rights, located in Chicago, became a civil rights organization designed to oppose homosexual oppression and discrimination in much the same way that fifteen years earlier the National Association for

---

47. Ibid.

the Advancement of Colored People had been organized to oppose racial oppression and discrimination.[48]

The organization of the Mattachine Society, a quarter century later, would further address lesbian and gay oppression in a way that would contribute to the present success of the civil rights movement for lesbians and gays. The Mattachine Society, founded by Harry Hay in 1950, also established itself as an organization that opposed gay oppression. The efforts of this organization galvanized lesbians and gays into communities that advocated equal treatment.

The Kinsey and Hooker Studies

No other work can claim more responsibility for challenging long-held and unfounded notions about homosexuality than the studies initiated by social scientists Alfred Kinsey and Evelyn Hooker. Their studies debunked negatively biased theories designed by psychologists Edmund Bergler and later Irving Bieber.[49] Not only did these studies parallel the fabricated psychological studies that "defined" blacks as inherently inferior to whites, some studies, like Bieber's, set out to depict gays as sick individuals just because of their sexual difference, regardless of function. In most cases, sick homosexuals were used to represent the entire group. An investigation into the subjects of Bieber's study found that 101 of 106 homosexual subjects were already being treated for a psychological disorder or "preselected for psychopathology, so the question of emotional disturbance of the homosexual population at large could not be addressed."[50] During the mid-twentieth century, the argument that homosexuality is a mental illness received a number of serious challenges. One of the first challenges to homosexuality

---

48. Ibid., 385.

49. See Bergler's "Differential Diagnosis between Spurious Homosexuality and Perversion Homosexuality," *Psychoanalytic Quarterly* 31 (1947): 399–401.

50. K. Lewes, *The Psychoanalytic Theory of Male Homosexuality* (Markham, Ont., Canada: Penguin Books, 1988), 209.

as pathology came from Alfred Kinsey's research in 1948, followed by the Ford and Beach anthropological studies in 1951 and Evelyn Hooker's work in 1954. The Kinsey and Hooker studies exposed the culture's dishonesty about homosexuals as a vile and pathological group of individuals.

Alfred Kinsey

Directly responding to the negative "studies" on homosexuality, in his expansive studies on human sexuality in *Sexual Behavior in the Human Male* and *Sexual Behavior in the Human Female*, Kinsey asserts that much of the pathology of homosexuals is a result of the hostile conditions and negative social teachings they experience. The reality of an oppressive social environment leading to pathology had also been noted by black and women psychologists about African Americans and women. Psychologist Karen Horney emerged as one female psychologist to identify gender oppression as harmful to women, followed by Kenneth Clarke's famous doll study that identified the adverse effects of segregation in *Brown v. Board of Education*, overturning "separate but equal" as constitutional.

Kinsey, an Indiana University zoology professor, encountered insufficient and unscientific claims about homosexuality when he studied sex research for class lectures. The Kinsey studies exist as a result of Kinsey's frustration with limited sex research of the early twentieth century.[51] Kinsey argues that his study, unlike previous studies on sex which imported normative claims and assumptions, simply informs communities about the sexual pluralism of human beings. In other words, Kinsey argues that Bergler and Bieber allowed their personal judgments to interfere with their scholarship. Kinsey points out that "in many of the published studies on sex there was obvious confusion of moral values, philosophic theory, and the scientific fact."[52]

---

51. A. Kinsey et al., *Sexual Behavior in the Human Male* (Philadelphia: W. B. Sanders, 1948), 9.
52. Ibid.

Perhaps the two greatest contributions of this study were the finding of how large a percentage of people enjoyed same-sex sexual expression and the degree to which most people have some level of erotic desire for the same and opposite sex. Kinsey reports, for example, "thirty-seven percent of the male population had engaged in physical contact to the point of orgasm with other men at some time between adolescence and old age."[53] Data such as this are used in the Kinsey studies to inform the public of the prevalence of same-sex sexual behavior. Neither Kinsey nor his team of researchers argues that 37 percent of the male population is homosexual. Considering that similar sexual responses were found among the female population, Kinsey and his researchers do, however, wish to raise the awareness of society concerning human sexuality and the plurality of sexual desire, informing the public — including religious leaders — that the "incidence and frequency of homosexual [expression] apply in varying degrees to every social level, to persons in every occupation, and of every age in the community."[54]

This discovery is the matrix of the Heterosexual-Homosexual rating scale. Commonly referred to as the "Kinsey scale," this scale measures the wide range of sexual desire in human beings. It is most helpful in that it attributes some degree of same- and opposite-sex attraction in most individuals, but allows for a wide range of variation in regard to the degree of attraction to one or the other sex.[55] Kinsey constructed this scale as a way of demonstrating sexual variance in humans.

Prior to this study, the common social (and I would add religious) understanding of homosexuals cast male homosexuals as not fully male, but quite similar to females with "fine skins, high-pitched voices, obvious hand movements, a feminine carriage of the hips and peculiarities of walking gaits."[56] Such generalizations set up two distinct categories of men, reinforcing past negative stereotypes that men who display nonmacho behaviors are pathological and not

53. Ibid., 43.
54. Ibid., 665.
55. Ibid., 638.
56. Ibid., 637.

real men. This scale challenges such claims by showing the overlap of opposite and same-sex desire in males, and that "the histories which have been made available in the present study make it apparent that heterosexuality or homosexuality of many individuals is not an all-or-none proposition."[57] Kinsey outlined his scale using numbers 0–6, with 0 representing exclusive heterosexuality, 1 and 2 showing a few cases of satisfying same-sex sexual attraction, 3 representing a relatively equal attraction to both sexes, 4 and 5 identifying a few satisfying opposite-sex sexual experiences and 6 representing exclusive homosexuality.

Without question, this important study made a dent in the old notion that homosexuals, especially gay men, were in and of themselves sick individuals, freaks of nature, wholly different individuals who preyed on the weakness of young boys by molesting them. In a day when almost no one "came out," it was easier to associate homosexuality with a sickness since child molesters became the example that most people had of homosexual men.

This notion fits perfectly with black church indoctrination that homosexuals are like the men in the biblical story of Sodom and Gomorrah. Wrestling with the social and religious messages that taught them that they were bad and should be ashamed of themselves, one can understand why notable black church homosexuals like George Washington Carver and James Cleveland concealed their homosexuality. Social and religious views about homosexuals have remained negative in history. The few known historical figures such as Michelangelo, Socrates, Oscar Wilde, Sappho, Virginia Woolf, Walt Whitman, or Aaron Copland were either dismissed or felt to be lacking in adjustment or spiritual quality.

Evelyn Hooker's Study

In the 1950s, psychologist Evelyn Hooker launched a social scientific investigation to see whether homosexual men were indeed inferior to heterosexual men in their morality and adjustment. In response to Bergler's pseudoscientific studies on pathological

---

57. Ibid., 638.

homosexuality, Hooker began her research on male homosexuals. The ultimate goal of her research was to reveal the validity, if any, of a higher degree of pathology in homosexuals. The result of Hooker's findings, however, presents a stark contrast to Bergler's claims that homosexuals are severely disturbed and distinguishable. Contrary to Bergler's view, clinicians in Hooker's study discovered that they could not distinguish the case material and Rorschach test responses of heterosexual males from the homosexual males. Both groups displayed similar levels of pathology and adjustment, with many homosexuals scoring very high and many heterosexuals scoring very low. Her findings — published in the 1957 *Journal of Projective Techniques* as "The Adjustment of The Male Overt Homosexual" — also validate that a hostile society contributes significantly to the pathology of homosexuals. Hooker's work became a crucial element in rethinking homosexuality and in 1973 contributed to the removal of homosexuality from the list of mental disorders in the American Psychiatric Association's *Diagnostic and Statistical Manual of Psychiatric Disorders*.

Stonewall, African American Gay Consciousness, and Rethinking Homosexuality in the Church

Just as the challenges to racism instilled racial pride in African Americans and emboldened African Americans to demand equality, African American along with Anglo-American gays and others found encouragement from modern research that offered an accurate assessment of homosexuality, rather than statements based on prejudice. This research raised their consciousness and compelled them to demand equal treatment from the society and later the church. Likened to Rosa Parks's defiance of racial bigotry, the 1969 Stonewall Rebellion, the first militant protest of gays against homophobia in the United States, set in motion a movement dedicated to promoting lesbian and gay equality in the United States. Black and white lesbian and gay leaders (many of whom had participated in

protests and demonstrations against racial segregation and discrimination) modeled their nonviolent protests on the women's protest
for suffrage and equality in the 1920s and the black activism of the
1950s and 1960s. By the 1970s, lesbian and gay awareness became
a part of many discussions taking place within social, educational,
political, and mainly white religious arenas.

During this same period, gay Christian church leaders found inspiration from the courageous efforts of a gay Pentecostal preacher,
Troy Perry, and began to oppose the homophobia and heterosexual
supremacy of mainline churches. Perry founded the first historically gay Christian denomination, the Universal Fellowship of
Metropolitan Community Churches, in Los Angeles in 1968. He
was later joined by other dedicated gay and lesbian Christian ministers such as Malcolm Boyd, James Tinney, Carl Bean, Janie Spahr,
and Mel White, who oppose church oppression and are civil rights
leaders of gay equality.

Frustrated with the continued homophobic practices of black pastors, in the 1980s a few black lesbians and gays began forming black
lesbian and gay churches.[58] Like their white counterparts who refused to accept the homophobia in mainline churches, a number of
black gay ministers formed churches for other black gay Christians
after challenging homophobia in black churches. Today, a growing
number of African American lesbian and gay Christians are refusing to accept black church oppression and consider homosexual
condemnation as contrary to the message of love and liberation presented in the gospel of Jesus. Drawing from liberation theology, this
group of African American lesbian and gay Christians and others
challenge black churches and the larger Christian church with this
question: If the majority Christian culture today recognizes that
earlier Christians should not have adhered to certain biblical passages on slavery and should not have supported the subsequent

---

58. In chapter 7, I discuss Troy Perry's work in detail, along with James
Tinney's and Carl Bean's pioneering work for African American lesbian and
gay Christians in the establishment of Faith Temple and Unity Fellowship
congregations, respectively.

racial oppression, how does the same Christian culture justify the present adherence to a few biblical passages that allegedly depict gays as immoral and, as a result, deserving of denigration and unequal treatment? Given this problem, it is here that we take a closer look at the black church's biblical responses to homosexuality and the tension that presently exists for lesbian, gay, and heterosexual congregants.

Chapter 2

The Black Church, the Bible,
and the Battle over Homosexuality

RELIGION PLAYS A VITAL ROLE in the lives of African peoples, providing them with a moral compass in their families and communities. Black church historian Albert Raboteau reminds us that Africans came to the Americas religious but not Christian; most entered this land as practitioners of the traditional African religions and Islam. When examining African cultures, "scholars have always agreed that religion permeates every dimension of African life."[1] As a culture, Africans and their descendants are of course not alone in valuing religion; Europeans, as well as other groups, also value religion, and indeed share some similar spiritual beliefs. Both groups came to America believing in a spirit world, the power of dead ancestors, and godly retribution.[2] In some cases, Christian practices paralleled those of the traditional African practices so much that Christianity had a great appeal to Africans and allowed for a continuation of their religion. This blending or syncretism of traditional African religion with Christianity enabled the transition from African religion to Christianity.

Even after being converted to Christianity in the context of slavery, Africans generally considered religion and religious practice important aspects of their lives. They always valued religion and understood God and Jesus as having sustained them through slavery and having given them the hope for and the experience of a

---

1. Peter J. Paris, *The Spirituality of African Peoples: The Search for a Common Moral Discourse* (Minneapolis: Fortress Press, 1995), 27.
2. Ibid.

liberated life. It is therefore no surprise that religion plays such a big role in the lives of contemporary African Americans.

African American slaves maintained elements of their traditional African beliefs and Islam for decades, but in a slave culture that largely controlled their religious practice, they eventually adopted Christianity as their primary religion, dismissing African religions as illegitimate. Raboteau characterizes this transition as "death of the gods."[3] Phyllis Wheatley's own words about herself as a Christian would later become a common representation of African Americans' religious worldview:

> 'Twas mercy brought me from my Pagan land,
> Taught my benighted soul to understand
> That there's a God, that there's a Saviour too....[4]

Despite the initial reluctance by many white slave owners to Christianize African slaves due to their anxiety that a Christian status could disrupt the master-slave relationship, white Christian ministers later received African American slaves into Christianity, indoctrinating them with a selective biblical ethical code that emphasized subordination, slave ethics, and sexual immorality.

The Making of Black Christians

African Americans looked for other similarities in the religion of their white masters. The first and second Great Awakenings and the evangelism of the Baptist and the Methodist denominations in particular had the greatest appeal for African Americans due to their more demonstrative and less rigid style of worship as well as their emphasis on the Bible. As a consequence, African Americans primarily identified with these two communions during and after slavery. Hence, "the majority of the black preachers and separate black churches were Baptist, which helps to explain why the Baptists attracted as many members as they did. Baptists simply

---

3. Raboteau, *Slave Religion*, 44.
4. Paris, *Spirituality of African Peoples*, 46.

offered more opportunity for black participation than any other denomination."[5] When African Americans found themselves in other denominations, like the Episcopal Church of their masters, they often exercised their freedom after slavery and united with black Baptist and Methodist denominations.[6] Slaves soon valued Christianity as the invisible institution that fostered their ability to cope with the atrocities of slavery. Religion established a dominant presence in the lives of most black people.

Since the majority of African American slaves became Christian through the evangelical efforts of Methodists and Baptists during the Great Awakening revivals and plantation missions, they also adopted the conservative Christian traditions and strict adherence to the Bible characteristic of these denominations. This particular strain of Christianity differed from the liberal Quaker tradition that opposed slavery and emphasized gender equality and an "inner light" in all people, and the Roman Catholic, Congregationalist, and Episcopal traditions that placed less emphasis on scripture and proselytizing. Despite Quakers' and Congregationalists' dedicated efforts to abolish the slavery endured by blacks, African American slaves found the quiet, nondemonstrative worship style of these denominations less familiar and therefore less appealing.

The Bible in "Black and White":
Baptists and Methodists

The theological perspective of slavery as unchristian rarely impressed white conservative Protestants; indeed, they found biblical sanction for their participation in slavery. The importance of scripture within white conservative Protestant circles found similar appreciation and symbolic meaning among African Americans, and was indeed valued as the word of God. Baptists, in particular,

---

5. Raboteau, *Slave Religion*, 187–88; also see Richard E. Wentz, *Religion in the New World: The Shaping of Religious Traditions in the United States* (Minneapolis: Fortress Press, 1990).

6. Gardiner H. Shattuck, *Episcopalians and Race: Civil War to Civil Rights* (Lexington: University Press of Kentucky, 2000), 8.

emphasized "the notion that ultimate authority resided in 'God's word,' the Bible," unlike Catholic Christianity where "neither the Bible nor the sermon played as important a role."[7] In light of this reality, the lack of other educational resources, and the seriousness with which blacks approached their faith, African Americans highly regarded this sacred book as God's intention for them. African Americans listened attentively to the sermons taken from the Bible by white and black preachers. Through reading the Bible and listening to the passages taught to them through sermons, African Americans typically became "Bible Christians."[8]

African Americans, the Bible, and the Invisible Institution

This biblical indoctrination by conservative white Protestants laid a foundation for African Americans' understanding of scripture in strict literal and legalistic ways. Conservative white Protestants generally taught blacks that it was the Bible itself that insisted they were to be slaves to whites. Among the African American Christian slaves who accepted this perspective was the famous preacher Jupiter Hammond.

A poet and preacher, Hammond did not condone the institution of slavery and, despite his doubts about whether blacks could handle freedom, hoped for black emancipation. Nonetheless, he thought that physical freedom should not take precedence over spiritual freedom and that there should be "reinforcement of the master-slave relationship."[9] If Hammond's view seems contradictory, it is a reflection of the quandary in which many black

---

7. Raboteau, *Slave Religion*, 272.

8. The term "Bible Christian" is used here to suggest that African Americans became affiliated with denominations that emphasized a strict adherence to scripture. This should not be read, however, that blacks, like white Bible Christians, did not emphasize certain passages over others and, in some cases, interpret passages as not being applicable to them.

9. Milton C. Sernett, ed., *Afro-American Religious History: A Documentary Witness* (Durham, NC: Duke University Press, 1985), 35.

Christians found themselves: at one and the same time understanding God to be the arbiter of justice and freedom and yet also aware of scriptural passages that they understood as identifying God as upholding the institution of slavery and thus their slave status.

However, most African American Christians did not find the slavery passages compelling. As African American biblical scholar Vincent Wimbush notes,

> ... from the beginning of their engagement with [the Bible] African Americans interpreted the Bible differently from those who introduced them to it, ironically and audaciously seeing in it — the most powerful of the ideological weapons used to legitimize their enslavement and disenfranchisement — a mirroring of themselves and their experiences, seeing in it the privileging of all those who like themselves are the humiliated, the outcasts and powerless.[10]

As black Christians embraced biblical stories of Jesus' love and God's liberating power, it became more and more difficult to reconcile a God who delivered Israelites from oppressive Pharaohs with a God who was apparently keeping them enslaved. In this approach to scripture, blacks, like other groups, demonstrate a practice of selectively choosing scripture. This selection bias attends to information that confirms what is already believed (based on teachings and interpretations of that community) and offers validation while viewing other biblical injunctions as irrelevant to their present status. Thus, the Bible can and historically has been used by the oppressors and the oppressed, each for their own liberation and benefit. Yet it is much too simplistic to refer to the Bible in binary ways as either an oppressive book or a liberationist document. As noted by African American biblical scholar Dr. Renita Weems, the Bible has less to do with either oppression or liberation. Rather, Christians read the Bible and assign meaning to create oppression or liberation in their lives and the lives of other human beings.

---

10. Vincent L. Wimbush, ed., *African Americans and the Bible: Sacred Texts and Social Textures* (New York: Continuum, 2000), 17.

Nancy Ambrose, the slave grandmother of African American theologian Howard Thurman, expressed this reality in the following case:

> During the days of slavery, . . . master's minister would occasionally hold services for the slaves. Always the white minister used as his text something from Paul. Slaves be obedient to your masters as unto Christ. Then he would go on to show that if we were good and happy slaves, God would bless us. I promised my maker that if I ever learned to read and if freedom ever came, I would not read that part of the Bible.[11]

This example points to the limitations of scripture and the different hermeneutical or interpretive lenses that a Christian culture may bring to a passage. As Wimbush's analysis and Ambrose's Christian experience affirm, black people's experience of God's grace and Christ's presence in their lives made them full and equal children of God. In Ambrose's mind, Paul's biblical writing suggesting that as a slave Ambrose was subordinate to free whites failed in its meaning and reflection of God's intention. For her, faith and relationship with God told her that she was a child of God and should be treated the same as whites who claimed God's favor, regardless of what was stated in the Bible.

The Bible and African American Christian Resistance to Slavery

The above example also shows that African American Christians demonstrate that you can be faithful Christians without accepting all scripture as authoritative. The rejection of scriptures that support slavery is the clearest example. So in the context of slavery, two theologies emerged from the same Bible and Christian religion: one initially supported by a majority of white Christians who promoted slavery, and the other supported by a majority of blacks

---

11. Howard Thurman, *Jesus and the Disinherited* (New York: Abingdon-Cokesbury Press, 1949), 30–31.

who opposed slavery. Both groups used the Bible to endorse their cultural views and practices.

Many black Christians, like Frederick Douglass and Ambrose, refused any theological doctrine that subjugated them, and protested white supremacy both privately and publicly. In 1787, the first such protest of white racism in the church came from African American Methodist minister Richard Allen and others. After experiencing racism in the white Methodist Church, Allen, Absalom Jones (the first ordained black priest in the Episcopal Church), and others left, and instead organized the Free African Society. Twenty-nine years later, Allen would organize the first black denomination, the African Methodist Episcopal Church.

One of the most powerful displays of this kind of Christian protest came from Bostonian David Walker, a young free African American abolitionist. In his now-famous *Appeal to the Colored Citizens of the World*, Walker uses the biblical Exodus story to declare that God's judgment on white America would be like the destructions inflicted upon the thousands of Egyptians whom God hurled into the Red Sea for afflicting his people in their land. He called on blacks to "prepare the way of the Lord" by "throwing off the yoke of slavery."[12]

Some African American Christians, like Nat Turner, believed that biblical passages of this sort revealed God's intention that they overthrow the evil system of slavery. In 1831, Turner took the Bible at its word and executed the most deadly protest of slavery. Unlike the attempted insurrections of Prosser and Vesey, Turner's revolt was largely successful. A slave preacher and visionary of "righteous vengeance," Turner confessed before his execution that God had directed him to lead a bloody slave revolt that claimed the lives of some fifty-five whites.[13] The publication of *The Confessions of Nat Turner* reveals that Turner never repented for the revolt, since in his mind it was a God-inspired act revealed in scripture as

---

12. Sernett, *Afro-American Religious History*, 31.
13. Ibid., 88.

"the hosts of good would meet the armies of evil."[14] Though these biblical interpretations were viewed as extreme by most African American church leaders, these leaders still viewed scripture regarding slavery and black subjugation in fundamentally different ways than whites, and taught this interpretation to generations of blacks. African Americans identified with the Israelites in the Bible and interpreted the Civil War as God creating dramatic events to bring about their liberation from slavery. As such hermeneutics created a community of black people, it also demonstrated that God was on their side and would take care of them.

African Americans, the Bible, the Visible Institution, and Homosexuality

The black church has functioned as the center of black people's lives from its origins as an invisible institution during chattel slavery to its present day as a highly visible institution. Being one of the few institutions owned by black people for black people, the black church, at its best, has not only served as a house of worship, but has also provided social status, hope, and stability for the millions of Africans who have lived in America. As black sociologist E. Franklin Frazier notes, the black church is "a nation within a nation . . . [the impetus for other] institutions such as schools, banks, insurance companies, and low income housing . . . an academy and arena for political activities [and a place that] nurtured young talent for musical, dramatic and artistic development."[15] It has provided places of worship that black people could own and offered a community of "comfort, nurture and care among an outcast people, a refuge in a hostile white world, where they could sing, shout and laugh and cry among those who understood and shared the pain [of racism]."[16]

---

14. William Styron, *The Confessions of Nat Turner* (New York: Random House, 1967), 88.

15. Lincoln and Mamiya, *The Black Church in the African-American Experience*, 8, citing E. Franklin Frazier.

16. Ibid., 272.

Despite this rich history of using the Bible to oppose oppression, black church leaders have ironically not taken a similar approach on sexual oppression and oppressive religious and societal actions against black women, lesbian and heterosexual, and gay men. Instead, blacks often internalize this country's racist sexual depictions of a black sexuality that is out of control and in need of salvation by Christianity. As a consequence, black bodies have been devalued, bought and controlled in slavery by whites who "[felt] no compunction about exploiting those bodies for their sexual gratification, . . . [subjecting] black women . . . to sexual abuse and black men . . . as progenitors of new slaves through siring."[17]

Womanist theologian Kelly Brown Douglas asserts that whites in general still perceive "black men and women as [being] highly sexualized, lascivious beings . . . prone to a 'sexual prowess' or 'sexual promiscuity.'"[18] Such representations are not uncommon within black communities and pop culture of rap and hip-hop videos. In this respect, African Americans have internalized some of the racist sexual depictions of themselves as sexually obsessed individuals or sex predators. Even when there is acknowledgment of being sexually active, African Americans may not feel good about sexual expression, even when it is in loving, caring relationships.

Douglas goes on to say that African Americans are inheritors of a racist past that victimized all aspects of their lives, not the least of which was their sexuality. Following slavery, the racist attitudes that defined black men as sex predators caused black men extreme hardship and death. By appealing to the age-old stereotype that black men harbor an insatiable sexual desire for white women, black men existed as targets to be blamed for raping white women. Rape was used more than any other reason as the cause for lynching black men.[19] Indeed as Paula Giddings notes, it was black women

---

17. Samuel K. Roberts, *African American Church Ethics* (Cleveland: Pilgrim Press, 2001), 229.

18. Kelly Brown Douglas, *Sexuality and the Black Church: A Womanist Perspective* (Maryknoll, NY: Orbis Books, 1999), 11.

19. David Lewis, *W. E. B. DuBois: The Fight for Equality and the American Century, 1919–1963* (New York: Henry Holt, 2000), 296–97.

themselves and not white men who were identified as the culprits for their own rape due to the purported insatiable appetite that blacks had for sex. This mythical construction by white racist men became an excuse for lynching black men. Lynching functioned as the white male solution to protecting white women from the sexual savagery of black men. Given the majority culture's racism and sexual attitudes, African Americans soon learned that their very survival depended on distancing themselves from any representation of "sexual perversions." Much of black heterosexuals' antihomosexual sentiment exists as a means of countering the perception of black sexuality being perverse in order to survive and gain respectability and acceptance by the majority. Thus, it is understandable that African Americans would approach homosexuality with more dread and disdain than others, often denying a black homosexual presence to avoid being further maligned in a racist society.

As in the days of slavery, the black church maintains a conservative theological approach to issues of gender, sexuality, and sexual expression. All of the historically black denominations — the African Methodist Episcopal; African Methodist Episcopal Zion; Christian Methodist Episcopal (formerly Colored Methodist Episcopal); National Baptist Church, USA, Inc.; National Baptist Church of America, National Progressive Baptist Church; and the Church of God in Christ — have restrictive doctrinal views about sexuality. All of these church bodies promote a theological view that homosexuality is sinful and that the only legitimate sexual expression is toward the opposite sex in marriage.

It is difficult to determine exactly when Africans and African Americans integrated negative views about homosexual expression into their theology and espoused antihomosexual pronouncements in black religious and social communities. History shows that it was Europeans who strongly influenced Africans and African Americans to adopt puritanical views about sexuality and homosexuality.[20] As European Christian missionaries encountered black

---

20. For a full discussion of this indoctrination to sex-negative and antihomosexual views by white conservative Protestants, see Murray and Roscoe, *Boy Wives and Female Husbands.*

Africans, it was common for them to identify Africans as unholy and uncivilized, as "lewd, lascivious, and wanton people."[21] This racist sexualizing of black people impacted African Americans in a variety of negative ways, leaving black leaders in a perpetual reaction of hiding black sexuality.

Black leaders adopted a rigid biblical theology of sexuality and transmitted it to black Christians and black culture. Whereas from the beginning blacks refused to simply accept whites' interpretation of scripture, the same "hermeneutic of suspicion" did not occur regarding scripture and sexuality. Wimbush is correct that the understanding of sexual mores outside of heterosexual marriage and the understanding of gender roles is hardly different between the predominantly white Southern Baptists and the predominantly black National Baptists.

The sex-negative Christian tradition and demonized black sexuality make the issue of sexuality especially onerous for African American lesbians and gays in black churches. For the past century, in an effort to gain respectability, African American pastors, college presidents, and educators like W. E. B. DuBois promoted dualistic notions of sexuality and conservative sexual mores in order to gain respectability from the mainstream white ruling class.[22] On black college campuses and in black elite social clubs, Victorian sexual mores reigned supreme.

So how did this come to be? Following slavery, many of the African American leaders received their education about the body from "Puritan" New England missionaries (founders of the first

---

21. Douglas, *Sexuality and the Black Church*, 33.

22. In *Black Bourgeoisie: The Rise of a New Middle Class in the United States* (New York: Collier Books, 1957), E. Franklin Frazier documents that educated blacks led this sexual purity/respectability campaign to win favor from whites and lower the risk of sexual violence (rape and lynching) directed against blacks by proving they were not the oversexed sexual brutes that they had been portrayed as by racist whites. Thus, the historically black college campuses were patrolled by austere New England spinsters and DuBoisian gentlemen and ladies who imposed severely strict sexual codes, expunging any young woman or man who refused to abide by the rules and present pristine behavior. The remnants of this era can be witnessed on black college campuses today.

black colleges); later black educators instilled in young black minds negative messages about the sexual expression of black bodies by stressing that "it was only 'common' Negroes who engaged in premarital and unconventional sex relations. . . ."[23] As famed black sociologist E. Franklin Frazier notes in *Black Bourgeoisie*, black educators on black college campuses put forth this image of the "chaste" black body as "proof of respectability in the eyes of the white man, who had constantly argued that the Negro's 'savage instincts' prevented him from conforming to puritanical standards of sex behavior."[24]

Douglas argues that this internalized negativity about black bodies can still be observed in behavior expressed by black church members, such as women covering their legs when sitting in the pew.[25] For generations black people lived under the assumption that because they were perceived as sex predators they would also pay the ultimate price. In order to gain respectability and simply to survive, black people adopted a sexual conservatism, if not sexual prudishness. So while it is understandable that blacks would distance themselves from society's "sexual perversions" such as homosexuality, it is unfortunate that such a reaction has led a black majority to adopt harsh attitudes toward lesbian and gay people, their relationships and equality.

Homosexuality in Black Churches

In most black churches, parishioners experienced sermons identifying homosexuality not only as a sin, but with a rage that placed it as an even greater sin, as a monstrosity, a part of a wicked spirit. One of the first recorded accounts of a black minister leading an organized protest against homosexuality and black gays is from the early twentieth century. In 1929, during the Harlem Renaissance that gave birth to a number of gay African American artists, including Richard Bruce Nugent and Alain Locke, African American pastor

---

23. Ibid., 71.
24. Ibid.
25. Douglas, *Sexuality and the Black Church*, 31, 83.

Adam Clayton Powell Sr., of Harlem's famous Abyssinian Baptist Church, "initiated a vigorous crusade against homosexuality."[26] Powell's "crusade" is the first of what would become a common response of African American ministers. Messages that would ordinarily be considered messages of hate were justified by black ministers as being faithful to their calling to preach against sinful behavior.

More than fifty years later, on May 5, 1985, at another famous New York City church — Riverside — the Reverend Dr. Channing Phillips, an African American heterosexual supremacist minister, used the Bible (Gen. 1:27) to denounce gay love relationships:

> Male and female God created them... it is difficult to avoid the conclusion that heterosexuality... is being lifted up as the model of human sexuality.... Those are hard words... that imply that deviation from the parable of heterosexual relationship ordained by marriage is contrary to God's will — is sin.... And no theological or exegetical sleight of hand can erase that word of the Lord.[27]

Just as pastors Adam Clayton Powell Sr. and Jr. had railed against homosexuality decades earlier (the present pastor, the Reverend Calvin Butts, has also followed in this manner), Channing Phillips made it clear to the gay Christians present that he understood their

---

26. Thomas Wirth, ed. *Gay Rebel of the Harlem Renaissance: Selections from the Work of Richard Bruce Nugent* (Durham, NC: Duke University Press, 2002), 22; also Jervis Anderson, *Bayard Rustin: Troubles I've Seen: A Biography* (New York: HarperCollins Publishing, 1997), 229–30, notes that Congressman Adam Clayton Powell Jr. (also a minister) would follow in his father's footsteps of anti-gay sentiment by attacking long-time gay African American civil rights activist, King advisor, and architect of the 1963 March on Washington Bayard Rustin, which eventually led to Rustin's resignation from the Southern Christian Leadership Conference (SCLC). Rustin's resignation from SCLC was prompted amid threats from a Powell source that if he did not resign "Powell would announce publicly that King and Rustin were involved in a sexual relationship."

27. James B. Nelson, *Body Theology* (Louisville: Westminster/John Knox Press, 1992), 55.

relationships to be inconsistent with God's intention for human-kind.[28] However, unlike fifty-five years earlier when Powell Sr. led his crusade against black gays, this time there was a counter-response by a white heterosexual man who invited congregants to join him at the front of the church at the end of the service. Singing the last hymn, over five hundred worshipers stood with him as a demonstration of the love, justice, and equality that they felt for their lesbian and gay sisters and brothers.

Dr. William Sloane Coffin, the white heterosexual senior pastor at that time, disturbed by the bigotry, preached a sermon the following Sunday that was in sharp contrast to the message delivered by Dr. Phillips. Coffin acknowledged the pain and struggle that Christians on both sides must feel:

> I can only begin to imagine the hurt and anger felt by those of you who thought you had found here at Riverside what you had almost despaired of finding anywhere: a church where, despite the misinformation, superstitions and prejudices of our culture, not only black and white could feel at home, celebrating and affirming each other's existence in the name of Jesus Christ, but also gay and straight. I can also understand the pain of others who thought that what they had heard confirmed their moral apprehensions about homosexuality, only to have these apprehensions questioned by a demonstration. . . .[29]

Nonetheless, Coffin did not hesitate, declaring that "we now have a sharply divided church . . . [over] homosexuality . . . the most divisive issue the churches of America have encountered, or evaded, since slavery."[30] He stated, "I do not see how Christians can define and then exclude people on the basis of sexual orientation. . . ." The following two Sundays, other Riverside clergy made "clear

---

28. In a 1988 *Amsterdam News* article, Butts declared that "while the church has a 'divine responsibility' to those who live with AIDS, drug addiction and homosexuality are still against the will of God" (Cathy Cohen, *The Boundaries of Blackness* [Chicago: University of Chicago Press, 1999], 101).

29. Ibid., 56.

30. Ibid.

their convictions affirming the church's inclusiveness of all sexual orientations."[31]

Though his was a common black ministerial response, Channing Phillips's example is not to suggest that all African American ministers are heterosexual supremacists. Some African American heterosexual ministers disagree with the position of many fellow African American clergy in the same way that they oppose white homophobic ministers' condemnation of gays. However, an overwhelming number support Phillips's theological understanding and resist viewing this perspective as oppressive. Such uncritical responses send forth a message that concern for oppression is only a concern when the oppression is racial oppression. Regarding issues of sexual equality within the church, many of the proponents are white and many of the opponents are black, with very few black heterosexuals advocating for gay equality in black churches.[32]

Like the parishioners at the Riverside Church, African American Christians also find themselves presently in the middle of what has become a moral dilemma. Although a black church Christian majority continues to view homosexuality as immoral, some find themselves conflicted with the traditional perspective of identifying homosexuality as sin. Others attempt to sidestep the issue by resorting to a Christian view of "love the sinner, hate the sin." Many find this perspective illogical. They argue if same-sex sexual attraction or expression is what makes the person gay, then what is being loved? With sexuality being an inextricable part of one's being, the

---

31. Ibid.

32. In 2000, Rev. Jimmy Creech, a white heterosexual United Methodist pastor, was stripped of his credentials because he opposed the injustice of the denomination that denies its lesbian and gay Christian members the rite of marriage. Although many white heterosexual Christian ministers continue to deny lesbian and gay Christians ordination and marriage, there are some who have ordained and married gays. This is not the case in the historically black denominations. While no black denomination has ordained an openly gay black minister, recently the oldest black denomination, the African Methodist Episcopal (AME) church, became the first black denomination to deny ordination to an openly gay black man, Tommie Watkins.

popular saying has as much success in reality as loving brown-eyed people while hating brown eyes.

African Americans' rage and silence about homosexuality reflect this pervasive black cultural sexual shame and often leads to pain and abuse for both gays and heterosexuals. Yet it is striking that most of these perceptions have been constructed from the often vitriolic anti-gay sermons by black ministers. With so few resources on homosexuality and the black Christian faith, African Americans experience difficulty adopting progressive Christian views that place homosexuality on par with heterosexuality. Almost nothing has been written on the subject from a black religious standpoint and even less engaging social scientific and theological perspectives. This is a problem. It has only been within the last decade that a few scholarly resources emerged addressing homosexuality and black faith.

In *Sexuality and the Black Church* and *One More River to Cross*, authors Kelly Brown Douglas and Keith Boykin, respectively, assert that a significant number of African American heterosexuals are moving from some of the past derisions and beginning to accept African American lesbians and gays. And while Douglas and Boykin correctly point out that a decade ago African Americans supported civil rights for gays more than other groups, more recently the tide has turned.[33] As pointed out earlier, African American heterosexuals no longer provide solid support for the civil rights of black

---

33. At the time of their work, Boykin and Douglas documented that in terms of civil rights for lesbians and gays, African American heterosexuals held a slightly better track record than their white counterparts. They supported this claim not simply in terms of support for civil rights legislation for gays, but also based on community responses, contrasting the hostile attacks made by Irish American heterosexuals toward Irish American gays at the infamous St. Patrick Day parades in Boston and New York with the relative acceptance of black heterosexuals toward black gays at Chicago's Bud Billiken parade in 1992 and the 1994 Million Man March. Such citations are important and perhaps allow blacks to move from mere tolerance and benign acceptance of a gay presence, as in the above examples, to a position that publicly recognizes same-sex sexual relationships as moral and equal to heterosexual unions. Since neither the parade nor march affirmed black lesbians and gays and their concerns or included gay speakers, there is considerable work that must be done in this area.

and other gays. Undoubtedly, this change in support is related to a resurgence of gay demonizing and the religious and political opposition to gays' civil rights for marriage by black clergy and leaders such as G. E. Patterson (Church of God in Christ). To be sure, African American heterosexual Christians as a group support a number of civil rights for gays, but as a result of black church teachings on the matter, they lag behind other groups in their support of gays more broadly. Thus, the group may feel that gays deserve civil rights relating to fair housing and employment, but given the common view that homosexual relationships are immoral, would be conflicted in their support for civil rights protection for such relationships, even in the privacy of the home. The following is an example.

In a study that followed the 2003 *Lawrence v. Texas* Supreme Court ruling legalizing private consensual sexual expressions between lesbians and gays (a right granted to all heterosexuals), African Americans were identified as the group least accepting gay marriage and homosexuality as a moral expression (only 36 percent of African Americans, compared to 48 percent of non–African Americans, feel that African American lesbians and gays and other gays should be allowed to marry).[34] African Americans, even those who may not be regular churchgoers, typically base their refusal to accept homosexuality in biblical authority.

The Bible and Homosexuality in Black Churches

Today, many religious scholars suggest that — given the cultural and time limitations of the Bible — the Bible is not an adequate source for responding to the issue of homosexuality any more than it sanctions organizing a free society or providing women and men with equal authority in the home and church. African American Christians, like other Christians, "treat so literally the references to homosexual practice in the Bible, while at the same time they

---

34. *USA Today* poll, "Americans Less Tolerant on Gay Issues," July 29, 2003.

interpret biblical texts on almost every other topic with considerable flexibility and non-literalness."[35] Since few African American Christians have been encouraged to read all the passages related to homosexual activity, engage in a discussion about these passages, and provide a context for why these passages likely were written, they generally find it difficult to accept the morality of homosexuality and move toward viewing gay relationships as equivalent to those of heterosexuals and worthy of the religious and social sanction of marriage.

Wimbush argues that it is not just what is in the Bible that makes black Christians passionate about following certain passages, but rather the pastor's emphasis on certain passages as authoritative. Few blacks raise this logic: since whites were wrong on their use of the Bible to support the practice of slavery, perhaps the majority of whites are also wrong on their use of the Bible to support a view that homosexuality is sinful.

The first reality about homosexuality in the Bible is that the biblical writers were not as preoccupied with the issue of homosexuality as the present-day black church and larger Christian church. There are no more than six or seven passages that address homosexual activity: Genesis 19:1–29 (Judg. 19); Leviticus 18:22; Leviticus 20:13; Romans 1:18–32; 1 Corinthians 6:9–11; and 1 Timothy 1:8–11. Moreover, these "biblical passages reportedly relating to homosexuality had little to do with early Christian misgiving on the subject."[36] The writers refer to homosexual activity (a practice that was assumed to be a deviation from a "natural" heterosexual construction), but there is no specific reference to — or for that matter condemnation of — two people of the same sex cohabitating in a loving, committed, and long-term sexual relationship.

Many point out with good reason that it is anachronistic to use the Bible to address the homosexual reality of the twenty-first century unknown to ancient and first-century biblical writers.

---

35. Nelson, *Embodiment*, 181.
36. Ibid., 92.

New Testament scholar Robin Scroggs offers the following brilliant summary:

> The basic model in today's Christian [gay] community is so different from the model attacked by the New Testament that the criterion of reasonable similarity of context is not met. The conclusion I have to draw seems inevitable: *Biblical judgments against homosexuality are not relevant to today's debate.* They should no longer be used in denominational discussions about homosexuality, should in no way be a weapon to justify refusal of ordination, *not because the Bible is not authoritative,* but simply because it does not address the issues involved.[37]

Finally, Jesus' silence on homosexuality in all four Gospels ought to make African American Christians think twice before assuming that homosexuality is the great sin that the majority of black and white churches declare it to be.[38] A reasonable response is that if homosexuality were a great sin or a sin at all, at some point during his ministry, Jesus would certainly have addressed this terrible way of life, as he did other sins. The fact that the black church has been able to assert the dominant position that "the Bible opposes homosexuality and is definitive for what the church should think and do about it" supports Wimbush's point of the culture's interpretation rather than a biblical emphasis against homosexual relationships.

Some African American heterosexual pastors and academics, like Drs. A. Cecil Williams, James Forbes, Michael Dyson, Dwight Hopkins, and Kelly Brown Douglas, differ with this common cultural response to scripture and — like their response to passages sanctioning slavery — view biblical passages on homosexual activity as culturally and time bound. In addition to hermeneutical considerations, this view recognizes that the writers wrote with a limited

---

37. Robin Scroggs, *The New Testament and Homosexuality: Contextual Background for Contemporary Debate* (Philadelphia: Fortress Press, 1983), 127.

38. This statement should not be read to imply that predominantly Asian and Latino churches do not have similar views. However, the level of emotion, attack, and politicization of this issue tends not to be as high as is true in black and white congregations, especially in the conservative Protestant denominations.

understanding of human sexuality. Our early twenty-first-century understanding of science, social science, and human sexuality offers insight regarding gender, sexual expression, and activity in ways unavailable to first-century writers like Paul.

So, for example, in *Heterosexism: An Ethical Challenge,* authors Patricia Jung and Ralph Smith argue that Paul's writing in Romans 1, the most commonly cited New Testament passage for identifying homosexuality as immoral, must be placed in context. It is important to note that "Paul presupposed that all same-sex desires and behaviors among the Gentiles resulted from their insatiable lust for sexual variety, rooted intimately in their idolatry."[39] People living at that time did not share the contemporary notion of sexuality that someone's sexual attraction toward persons of the same sex might be deeply ingrained and natural, in the same way that heterosexual desire is directed toward the opposite sex, implied in the phrase "sexual orientation."[40]

Paul's invoking of the word "natural" in the twenty-seventh verse leaves no doubt that he understood everyone's sexual constitution to be directed toward the opposite sex. Many African American heterosexuals also use the term "natural" when referring to themselves and use "unnatural" to identify homosexuality as an illegitimate sexual expression. Since much of the present resistance to accepting homosexuality as a Christian perspective has to do with the "unnatural" language found in Romans, it is important to keep in mind that when the passages about homosexual activity were written, the biblical writers also understood that in nature certain humans were naturally slave and naturally free. Thus, it would not register as odd for most white Christians of the eighteenth century to view "[African Americans] as biologically inferior to...white[s] — that race determined mental and *moral* traits. [African Americans] as...member[s] of an inferior

---

39. Patricia Beattie Jung and Ralph F. Smith, *Heterosexism: An Ethical Challenge* (Albany: State University of New York Press, 1993), 80.

40. Ibid.

race, [were] meant to be . . . slave[s], [their] normal and natural condition."[41] This example allows us to see that what is perceived as
natural does indeed change over time.

Also worthy of further analysis is Paul's reference to idolatry and
the fall in this passage. In verses 20–23, Paul refers to creation in
the Hebrew Bible to discuss the fall. In Paul's mind, idolatry and
the fall are causal in homosexual practice, a manifestation of this
disordering. What is in question here is not Paul's understanding
about homosexual practice — Paul does not look favorably upon
homosexual acts and attributes — but the way black church Christians and others uphold Paul's position on homosexual practice as
pure and infallible to be followed by all people throughout time and
space. Jung and Smith argue that "Paul might well conclude that
the fall results in both the sexual disordering of desires and behaviors and the sexual disorienting of some of us. However, were he
a part of our world, it is also possible, and we think theologically
consistent, for Paul to conclude that although sin has disordered
everyone's sexuality, it has disoriented no one's."[42]

This approach to Paul's writings does not mean, however, that
black gay and heterosexual Christians disregard scripture altogether
or refrain from judging right and wrong behaviors. Like other Christians, I regard sin as those behaviors that violate, destroy, and
abuse our fellow human beings and our relationships with them.
In this respect, homosexuality does not belong in the category of
sin any more than heterosexuality does. Abusive and destructive
sexual relationships between two men or two women are just as
wrong as, but no more wrong than, abusive and destructive sexual
relationships between a man and woman. The affirmation of gay
relationships is in no way intended to disregard or diminish heterosexual relationships but rather to broaden the concept of family
in black faith and social communities. This will mean adopting a
different understanding of traditional antihomosexual passages.

---

41. Benjamin Quarles, *The Negro in the Making of America* (New York: Collier
Macmillan, 1987), 66.
42. Jung and Smith, *Heterosexism*, 82.

A Tragic View

Many black heterosexual Christians erroneously understand the Sodom and Gomorrah story as representative evidence that gay men are more inclined to rape. As noted earlier, the Genesis 19 passage of Sodom and Gomorrah continues to be misused widely by black preachers, exacerbating the pain and tension between gays and heterosexuals. Sermons on this text are largely responsible for heterosexuals' perception that gay men are sex predators and child molesters. Such preaching further contributes to the crisis faced by gay men, already perceived as flawed by many in the church. For some heterosexual men, this preaching fuels their loathing toward gays. At the heart of this homophobia is the fear that gays, already deemed to be unnatural, if not controlled will harm good heterosexuals with their sinister and sinful predatory sexual behavior.

This thinking about sexual predatory behavior is not unlike the racist thinking that black men are innately sex predators and will prey upon good white women. Such unchecked cultural thinking cost many innocent black men their lives and still causes pain and injustice for black men today. Unfortunately, many African Americans rarely reflect upon the similar flawed "sex predator" labeling of gay men and the moral injustice that comes with such labeling on an innocent gay majority. This is why black church minister and gospel artist Donnie McClurkin's story about his molestation as a child and its connection with homosexuality did not cause a stir among black Christians.

The Tragic Donnie McClurkin Story

The Reverend Donnie McClurkin, an award-winning songwriter and gospel singer of hits such as "Stand" and "We Fall Down but We Get Up," has spent the last half decade talking about his success and perpetuating the oldest myth about homosexuality: that it results from child molestation by an adult male. In a 2001 interview, McClurkin shared his story about his childhood sexual abuse, which is detailed in his book *Eternal Victim, Eternal Victor.*

McClurkin is one of the few African American men in the country who has shared this type of story: being raped by an uncle at eight and sexually abused by male relatives while growing up in New York. Rape should never be understood as the cause of one's homosexuality any more than the more common rape of heterosexual girls should be equated with having caused their heterosexuality. Since the interview, however, McClurkin has related the early years of abuse as his brush with homosexuality. He goes on to report that he experienced subsequent "deliverance."

While I am sorry about this horrible evil that occurred in McClurkin's childhood, I find it regrettable that his bitterness and inability to work through this trauma lead him to generalize that homosexuality is a bad "choice" that should be overcome. This understanding of homosexuality does not consider that most gay men and lesbians were not raped and are not rapists. Even for gay men raped at an early age, there is no more reason for them to "change" their love relationships with men to be with women because they experienced rape by some abusive men than it is for heterosexual women to "change" their love relationships with men to be with women because of violent sexual encounters with men. McClurkin's advice to adolescent gay boys "that homosexuality is a choice they can overcome" is without merit. No reputable scientific study concludes that homosexuality is a choice and can be overcome.[43] Even if homosexuality or heterosexuality were a choice, there is no reason that either should be avoided. Both expressions possess the potential to offer sexual fulfillment and spiritual wholeness.

The two remaining Hebrew Bible texts in the book of Leviticus (Lev. 18:22: "you shall not lie with a male as with a woman; it is an abomination"; and 20:13: "If a male lies with a male as with a woman, both of them have committed an abomination; they shall be put to death; their blood is upon them") pertain to male homosexual activity as prohibitive and punishable by death. The fact that

---

43. Keith Boykin, "Confessions of Donnie McClurkin," *www.keithboykin.com* (November 19, 2002).

only men are mentioned points to the lack of scientific knowledge about reproduction. Such activity for males also carried with it a stigma of at least one of the men being placed in what was understood to be the sexual position appropriate for a woman. In the sexist cultures of the time, "to lie with a man as with a woman" "became a powerful symbol of scorn in societies where the dignity of the man was held in such high esteem."[44]

Noting Wimbush's claim that the culture interprets the importance of the text, it is because we live in an antihomosexual culture that we are more aware of the texts from Leviticus that address homosexuality rather than those that enumerate other sins and their punishments: death to children who curse their father or mother (Lev. 20:9) or death to men who commit adultery with another man's wife (20:10). Furthermore, those in the black church generally do not think that it is sinful to eat shrimp (Lev. 11:10) or pork (11:7), or to wear clothes with mixed fabric (19:19), as the Levitical code describes along with male homosexual activity.[45]

The meaning of the remaining two New Testament passages (1 Cor. 6:9–11 and 1 Tim. 1:8–10) used to express God's condemnation of homosexuality is also not as clear as many black Christian opponents of homosexuality claim.

> Do you not know that wrongdoers will not inherit the kingdom of God? Do not be deceived! Fornicators, idolaters, adulterers, male prostitutes, sodomites, thieves, the greedy, drunkards, revilers, robbers — none of these will inherit the kingdom of God. (1 Cor. 6:9–10)

> Now we know that the law is good, if one uses it legitimately. This means understanding that the law is laid down not for the

---

44. Nelson, *Embodiment*, 185.

45. The practice of raising the homosexual passages in Leviticus by black ministers and their relative silence on heterosexual adultery, as in the 1990s cases of Rev. Jesse Jackson and Dr. Henry Lyons (former president of the largest black Christian body, the National Baptist Convention USA, Inc.) indicate black Christians' unwillingness to treat scripture with consistency, making Leviticus only relevant when it comes to homosexuality. The Levitical laws do not allow for adherence to one offense over others.

innocent but for the lawless and disobedient, for the godless and sinful, for the unholy and profane, for those who kill their father or mother, for murderers, fornicators, sodomites, . . . and whatever else is contrary to the sound teaching that conforms to the glorious gospel of the blessed God, which he entrusted to me. (1 Tim. 1:8–11).

First of all, these are the writings of Paul or a writer using Paul's name. Since Paul's admonition regarding slavery is rightfully questioned and opposed, one can raise similar questions about Paul's view of sexuality. Moreover, cultural translations or mistranslations further problematize what is being communicated in these texts. In the original Greek, the terms that seemed to imply homosexual practice for some translators were the words *malakoi*, actually meaning soft male, and *arsenokoitai*, meaning lying with or sleeping with a male.[46] There is no reference to loving relationships or to women at all.

Jung and Smith further point out that in the 1611 King James Version of the Bible, the Corinthian passage is translated as "effeminate" and interpreted to mean homosexual.[47] Herein lies the problem. A general definition of effeminate means "having feminine qualities, and inappropriate to a man." Not only is such a description culturally subjective, but the greater problem is that there is no necessary correlation between effeminate behavior and homosexuality. There are butch men who are homosexual and effeminate men who are heterosexual. If effeminacy is the issue, many heterosexual men in the world (a majority based on U.S. definitions of masculinity) would be guilty of this sin, while masculine homosexual or gay men would not be sinful.

Jung and Smith also note the homophobic bias of later translators (1946–65) to insert the word "homosexual" in this passage, even though there is no word "homosexual" in the Greek language.[48] Other versions like the Revised Standard Version and the Jerusalem

---

46. Jung and Smith, *Heterosexism*, 75.
47. Ibid.
48. Ibid.

Bible include words like "sexual pervert" and "call boys," clearly reflecting a twentieth-century cultural derision of gay males rather than the accurate, if unclear, translation of "abusers of themselves with mankind." Considering that the New Testament passages written by Paul (or attributed to Paul) are the most relevant concerns for black church Christians, Paul must be examined if we are ever going to place Paul and the texts in question in an appropriate context.

There is a striking irony that African American Christians are so uncritical of Paul's writing about homosexual activity but have maintained a critical attitude or simple rejection of Paul's injunctions on slavery. For such a Christocentric culture as the black church and its tendency to call on Jesus more than any other culture, it is especially curious that they would follow Paul's response to homosexual activity rather than Jesus'. The use of Paul in the continued denigration of gays as immoral people raises the question, at least on the issue of homosexuality, as to whether black church Christians are followers of Christ or of Paul.

Although Elliott may go too far in *Liberating Paul* by placing Paul as an opponent of gender and sexual exclusions, he is absolutely correct that throughout history people and groups have invoked the apostle Paul, often inappropriately, to justify the worst kinds of oppression, including oppression against all African Americans, women, gays, and Jews.[49] What is therefore curious is why so many black church Christians accept the limitations, the flaws, and failures of a human Paul. They seem intent on making Paul more infallible than Paul ever claimed to be. By Paul's own admission in his first letter to the Corinthian church, he declares that he, like everyone else, saw through a dark glass, which allowed him to know only in part (1 Cor. 13:12).

Knowing that sexuality can be mysterious even when it is revealing, and recognizing that scientific and social scientific research informs us about our bodies and sexual expression in ways that

---

49. Neil Elliott, *Liberating Paul: The Justice of God and the Politics of the Apostle* (Maryknoll, NY: Orbis Books, 1994), 4, 23, 217.

were hidden from those who lived twenty centuries ago, it is reasonable that Paul could not have known about homosexuality as we know about it today. To accept this reality as responsible, reasonable Christians, we can conclude that the apostle makes an uninformed judgment limited by his time and space.

Christians of the nineteenth and twentieth centuries eventually considered this point when they moved away from other Pauline injunctions about slavery and women. Black church leaders' present knowledge about lesbians and gays as living spirit-filled lives and serving faithfully in church (a counterclaim to Paul's description of such individuals in Rom. 1) demands a different treatment of scripture about and theological reflection of those engaged in homosexual practice. Certainly, "if the norm of the new humanity in Jesus Christ together with our best current moral wisdom and empirical knowledge would cause us to question some of Paul's moral convictions about the status of women and about the institution of human slavery, surely his moral judgments about homosexual acts ought not to be exempt."[50]

So I wonder: If Paul had been able to write about homosexual activity today with our level of knowledge, exposure, and critical thought, would he have drawn the same conclusions about homosexuality? If he had experienced the Christian witness and dedicated church work of the millions of lesbian and gay Christians in relationships serving congregations, shelters, choirs, youth programs, seniors, and community outreach services, could he still write about homosexual activity as producing "wickedness, evil, covetousness, malice, full of envy, murder, strife, deceit, craftiness, ... gossips, slanderers, God-haters, insolent, haughty, boasters, inventors of evil, rebellious toward parents, foolish, faithless, heartless, ruthless" (Rom. 1)? I say a resounding no. Given how he worked to change the attitude of former Jews toward gentile Christians, I can only imagine that his experience of God's lesbian and gay people, in black churches and beyond, would not allow him to draw the same conclusions. On what grounds could he dismiss the

---

50. Nelson, *Embodiment*, 188.

Spirit of God in their lives? By the same token, I believe that Paul would not support slavery if he were living among us.

While I share with my black church sisters and brothers that scripture is an important part of our faith and a valuable symbol and tool from which we make meaning of our religion, I also strongly believe that we are called to be faithful to how the present context educates us in understanding the text. This present knowledge about our sexuality also calls for a different response to the scriptures. Scriptures demanded that women be removed from the community when they menstruate. Just as it would be irresponsible and frankly unconscionable to continue this practice with our knowledge that menstruation is a normal biological function of women and does not make women unclean, it is equally irresponsible if we interpret texts having to do with same-sex sexual expression as prohibitive when we know that lesbians and gays can and do reflect the same Christian moral character found in heterosexuals.

These above passages are not the only weapons used by African American church people in their battle against homosexuality. A number of popular cultural arguments strongly influence black church communities. In the next chapter, I explore some of the more popular arguments.

Chapter 3

Natural Law, Choice, Procreation, and Other Black Church Arguments against Homosexuality

T HE OPPOSITION to homosexuality and gays in black churches is largely an opposition led by black men. Studies show that antipathy toward homosexuality is primarily male, driven as a result of male socialization and the machoism and sexism learned by males at a young age. The gender difference can be clearly observed in the way that black women and men in the military responded to this issue during the gays-in-the-military debate. Black women generally accepted lesbians in the military without advocating their exclusion. Black men, on the other hand, generally preferred discrimination against gays in the U.S. military. Within black churches, male clergy also provide evidence for this claim. Black heterosexual women clergy have been reluctant to join their fellow male clergy in an attack on homosexuality by using the Bible. Perhaps this is because women are familiar with having the Bible used by many of these same men to invalidate their call to ordained ministry and subjugate them in the church and home.

The opposition is not always from men and clergy. A significant number of black church Christians opposing gays are found not only in churches and communities but also at the school board and state legislatures. The Rainbow Curriculum in New York experienced its demise in large part because black women fought against including the history, culture, and contributions of lesbian and gay people in the educational curriculum of New York public schools. Alveda King, the niece of Martin Luther King Jr., has unleashed some of the most vitriolic rhetoric against gays, including black lesbians and gays, as she has untiringly advocated the discrimination against and exclusion of gays within society. In her campaign, "King for America," she identifies homosexuality as immoral and argues that lesbians and gays are not deserving of the civil rights fought for by her uncle, Martin Luther King Jr.

The Mutability (Choice) vs. Born-That-Way Argument

In their recent work on homosexuality, Janet Jakobsen and Ann Pellegrini point out that homophobic individuals like Alveda King use any number of arguments and tactics in order to silence or impose injustice on lesbians and gays. In their carefully detailed study, Jakobsen and Pellegrini argue that

> Biblically based homophobia can have it both ways. It can object to homosexuality on the grounds that homosexuality contravenes divine purpose . . . [and] that it is contra [or against] nature. . . . A fascinating and revealing example of this rhetorical shuttling between scientistic appeals to nature and religious appeals to God's law is found in Alveda King's testimony, in May 1999, before a joint House-Senate Judiciary Committee of the Massachusetts legislature.[1]

In their recounting of King's appeal for marriage to be a special right for heterosexuals in Massachusetts, they note that

> King cited scripture to make her case for DOMA [Defense of Marriage Act] and against same sex marriage. The biblical passages she selected were, in her view, unambiguous condemnations of homosexuality and by implication of same sex marriage. A member of the joint committee pressed King on her use of the Bible and asked her to respond to the striking coincidence that opponents of civil rights for African Americans in the fifties and sixties had also drawn upon the Bible — and indeed on some of the very same passages King

1. Jakobsen and Pellegrini, *Love the Sin*, 77.

was citing — to justify their racism as divinely sanctioned. In reply, King shifted the ground of her objection to homosexuality and same sex marriage from theology to biology. She told lawmakers that they should not "confuse skin color with sexual orientation." The comparison between homosexuality and race was invalid; African Americans, she argued, were denied civil rights because of an immutable characteristic, something in their very nature, which they could not change. But homosexuality . . . is a behavior based identity, something homosexuals have chosen; it is not natural and thus, not deserving of protection.[2]

The Choice Argument

Of the many illogical arguments against homosexuality the argument about choice is the one that defies all reason. How does one choose to make one's sexual impulses respond to the same sex? If sexual attraction were simply a matter of choice, wouldn't gays experiencing torment and suicide attempts just simply choose attraction toward the opposite sex and resolve their problem? Given that choice is only relevant if there is interest or desire, are heterosexuals saying that they are also sexually aroused by the same sex? If one were simply "trying it out," this individual would not stay with the same sex if her or his sexual and emotional needs were not being met.

The argument that there is choice in the motivation for one's sexual stimulation presupposes that sexual desire can be selected as one selects a profession, clothing, or food. In other words, "one never sees anyone setting out to become homosexual, in a way one does see people setting out to become doctors, lawyers, and bricklayers." The experience is just the opposite. By and large, "gay persons-to-be simply find themselves having homosexual encounters and yet at least initially resisting quite strongly the identification of being homosexual," not because same-sex sexual expression is repulsive, but because no one wants to live in a

---

2. Ibid., 77–78.

world that despises and attacks them for who they are.[3] Even when one chooses a profession, there is still some interest prior to the choice. If homosexual expression were the disgusting experience many claim, they would not have to spend so much time convincing others of its "filthiness" and enacting laws to keep people away from homosexuality. No one would want to remain in such an unpleasant encounter.

Heterosexuals who make the choice argument also fail to recognize the implications of such an argument with which they would fundamentally disagree. By the fact that King and others position themselves as heterosexuals, they contradict their own claim. If they are not attracted to the same sex, it is not an option for them to choose the same sex. Since humans generally experience sexual feelings before they declare a sexual identity, King and other anti-gay proponents make it clear by their argument that lesbians and gays must have been nongay in order for them to have "chosen" homosexuality. If heterosexuals could choose their sexual desire, then all heterosexuals should also be able to choose the same sex. For those heterosexuals arguing that they have absolutely no sexual interest in the same sex, then homosexuality is not optional. They cannot choose to be gay any more than gays can choose to be heterosexual. Thus, the claim that lesbians and gays chose their attraction is a contradiction. They have been gay or attracted to the same sex and are simply admitting that fact.

If Alveda King and heterosexuals are saying that gays chose to be honest and act on their sexual feelings, rather than live a lie about their opposite-sex attraction, should they expect black lesbians and gays to do otherwise? Expecting or coercing someone to give up a loving sexual response is insensitive and unjust to the person's humanity. No one deserves this treatment. The response that such persons should change through change therapies is inadequate and unnecessary.

As I have argued in the past, it is unreasonable and simply untrue that black lesbians and gays choose this "lifestyle" (a misnomer)

---

3. Mohr, *Gays/Justice*, 40.

and as a result get what they deserve. In other words, the argument goes, if gays would not choose to be gay, they would not encounter this suffering. This response fails to recognize the following: (1) human beings, whether heterosexual, homosexual, or bisexual, generally do not experience their sexual desire as choice;[4] (2) given the unending trials of a racist society, African American lesbians and gays would gain nothing by "choosing" a sexual identity and relationship so despised by the church and society; and (3) if heterosexual relationships were fulfilling for all people, there would be no need to "choose" same-sex relationships. To further simplify what amazingly does not appear as such, "picking the gender of a sex partner is decidedly dissimilar to picking a flavor of ice cream. If an ice cream parlor is out of one's flavor, one simply picks another. And if people were persecuted, threatened with . . . shattered careers, loss of family and housing . . . and the like for eating, say, rocky road ice cream, no one would ever eat it; everyone would pick another easily available flavor."[5]

This argument should not be interpreted as saying that if given a choice, one would choose heterosexuality because it is better and not choose same-sex sexual attraction because it is neither pleasurable, fulfilling, nor a complete sexual/emotional experience. To the contrary, because this sexual experience takes place with members of the same sex with similar arousal patterns of body parts, some sex researchers suggest that the partners in a homosexual relationship may actually have an advantage over their heterosexual counterparts as far as the production of pleasure is concerned.

Sexologist Helmet Katchadourian supports this claim by stating that "same-sexed persons are generally more effective in sexually stimulating their partners; being of the same sex they know from their own body what is likely to be more pleasurable rather than dealing with the more mysterious body of a member of the opposite sex."[6] This is not to say that many heterosexual relationships

---

4. Helmet Katchadourian, *Fundamentals of Human Sexuality* (Orlando: Holt, Rinehart and Winston, 1989), 379.

5. Mohr, *Gays/Justice*, 39–40.

6. Katchadourian, *Fundamentals of Human Sexuality*, 370.

do not provide sexual stimulation and pleasure for the opposite sex, since such a statement would be clearly false. This is stated simply to make clear once again that a statement from gays that they would not choose to be gay has nothing to do with the sexual experience and everything to do with desiring to avoid additional hardships in life from the anti-gay loathing, discrimination, and exclusion of church and society. Jung and Smith explain, "Homosexuality . . . is not just the absence of heterosexual desires but the presence of desires for the same sex. . . . Homosexual people are not 'sexually retarded' heterosexual people. Their sexual desires are not diminished. They cannot be aptly described as merely falling short of an exclusively heterosexual mark. They are clearly and simply oriented elsewhere."[7]

It remains unclear why there is so much preoccupation with the issue that homosexuality, unlike heterosexuality, is choice. Although Kinsey's research and subsequent sex studies point to sexual fluidity, these studies support the fact that most people do not experience their primary sexual attraction as choice. For bisexuals and homosexuals who meet their love with the same sex, there ought to be acceptance within black communities of faith for sisters and brothers to make choices and establish loving, caring, and spiritual relationships and families.[8] The question about choice is only relevant if one thinks that homosexuality is wrong. Those black Christians like King who insist that homosexuality is always a choice, and the wrong choice, demonstrate a supremacist thinking that being heterosexual is the only right way to be.

---

7. Jung and Smith, *Heterosexism*, 83.

8. Although it is true that individuals generally do not experience their sexual desire as choice, bisexuals have the capacity to choose to be with the same or opposite sex and experience wholesome sexual gratification. One should also keep in mind that largely due to Kinsey's research and that of other sexologists, sexuality, sexual attraction, and arousal are perceived as rather fluid. It is possible for people who are primarily heterosexual to have satisfying same-sex sexual experiences and for lesbians and gays to have satisfying opposite-sex sexual experiences. The degree to which one is heterosexual or gay is determined by the intensity of the sexual encounters with the opposite or same sex and the degree of interest that one displays toward them.

This thinking is no different from historical supremacist thinking of using New Testament scriptures to define other religions, such as Islam and Judaism, as wrong.

The Natural vs. Unnatural Argument

King also raised another common argument used by many black Christians in their antihomosexual rhetoric — the "it's not natural" argument. In 1998, African American Christians Debbie and Angie Winan, vocalists of the famous gospel recording Winan family, titled a song with just those words, "It's Not Natural." The Winan sisters, like King, "moved easily between a discourse of Christian morality to a discourse of nature."[9] Following Paul's discussion in Romans 1, they claim the appropriate or right way to have sex by appealing to nature. This claim assumes that one can know God's will and intention for humankind by simply following nature. Many black church lesbians and gays felt denigrated by this recording, and several expressed disagreement of this perspective to the recording artists.

The Winans' use of the nature argument follows an approach similar to that of those using the Bible to condemn homosexuality: they identify parts of nature that suit their purposes, while ignoring other parts of nature that the church and society disregard. Natural arguments have lost their appeal in the contemporary church and society and "the charge comes up now in ordinary discourse only against homosexuality."[10] During the early church and Middle Ages when the claim that homosexuality is unnatural gained prominence (largely as a result of Aquinas), Christians and others generally accepted this claim from church leaders without question. However, as one of my friends put it, "Aquinas had not looked at enough animals." Homosexual expression is not just a human reality; homosexuality is a part of the animal kingdom as well, especially in animals that are closest to human beings.[11]

---

9. Jakobsen and Pellegrini, *Love the Sin*, 90.
10. Mohr, *Gays/Justice*, 34.
11. Katchadourian, *Fundamentals of Human Sexuality*, 366.

The inaccurate view that since homosexuality is not present in animals or nature, it should not be expressed by humans is quite common. The argument that what is naturally present in animals should also be reflected in humans is neither prudent nor generally expressed. We do not, and should not, construct our lives as humans based simply on how animals live. We are human beings with the ability to reason; this attribute alone calls us to a distinctive existence, one other than that of animals — who as far as we know have very limited or no ability to reason. Humans' ability to reason can and does allow for a better existence.

If black Christians and others really believed that what is natural is determined by the animal world and thus humans ought to express themselves likewise, they would oppose circumcision (changing the penis from its natural state as found in male animals), demand that either males adorn themselves instead of females or look the same as females (many male and female animals look the same; when males and females are different, the male is adorned, e.g., peacock, lion, etc.) and follow the predominant sexual position of animals — stomach to back instead of face-to-face. Since a majority choose the opposite of these examples of nature, they follow "unnatural" practice. One can make just as strong an argument as the Winans that it is not natural for Christians to circumcise males, shave themselves, adorn females, and have face-to-face sex. These arguments only seem strange because we live in contemporary society that generally accepts circumcision, prefers more adornment on females, and identifies the face-to-face sexual position as normative. But in this respect, homosexuality is no more unnatural than face-to-face sexual positions.

In his book *Gays/Justice*, philosopher Richard Mohr highlights natural arguments against homosexuality on the grounds of nature's design that certain things function one way. One of the most common comments raised, primarily by black and other heterosexual men, is that "the parts don't fit." The "parts don't fit" argument is another layer used to support the view that homosexuality is unnatural. Mohr refuses the singling out of homosexuality by heterosexuals who accept not only other ways they can use their genitals besides penile-vaginal intercourse, but "that lots of bodily parts have lots of functions and just because some activity can be fulfilled by only one organ (say the mouth for eating), this activity does not condemn other functions of the organ to immorality (say the mouth for talking, licking stamps, blowing bubbles, or having sex)."[12] Again, black church leaders often oppose homosexuality because they are unwilling to accept the various ways genitals can be used for sexual pleasure with lesbians and gays, even though heterosexual couples in the church are not being criticized and condemned when they engage in the same kinds of oral and anal sexual expressions.

In *One More River to Cross*, Boykin gives an example of a heterosexual minister exercising this double standard. Boykin writes, "Like so many homophobes, [Rev. James] Sykes obsesses on a stereotypical image of male homosexuality. 'Don't come to me and tell me that they deserve some special rights, because . . . you got two men in the same thing and they're sticking their thing up their rump and they got all kind of semen coming out of their mouth.'"[13] This attempt by Sykes to cast these forms of lovemaking in a derogatory fashion omits the fact that heterosexuals in his congregation and throughout the world engage in the same oral and anal sexual expressions. If oral and anal sexual activity are inappropriate and unchristian acts for Sykes and other heterosexual ministers, then Sykes and those ministers should be consistent and not make this a gay issue but tell black church heterosexual Christian women and men that they are also wrong when they have semen in their mouths and "stick their things" in women's "rumps," respectively. As more African American gay and lesbian families come out and confront ministers' disparaging comments about their loving relationships, they, like Sykes, are finding it difficult to make the case against same-sex marriage.

---

12. Mohr, *Gays/Justice*, 36.
13. Boykin, *One More River to Cross*, 128.

Same-Sex Marriage

The recent marriage debate has divided African Americans largely into two camps: marriage traditionalists and marriage advocates, with a third group consisting almost exclusively of politicized lesbians and gay men who find the entire institution problematic due to its patriarchal and exclusivist structure.[14] Black Christians stand as some of the most ardent defenders of the notion that marriage should remain as a special right for heterosexual couples, both civilly and religiously. Their position has won them many friends from conservative white Protestant Christians who ordinarily are not interested in hearing from African Americans or black clergy on other important issues of the black majority, including affirmative action programs, better schools for black children, black poverty, and the racism of our penal system.

In February 2005, ministers who worked on the reelection of President George W. Bush urged conservative black ministers in California to join them in a campaign against gay marriage entitled "Black Contract with America on Moral Values." A summit held at the twenty-seven-thousand-seat Crenshaw Christian Center in Los Angeles and hosted by renowned televangelist Fred Price included the showing of a video designed to present all gays as nothing more than sex fiends, invoking Martin Luther King's name. Price commented: "The marriage issue has moved [me] to act." The purpose of this event was to present gays in a negative light and exacerbate the homophobia of the black pastors assembled. Seventy black pastors "nodded affirmatively" as they pledged allegiance to this campaign. Frank L. Stewart, an African American bishop, argued, "Black people have to change their whole paradigm of thinking. This is a philosophical war going on." The tactics resurrected the language and actions of former segregationists and Klan members of the 1950s and 1960s. Black lesbian activist Jasmyne Cannick

---

14. Marvin M. Ellison, *Same-Sex Marriage: A Christian Ethical Analysis* (Cleveland: Pilgrim Press, 2004), 1.

questioned how black leaders who have experienced discrimination could challenge the rights struggles of others, especially gay blacks.[15]

Across the country, in every denomination, black church leaders can be heard defending marriage from the Bible in the same ways that white ministers defended slavery, pointing out that the Bible only sanctions marriage between a man and woman. Like past efforts to keep marriage as an institution only for free white people or members of the same race, the Bible is once again the main defense used to prevent marriage from being extended to another group of citizens. The irony this time is that African American heterosexuals are leading the charge of denying marriage to another oppressed group, African American lesbians and gays and other gays.

On March 22, 2004, in a historic stand against marriage for gays, "the Reverend Clarence James and 29 other [African American] pastors . . . signed a declaration outlining their beliefs on marriage. . . . The declaration [stated] that marriage is not a civil right, and marriage between a man and a woman is important because it's necessary for the upbringing of children."[16]

This stand was no different from the actions of black pastors for the last two decades. In major cities throughout the country, black pastors have consistently organized protests by showing up at legislative hearings and government buildings opposing the civil rights of gay citizens of all races. By casting themselves as the only true heirs of civil rights protections, many black heterosexual ministers have been successful in drawing a wedge in the argument that the petitions of lesbians and gays are also civil rights.

In a statement to the press about this gathering, James stated, "When the homosexual compares himself to the black community, he doesn't know what suffering is."[17] Though James reflects a common response of black pastors, there are many problems with this

---

15. Peter Wallsten and Tom Hamburger, "Black Clergy Wooed for Values Fight," *Los Angeles Times*, February 2, 2005.

16. "Black Ministers Protest Gay Marriage," *New York Times*, March 23, 2004, A21.

17. Ibid.

perspective. First of all, James makes an untrue statement about gay people. By contrasting "the homosexual" with "the black community," his word choice identifies gays as white and as all the same. James conveniently ignores the millions of African American lesbians and gays in order to keep "gay rights" solely as a property of privileged wealthy white men (notice the use of the pronoun he), a group that is perceived as having it all and having been spared discrimination.

Furthermore, the language in the declaration is flawed. The sentence, "To equate a lifestyle choice to racism demeans the work of the entire civil rights movement," makes some false claims about both homosexuality and the civil rights movement. Homosexuality is no more a "lifestyle choice" than heterosexuality, and the civil rights movement is an effort to ensure *all* Americans equal rights under the Constitution. Indeed, some of the most committed leaders of the civil rights movement of the 1950s and 1960s were also lesbians and gays, those such as Bayard Rustin (King advisor and organizer of the March on Washington, 1963), James Baldwin, Audre Lourde, and white gay priest, the Reverend Malcolm Boyd.

The present injustice against lesbians and gays has everything to do with the civil rights movement. To reduce the movement to racism is a gross misunderstanding of the movement. The leader of this movement, Martin Luther King Jr., understood that while the movement committed itself to transforming evil racist structures of churches and society into systems of equality, he also knew that any injustice threatened other claims for justice. His work with the Poor People's Campaign and broader nonviolent work attested to his belief that "a threat to justice anywhere is a threat to justice everywhere." In other words, if a society can justify discrimination toward a group of lesbians and gays, similar reasons can be constructed to justify discrimination against skin color, gender, religion, or any other categorization of human beings.

Perhaps Martin King knew the limits of using the argument of choice to deny civil rights and marriage. For those who continue to argue that gays can be discriminated against because they chose their homosexuality, they should remember that in the days of Nazi

Germany, a group was discriminated against because of their religious choice. The argument that Judaism is a religious choice and one can simply choose another religion to avoid persecution highlights the injustice of discriminating against a group because a segment of the population feels that one group has chosen an expression that another group does not like. With such an approach, there would be an unending attack on groups that made choices that are disliked by another group. King knew that such an approach would never lead to a just society. The ugly history of denying marriage to individuals who chose someone of another race is too recent in our history for us not to have learned a lesson.

Finally, and perhaps the most disturbing, is James's claim about suffering. The claim that gays do not know what suffering is lacks credibility. Since gays experience pain from being disowned by their family members and denied their children, from lies about themselves, from losing their jobs within and outside the U.S. military, from housing discrimination, assault, ridicule, violence, and death just because they are gay, it is not true that gays do not understand suffering. If James cannot understand this as suffering, then it is he, and not gays, who does not know what suffering is.

On December 11, 2004, black heterosexual ministers led another anti-gay march in Atlanta. Considering King's unqualified position against any discrimination, the fact that the march began at the Martin Luther King Jr. Center for Nonviolent Social Change was especially problematic. Led by renowned televangelist Bishop T. D. Jakes ("whose name was recently added to the Traditional Values Coalition list of religious supporters against the right of gays and lesbians to marry") and the megachurch pastor Bishop Eddie Long, thousands of demonstrators turned out as a way of preventing gay couples from having the same right to marry as heterosexuals. Earl Hutchinson of Black News wrote that the sight of the daughter of Martin Luther King Jr., the Reverend Bernice King, "standing at the grave site of her father with thousands of demonstrators to denounce gay marriage was painful and insulting." Hutchinson feels "given [King's] relentless and uncompromising battles against discrimination during his life, it defies belief that he would back an anti-gay campaign." Even though Bernice King is an outspoken evangelical minister, many who know her would find it surprising that she has marched and written letters and petitions denouncing gay marriage.[18]

The antipathy black pastors have toward gay marriage is not only expressed in protest rallies. Two black denominations have provided official statements without devoting the same amount of energy to developing a perspective on the larger issue of homosexuality. Perhaps black denominational leaders feel that it is self-evident that all Christians would adopt the view that homosexuality is sinful. In a statement supporting the marriage traditionalist position, stating that it will "never allow the sanctioning of same-sex marriage by its clergy nor recognize the legitimacy of such unions," the patriarchal Church of God in Christ, led by Presiding Bishop Gilbert E. Patterson, expresses pride in exclusive heterosexual marriage, declaring on the denomination's website the following:

> Let it be known by men everywhere, that the General Assembly of the Church of God in Christ, Inc., has adopted this thirteenth day of April, year of our Lord, two-thousand four, in Memphis, Tennessee, this Proclamation of Marriage.
>
> We, the Presiding Bishop, the General Board and the Board of Bishops of the Church of God in Christ, solemnly proclaim that the institution of marriage was established and ordained by God (Genesis 2:24). Therefore, "God created man in his own image, in the image of God created him, male and female created he them" (Genesis 1:27). He created "the woman for the man" (1 Corinthians 11:9). Therefore, "marriage is honorable" (Hebrews 13:4).
>
> We believe that since the beginning of the recorded history, in most cultures throughout the world, marriage has been defined as the lawful union of one man and one woman. The traditional form of marriage is one of the bedrock institutions

---

18. Earl Hutchinson, *Hutchinson Report Newsletter*, December 13, 2004.

of most societies. We, therefore, affirm the preservation of the present definition of marriage as being the legal union of one man and one woman as husband and wife.

We believe that, "Children are a heritage of the Lord; and the fruit of the womb is his reward" (Psalms 127:3). In order to provide for the continuation of the species, God created within male and female the potential for bearing children. The first commandment given to Adam and Eve was to be "fruitful and multiply, and replenish the earth" (Genesis 1:28). Marriage between male and female provide the structure for conceiving and raising children. Compliance with the command of God is a physical and biological impossibility in same-sex unions. We, therefore, believe that only marriages between male and female, as ordained by God, is essential for the procreation of mankind.

We believe that the homosexual practices of same-sex couples are in violation of religious and social norms and are aberrant and deviant behavior. We believe that these unions are sinful and in direct violation of the law of God in that they are a deviation from the natural use and purpose of the body. "For this reason God gave them up to vile passions. For even their women exchanged the natural use for what is against nature. Likewise, also the men, leaving the natural use of the woman, burned in their lust for one another, men with men committing what is shameful, and receiving in themselves the penalty of their error which is due" (Romans 1:26–27 [all passages are taken from the New King James Version]). We believe that to legalize such unions will signal ecclesiastical and social approval of homosexuality and sexual deviancy as legitimate lifestyles.

Therefore, in spite of the progressive normalization of alternative lifestyles and the growing legal acceptance of same-sex unions, we declare our opposition to any deviation from traditional marriages of male and female. Notwithstanding the rulings of the court systems in the land in support of same-sex unions; we resolve that the Church of God in Christ stand resolutely firm and never allow the sanctioning of same-sex marriages by its clergy nor recognize the legitimacy of such unions.[19]

The other six historically black denominations hold similar versions of the Church of God in Christ's position; no black denomination supports marriage equality of lesbian and gay couples in the church with that of their heterosexual counterparts. The Church of God in Christ proclamation identifies all lesbian and gay unions as sinful. Black church communions resisting theological liberation by using certain texts prevent any possibility for offering a progressive Christian response to lesbians and gays presenting themselves as faithful loving people in relationships. Marriage advocates would say that a responsible theological response to marriage is more than just quoting selected scriptures that present one model of marriage as a way to exclude all others.

This approach by black church leaders does not address other biblical marriage models that most black church Christians would find immoral. One example is the biblical polygynous marriages (marriages with more than one wife) of God's patriarch, Abraham, and other men of God, e.g., Jacob or Solomon. These marriages are not found in the New Testament but neither are they ever condemned by God as sinful or inappropriate. This is not an advocacy for polygynous marriage but to point out that it is not true that Christians opposed to gay marriage are just opposed because they are not in the Bible. They are also opposed to polygynous marriages that are sanctioned in the Bible. In an attempt to end all discussion, the Church of God in Christ, nonetheless, uses the Bible as a last defense of exclusive heterosexual marriage and resistance to lesbian and gay marriage, much like most black denominations continue to resist women's equality and ordination.

While the Church of God in Christ represents the view of the majority of black Christians, recently a group of prominent African

---

19. Gilbert E. Patterson, *Marriage: A Proclamation to the Church of God in Christ Worldwide*, *www.cogic.org/marriageproclamation.htm* (October 12, 2004).

American heterosexual and gay clergy and politicians, including the Reverend James Forbes, the Reverend Dr. Kelly Brown Douglas, the Honorable John Conyers and Jesse Jackson Jr. (Jesse Jackson Sr. was not a part of this list), the Reverend Dr. Michael Dyson, Rev. Dr. Yvette Flunder, Rev. Irene Monroe, Dr. Randall Bailey, and Rev. Gilbert Caldwell issued a statement opposing the exclusion of lesbian and gay sisters and brothers from the institution of marriage as advocated by black clergy throughout the country.

The ministers who wrote the Church of God in Christ's proclamation use the Bible, like nature appeals, for opposing homosexuality. In so doing they overlook other biblical mandates, for example, stoning disobedient sons (Deut. 21:21), granting divorce only in cases of sexual unfaithfulness (Matt. 19:9), giving up wealth (Matt. 19:21), and greeting everyone with a kiss (2 Cor. 13:12). Interestingly, Paul's biblical injunction on kissing appears more times than his writing on homosexual activity. These are other examples of scriptures no longer observed by most Christians. I am not suggesting that Christians should observe these strict and even abusive habits, as in the case of stoning children, but rather that black Christians should also recognize the irrelevance of using the above passages on homosexual activity to address the present reality of lesbians and gays in today's black churches and communities.

Within black church advocacy for an exclusive heterosexual marriage structure, the "be fruitful and multiply" passage is also used. Despite the fact that heterosexuals engage in the same kinds of sexual behavior as lesbian and gay couples with heterosexuals also engaging in genital sexual intercourse, the Church of God in Christ Marriage Proclamation concludes that the problem that the heterosexual majority still has with lesbian and gay lovemaking is that "marriage between male and female provide the structure for conceiving and raising children. Compliance with this command of God is a physical and biological impossibility in same-sex union." This section ignores the fact that it is also impossible for many married heterosexual couples (elderly and otherwise) sanctioned by black church denominations to fulfill this command. In this respect, what can occur in a committed nonprocreative heterosexual relationship that cannot also occur in a committed homosexual relationship? Like the double standard of condemning the sexual activity of lesbian and gay relationships while heterosexuals engaged in the same sexual activity escape such ridicule, there is also a double standard between the two groups regarding the command to "be fruitful and multiply."

Gays, Heterosexuals, and Families

Much of the defense to keep marriage only between a man and a woman revolves around the procreation argument. Yet it is an argument that is not used in granting or denying marriage to heterosexuals. There are three categories of childless heterosexual couples receiving sanction and marriage rites in black churches. The first category is young African American heterosexual couples deciding not to have children. The other two categories — older black heterosexual couples (couples with women past childbearing age) and infertile heterosexual couples — are still allowed to marry in black churches, thus making the procreative argument for marriage invalid. In spite of the fact that infertility is typically unknown to the couple at the time of marriage, pastors rightfully do not make them feel inadequate because they cannot procreate.

With the acceptance of nonprocreative heterosexuals in black churches, one can see that marriage is not only celebrated for procreative couples. This reaction leaves us to consider that the reason black heterosexual Christians deny African American lesbian and gay Christian couples marriage is their problem with sexual expression between two women and between two men. Black church leaders fortunately can appeal to many seminary and some church resources for other Christian responses to lesbian and gay sexual relationships. These resources can facilitate dialogue and assist many heterosexuals in affirming the goodness of gay sexuality, launch a full-blown critique of hetero-supremacist norms and values, and reformulate a sexual ethic that does not presume that everyone is, or should be, heterosexual, married, and committed to procreation.

Considering that many heterosexual couples do not and cannot have children and that reproductive technologies allow for children in lesbian-headed households, the traditional card of procreative heterosexual coupling to trump all nonprocreating same-sex couples can no longer be used as the selling point for having families with children. This reality, along with studies that refute inherent qualities in one sex over the other and show well-adjusted children growing up in lesbian and gay-headed households, leave marriage traditionalists at a loss for why marriage should remain for heterosexuals only.

When confronted with the evidence about many infertile heterosexual couples, black church Christians and others shift the argument to marriage between a man and woman "for the upbringing of children," as stated in the declaration signed by the black pastors. Given the fact that in most black families a single mother rears children without the father's presence, the exclusive, one man-one woman model lacks relevance in black churches and African American communities. It is also disrespectful to those families that provide nurture, love, care, and the successful upbringing of black children to state that it is necessary for a man and woman to be present in order for successful upbringing of children. This does not mean that fathers and mothers cannot provide wonderful home environments for the upbringing of children — clearly they often do — but parent models must be broadened to avoid previous rigid and even racist assessments of family that place male-female–headed households as inherently superior to other family configurations.

In *Same-Sex Marriage: A Christian Ethical Analysis*, Christian ethicist Marvin Ellison describes that anti-gay marriage Christians and scholars like new natural law scholar John Finnis often find gay relationships lacking because they do not deliver the primary goods for marriage: the procreative and the unitive. Finnis argues that "the human mouth is not a reproductive organ" and the sheer pleasure derived from same-sex relationships is "morally worthless." Finnis believes that marriage is for the purpose of procreation and gender complementarity, ends that same-sex marriage cannot achieve. Thankfully, U.S. marriage today is not so limiting. If the church and society were to determine procreation to be a prerequisite for marriage, many heterosexual couples would be denied marriage. Throughout U.S. history, heterosexuals have been granted marriage without procreating, thus providing evidence that procreation is not a necessary function of the marital relationship. Likewise, the complementarity and balance of roles and functions within lesbian and gay relationships disprove Finnis's claim that complementarity is not achieved in same-sex relationships.

With the current abundance of black children living in adoption and foster homes after having being given up by their heterosexual parents, procreation becomes an unnecessary concern. African American gays do not in any way pose a threat to black communities, churches, or the common good. A recent study showed that of children waiting to be adopted, 90 percent are children of darker color.[20] Instead of disparaging comments about nonprocreative gay couples, what is needed from African American church leaders is encouragement for responsible adults, be they heterosexual, lesbian, or gay, to take care of needy black children. Rather than being a threat to black families and communities, African American lesbians and gays are often devoted to their families and communities and, because they generally have not had children, may be able to provide financial resources and care for parents and other family members with less difficulty than heterosexual family members committed to their own families.

When there are so many problems in black families and communities — heterosexual male violence in homes, heterosexual fathers absent from the majority of black homes, unfaithful marriages, gang violence, substance abuse, child support problems, large prison populations, troubled heterosexual parenting, teenage pregnancies, high rates of AIDS and other sexually transmitted diseases — it is difficult to understand why black pastors spend

---

20. Dan Woog, "Adopting a Family," *The Advocate*, January 20, 1998, 70.

so much time opposing gays for honoring their committed relationships by choosing marriage. This focus may be the result
of frustration from unsuccessfully trying to resolve these ills in
black churches, families, and communities. This conversation is
a diversion from such failures; it conveniently scapegoats African
American gays as causing the problems in black families and
communities rather than addressing those obviously caused by
heterosexuals.

The heterosexual supremacist approach to marriage by African
Americans can also be found in the work of African American divinity professor Dr. Cheryl Saunders, a Howard Divinity School
Christian Ethics professor. Saunders, also a pastor in the Church of
God (having rightfully chosen not to adhere to the biblical passages
that identify her role as a woman in church leadership as invalid),
finds that lesbian and gay relationships "severely undermine the
heterosexual family."[21] Like former divinity school professor Don
Browning, she supports the view that the church should continue
"to hold up the image of covenanted heterosexual marriage as the
normative pattern for organizing human sexuality."[22] Saunders and
other marriage traditionalist black pastors are finding that many
people are raising questions regarding heterosexual marriage as an
exclusive institution. They are finding that committed homosexual
unions can and do provide the same love and nurture present in
many heterosexual unions. Both unions provide a stable environment for the rearing of children. To make a claim that gays "severely
undermine the heterosexual family," as Saunders asserts, suggests
that the heterosexual family and heterosexuality are not as strong as
marriage traditionalists argue, but rather weak units that crumble
under a more powerful and attractive lesbian or gay configuration.

---

21. Cheryl Saunders, "The Black Church and Homosexuality," conference
paper. This paper was presented on February 12, 1998, at a conference sponsored
by the Carpenter Program in Religion, Gender and Sexuality and the Kelly Miller
Smith Institute of Vanderbilt Divinity School. The quotation is taken from the
Tennessean, February 13, 1998, 2b.

22. Don S. Browning, *Religious Ethics and Pastoral Care* (Philadelphia: Fortress
Press, 1983), 72.

Ironically, this claim does not speak favorably or convincingly to the stability and quality of heterosexuality. The "severely undermine" language used by Saunders creates hysteria among heterosexuals, perpetuating a negative image of gays as people to be feared because they threaten the moral fabric of society. This rhetoric has created a frenzied African American heterosexual population and influenced church leaders into one of the most public oppositional religious and political stands they have taken against the civil rights of lesbians and gays.[23]

Black church leaders by and large ignore this question and take an exclusivist approach to marriage, selectively using scripture as a justification for denying black gay Christian couples and creating a privileged status for themselves. They, along with many white conservative Protestants and Catholics, insist that heterosexual marriage provides a "unique legal, social, economic and spiritual union. . . . No other relationship transforms young men and young women into more productive, less selfish, and more mature husbands and wives, and fathers and mothers, than marriage."[24] In this uncritical view of heterosexual marriage, marriage traditionalists proclaim a correlation of society's ills, "such as divorce, illegitimacy, sexually transmitted diseases, and crime," with the decline in heterosexual marriage.[25]

Many black church Christians swept up in this thinking made alliances with the strange bedfellows of the Christian right and President George W. Bush during the 2004 presidential election. Given the history of white conservative Protestants and their fight against civil rights for African Americans and their support of segregation, it is ironic that African American heterosexuals make alliances with this group. Many black church Christians decided

---

23. Unlike black church leaders, many African American politicians have been wonderfully supportive toward all gays and their equality. Within the U.S. Congress, for example, blacks consistently support civil rights for lesbian and gay Americans, exemplifying the best expressions of liberty, justice, and equality for all people.

24. Ellison, *Same-Sex Marriage*, 57.

25. Ibid.

to join them in their opposition to and sometimes attack on gay relationships by advocating bans on same-sex marriage. Eleven states, including Georgia, with the support of over two dozen black ministers, included referenda prohibiting marriage for lesbian and gay couples. Through the efforts of many black heterosexuals who supported this discrimination, laws providing special rights for heterosexuals came into effect in all eleven states.

This historic action is at odds with a president who recently stated that "progress depends on the full protection of civil rights and equality before the law." He further stated he i committed to creating a nation that "values every member of society and provides people with equal opportunity to succeed."[26] It is indeed odd that so much energy would be spent by black people in supporting a president who has not been sympathetic to many black concerns and has denied others their civil rights. Such actions by black church leaders point to the human tendency and willingness to gain respectability at the expense of another group. In this opposition, there is a tendency to focus opposition toward white gays rather than face the reality of opposition to one's own.

Africa and Homosexuality

Another popular anti-gay argument used by African American heterosexuals, including many Africentrists, is the argument that homosexuality is not African and thus not African American. There is no reason why Africans would not express their sexuality like other humans. Yet this argument continues to be used to diminish and dismiss the lives of African American and African lesbians and gays.

When I was a professor at the historically black Fisk University, I was under constant siege from students decrying homosexuality as a perverse European sexual practice, unknown to Africans until Europeans imposed it on them.[27] Interestingly, these same students

---

26. "President Bush and Senator Kerry Tell What They Would Do for Blacks," *Ebony*, November 2004.

27. Marc Eprecht, " 'Good God Almighty, What's This!' Homosexual 'Crime' in Early Colonial Zimbabwe," in *Boy Wives and Female Husbands*, ed. Stephen O.

spent an enormous amount of energy "proving" that Europeans stole everything from Africa, from art to philosophy, from the advanced African cultures of Timbuktu and Mali. Everything, that is, except for homosexuality. With a number of scholars and researchers having documented a homosexual presence from ancient times to the present, not only in Europe, but also throughout the world and the animal kingdom, it becomes difficult to imagine that homosexual practice would not also have been present in Africa. Although black people, like others, have been dishonest about same-sex love in their lives, in our contemporary world, blacks are finding it more difficult to support the myth of homosexual absence.

Why are many Africans and African Americans resistant to a homosexual presence in Africa even when there is considerable evidence otherwise? What is the historical significance of this resistance and denial? There are a number of reasons for this response. In a world that continues to view Africans and African descendants as less developed, less moral, and perhaps less human, and given the stigma of homosexuality as an immoral expression, it becomes clear that the myth about homosexuality satisfies a cultural need — thus, the view that homosexuality is an outside aberration imposed on sacred African people.

In an effort to ensure moral credibility for African people, Africans and Africentrists ironically make a racist claim about Africans and African Americans when they assert the absence of homosexuality in African peoples before Europeans arrived. Since homosexuality is a part of human sexuality, identified in various forms on all continents by anthropologists and sociologists, it becomes a racist claim to state that Africans do not express themselves with same-sex love or sexual activity like the rest of the world. In their brilliant work, *Boy Wives and Female Husbands: Studies of African Homosexualities*, anthropologists Stephen Murray and Will Roscoe simply

---

Murray and Will Roscoe (New York: St. Martin's Press, 1998), 198–99; and Ron Simmons, "Some Thoughts on the Challenges Facing Black Gay Intellectuals," in *Brother to Brother* (Boston: Alyson Publications, 1991), 213.

refute this claim in the following statement: "Although contact between Africans and non-Africans has sometimes influenced both groups' sexual patterns, there is no evidence that one group ever 'introduced' homosexuality to another."[28]

The greatest mystery surrounding this issue is the myth that Europeans brought homosexuality to Africa under colonialism. Although Africans and African Americans are right to criticize European colonialism, the accusation that colonialism imposed homosexuality is without foundation. Despite the presence of homosexual expression in European countries, most of Europe, prior to and during the African slave trade, strongly rejected same-sex sexual practice. European Christians were generally sex-negative and antihomosexual. Hence, European Christian missionaries, slave traders, and colonialists who went into African countries were more prone to condemn homosexual practice rather than condone or encourage it. Under colonial rule in Mugabe's Zimbabwe, for example, "African men's own testimony also shows that they generally expected and often feared the stern disapproval of whites and sought for that reason, to keep their homosexual practices secret."[29]

The assertion that homosexuality is a perverse sexual practice of Europeans imposed on Africans is a reflection of the human tendency to attribute stigmatized behavior to a despised group. How could whites be responsible for sexual feelings in black Africans or black people anywhere? Are blacks granting that whites even have power over their sexual desires? Anthropologist Marc Eprecht had a similar question when he examined the hundreds of homosexual cases in Zimbabwe and surrounding African countries involving only a few whites. "Were this a white man's disease, how to explain that nearly 90 percent of all cases of homosexual crime involved African men [having sex with] other African men or boys?"[30]

---

28. Murray and Roscoe, *Boy Wives and Female Husbands*, 267.
29. Eprecht, " 'Good God Almighty,' " 218.
30. Ibid., 206.

The cultural teaching that homosexuality is a white perversion provides the convenience of disowning homosexual reality in black people. The courageous gay black South African Simon Nikoli stated that his mother, perceiving his homosexuality as a bad thing, told him, "I knew that I should not have sent you to that white school."[31] This common response prevents black Africans from re-assessing homosexual expression and its relevance to those within their families, communities, and themselves. Also, the harsh re-sponse toward fellow gay and lesbian Africans or those who engage in sexual relationships with the same sex, places many Africans in a similar position as the Europeans who colonized them. It is often difficult for previous victims to see themselves as victimizers. The following examples make the case.

In the spring of 2001, two women in Somalia were sentenced to death for "unnatural behavior." Also, "In Uganda, church leaders of the Uganda House of Bishops called on the government not to reg-ister a gay and lesbian group called Integrity Uganda. The church group reportedly described the gay organization as unbiblical and inhuman." Four years later, black Nigerian leaders tortured six young black same-gender-loving women by whipping them ninety times each with a cane (a rod for whipping) for having sex, and a black Nigerian man was "sentenced to death by stoning after he admitted to having had sex with men."[32] Precisely because of this cruelty, these hostile reactions and violent attacks on Africans prevent them from acknowledging their homosexual practice, con-tributing to the lie that there are no African homosexuals. Since no one is being violated, harmed, or killed by two people who share a loving sexual relationship, the hostile reaction by Africans and African Americans is confusing. Even if one understands homo-sexuality as sin that should be avoided, other sins and their sinners do not receive such rage, condemnation, and attack.

---

31. Murray and Roscoe, *Boy Wives and Female Husbands*, 45.
32. Kevin Hauswirth, "Meanwhile in Nigeria" in the *Advocate*, December 6, 2005, 32, and Patrick Murray, "Murder and Hypocrisy" in the *Advocate*, Jan-uary 31, 2006, 37.

Along with denial and misinformation about homosexuality, like their African American counterparts many Africans are simply silent about homosexuality and sexuality in general. African researcher Nii Ajen offers explanations for this "code of silence" regarding sex, arguing that "Victorian, colonial and Christian ideas of what is 'prim and proper'... have had such a great impact on Africans' sense of decency... they scarcely discuss certain issues that they consider unseemly."[33]

The scarcity of a record on homosexuality is not unique; Africans, generally, recorded very little about African culture. With the few exceptions in northern African countries, there are practically no writings about ancient African family life, social customs, government, and food and sex practices. The knowledge about African cultural practices is usually obtained from older African griots through word of mouth within an oral tradition. Thus, it is important to keep in mind that given the cultural taboos against speaking about sex, it would be virtually impossible for homosexual practices to have been recorded.[34] Yet this absence of records should not be interpreted as the absence of homosexuality. People can and do express themselves sexually, in a variety of ways, without ever writing or talking about it.

Regardless of the fact that African people did not leave their own records of homosexual practice, African same-sex sexual expression did not go totally unnoticed and undocumented by anthropologists. Their research indicates that homosexual expression has existed in Africa for a long time.

Murray and Roscoe identify many African homosexual practices and the moral condemnations of early European missionaries: "from late sixteenth-century Portuguese reports of 'unnatural damnation' in Angola,... John Burchardt's 1882 report of 'detestable vices' in Nubia, to the 1893 report of copulation contre

---

33. Murray and Roscoe, *Boy Wives and Female Husbands*, 130.
34. Baum, "Traditional Religions of the Americas and Africa," 19.

nature in . . . Senegal and the 1906 report of . . . Herrero men forsaking the natural use of a woman."[35]

As early as the sixteenth century, rather than condone same-sex sexual behavior, European missionaries frowned on different gender and sexual behavior in some African men. An example of this disdain is found in the writing of French Catholic priest Father J. B. Labat. In his *Relation historique de l'Ethiope occidentale*, he refers to the Congo's Ganga-Ya-Chibanda as "a bare-faced, insolent, obscene, extremely villainous, disreputable scoundrel, committing the foulest crimes with impunity."[36]

In his writing, it becomes clear that Labat assumes Chibanda's association with women to have derived from his "brutal passions" for them. However, "in most cases where males in alternative gender roles have been observed with women, the situation is the opposite of what Labat assumed: they enjoyed such access precisely because they lacked (or were assumed to lack) heterosexual desire [such as the Omani men, the mashoga of Mombasa and the mwanni of the Ila]."[37]

To be sure, there is physical affection and contact between the same sex in African cultures that has nothing to do with homosexuality. However, considering the difficulty in owning a sexuality that is so demeaned by many African societies, it is reasonable that homosexual expression would be denied. It is important to keep in mind that, just because someone says that homosexuality does not exist does not make it so. Twentieth-century anthropologist Kurt Falk substantiates this point.

In the 1920s, Falk documents that for Africans in West Africa and Angola "speaking about homosexual sex is considered disgusting. . . . Nevertheless, homoeroticism, gender variance (and exchanging sex for material goods) are not phenomena alien to Africa, just as silence does not mean absence."[38] He goes on to say

---

35. Murray and Roscoe, *Boy Wives and Female Husbands*, 11.
36. Ibid., 9.
37. Ibid., 10.
38. Cited in ibid., 168, 132.

We have spoken to all of the native tribes of Southwest [Africa] and found that active same-sex intercourse is engaged in by all.... Thus, the fear [expressed in some German publications] that "the morality of the natives thereby is done harm" [by contact with white homosexuals] is baseless. It would be more correct to say that the harm is to whites by their proximity to the natives.... In any case, given the present circumstances, the fear is unsubstantiated, because to the natives having sex is as normal as eating and drinking and, by all means, tobacco-smoking.... Because they view homosexual intercourse with unbiased eyes, they have known and practiced it from time immemorial.[39]

Behavior described as sexual between a man and a woman is often denied as being sexual if it involves two people of the same sex. Researchers find that in case after case, Africans have not been honest about their homosexual expression. His research shows that "even the man you may have just done everything with sexually will say no if you ask him if he is gay. And if you should ask that same man if there is homosexuality in Africa, a likely response will be 'no, there is nothing like that in Africa.' "[40]

In Lesotho, boarding-school girls form "same-sex couples composed of a slightly more dominant partner called a mummy and a slightly more passive partner called a baby.... The girls do not describe these relationships as sexual, although they include kissing, body rubbing, possessiveness and monogamy, the exchange of gifts and promises, and sometimes genital contact."[41] Some Basothu women in southern Africa also resist the idea that their interaction

---

39. Kurt Falk, "Homosexuality among the Natives of Southwest Africa (1925–26)," in *Boy Wives and Female Husbands: Studies of African Homosexualities*, ed. Stephen O. Murray and Will Roscoe (New York: St. Martin's Press, 1998), 195.

40. Ibid., 131.

41. Kendall, "When a Woman Loves a Woman in Lesothu: Love, Sex and the (Western) Construction of Homophobia," in *Boy Wives and Female Husbands: Studies of African Homosexualities*, ed. Stephen O. Murray and Will Roscoe (New York: St. Martin's Press, 1998), 231.

with each other could be construed as sexual in spite of the eroticism, intimacy, and "kissing each other on the mouth with great tenderness, exploring each other's mouth with tongues...for periods of time in excess of sixty seconds...[and] the longest kisses take place out of view of men and children."[42] This present context of dishonesty about same-sex sexual desire and practice has implications for an often-touted absence of homosexuality — past and present — in Africa.

One of the major disputes over the subject of homosexuality has to do with the various cultural differences and approaches to same-sex desire in African and other traditional societies as opposed to an industrialized West. While the use of rites and religion with homosexual expression may be virtually absent in the West, transgendered homosexuality in African tribal societies has been honored.

In "The Traditional Religions of the Americas and Africa," Robert Baum documents that "African religions reveal an importance in homosexual relations that goes far beyond ethical judgments of sin and propriety to include revelations about the nature of spiritual beings, religious authorities....In many instances spiritual beings and their religious specialists in the human community are seen as androgynous, or of an intermediate gender, and thereby provide an importance for a diversity of sexual orientations that remain peripheral to many other religious systems."[43] Baum goes on to say that "transgenderal forms of homosexual relations are fairly common among the peoples of southern and central Africa....Certain [biological] men assume a transgender role wearing women's clothes and hairstyles, performing women's work and marrying men."[44]

This data informs us of the diversity of African responses to homosexual and gender expression and challenges us to reexamine popular African and African American views about homosexuality.

---

42. Ibid., 231–32.
43. Baum, "Traditional Religions of the Americas and Africa," 2–3.
44. Ibid., 29.

Even if Africans uniformly oppose homosexuality, African Americans do not construct a moral code strictly based on African religious and cultural traditions. By and large, African Americans practice different religions and have organized different marital structures, with the latter rightfully refusing to participate in African female genital mutilation, which has caused damage and death to many African women and girls.[45] What is desperately needed in both cultures is an open and loving response that offers justice for all persons in community who care for and support the good of the community.

Like African Americans, some black Africans, like Bishop Desmond Tutu and Nelson Mandela, are challenging the traditional views that homosexuality is immoral and unnatural and therefore deserving scourge and opposition.[46] They recognize that the image of God is reflected in all creation and that our sexual expression is God's gift to us. We must recognize that each time an individual is coerced into denying that gift, the human spirit and soul are lost. Such denial whittles away at human creativity, imagination, and the erotic power that every human being needs in order to flourish and form relationships. When this is realized, we will be able to admit and celebrate that homosexuality also came out of Africa. This celebration will allow black church Christians to affirm all couples united in love and commitment for each other, continuing the African American tradition of affirming a diversity of loving families: extended, single parent, and nuclear.

In light of African American lesbian and gay Christian couples, relationships that sometimes include at least one child, the current restrictive practice of marriage being limited to heterosexual couples is a problem and must change.

Ellison states that E. J. Graff rightly notes, "Changing a given rule changes the very *definition* of marriage."[47] And it is true that church and political leaders are, once again, engaged in an expansion of this

---

45. Alice Walker, *Warrior Marks: Female Genital Mutilation and the Sexual Blinding of Women* (New York: Harcourt Brace, 1993), 105.

46. Murray and Roscoe, *Boy Wives and Female Husbands*, 248.

47. Ellison, *Same-Sex Marriage*, 74.

institution. Despite past religious and political opposition, most would agree today that the change in the nineteenth century to legalize all African American marriages and interracial marriages between blacks and whites in 1967 made a stronger society. As the best of Africentrism has taught us about appreciating and valuing African ways of being and doing, affirming the goodness of erotic love between women and men and their need to have the social and religious communities in which they live affirm and reward their families allows us another way of celebrating God's gift of sexuality for lesbian, gay, and bisexual sisters and brothers. In the next chapter, we consider the lives and Christian witness of those African American lesbians and gays in black churches and what they are asking members of the church community and human family.

Chapter 4

Black, Gay, and Christian
in the Black Church

He came unto his own and his own received him not.
— John 1:11

W AS SOJOURNER TRUTH a lesbian woman? Did a number of
black cult leaders such as Prophet Jones and gospel singers
of the early twentieth century find love and fulfillment with the
same sex? Why did Carter G. Woodson, historian and initiator of
Negro History Week, never marry a woman? When these questions are raised, the heterosexual majority rebuffs the implications
that African Americans held in high esteem as moral leaders and
Christian people could also be homosexual or even bisexual.

In their dread of homosexuality, many argue that it is insignifi-
cant to raise such matters. And that would be the case if we lived
in a world that did not emphasize heterosexuality while attacking nonheterosexuality. In today's culture, heterosexuals generally
believe that their sexual orientation and love relationships are significant and worthy of public mention. Gays have long felt the same
need and are now beginning to assert their love relationships in the
ways and spaces formerly claimed by heterosexuals.

Inasmuch as pre-twentieth-century individuals did not generally
understand sexual attraction as categorical, one could argue that
an inquiry about Sojourner Truth's or any other figure's sexual orientation is anachronistic. Many scholars, including gay scholars
like David Halperin, assert that humans simply experience sexual
drives and the fact that we have identities at all is a result of the
social constructionism of a postmodern world. Sexual categories,

like racial categories, are drawn in our attempt to form classes of people based on levels of pigmentation and sexual attraction.

Despite the valid claims in Halperin's assertion, we live in an age when sexual identity matters. One's sexuality is not simply a private matter, a part of one's private life, but it often is very much one's public identity. It is unrealistic that we would not *expect* to know about the sexual relationships, marriage, or family of politicians, celebrities, athletes, ministers, co-workers, friends, and family. When a person is especially silent about such matters, it is usually an indication that the person is not heterosexual. Gays are always conscious of the fact that there may be negative repercussions from revealing their gay identity.

Heterosexuals never live with this reality or fear. In contrast, heterosexuals experience affirmation and benefits from relationships and marriage. Thus, heterosexuals love to tell about their sexual attractions, dates, and romance. We see signs of this around us every day. A heterosexual privilege is the freedom from this silence, and many feel a sense of entitlement to such relationships, marriages, and benefits. The "private life" of a heterosexual shares a comfortable "public sphere" that is not criticized as "flaunting" but received as a very natural way of being in the world. The difference in "coming out" for the two groups is that homosexuals have a lot to lose while heterosexuals will certainly gain. In a society and world that celebrate heterosexuality, heterosexuals not only receive smiles and affirmation for announcing their sexual interests in the opposite sex, when they become married they receive gifts, money, benefits, and rewards for being heterosexual. Weddings, pictures, applications, census forms, discussions, introductions, commercials, movies, signs, parties, church groups, media, etc. make it clear that heterosexuals enjoy coming out as heterosexual.

Heterosexuals are so privileged in this regard that they may not understand that gays are often condemned when their actions are the same. Here is an example. When I taught at Fisk University, I cut out the society page from the local newspaper, and before attaching it to my bulletin board, wrote on the newspaper the question, should these people have come out? A number of students responded as I thought they would by asking whether all the heterosexual couples in wedding attire were gay. I said, "No. They are heterosexual and by their marriage announcement have come out about their sexual orientation, their sexual attraction. Before they announced this at some point in their lives, there would be no way of knowing they were heterosexual." Although the students understood my point, their demeanor and desire to change the subject made it clear that they felt marriage recognition existed as a sole right, privilege, and entitlement to heterosexuals. So contrary to the common negative response of heterosexuals to gays who identify themselves as gay, heterosexuals typically think that one's sexual identity is important and matters. They just want that identity to be heterosexual.

Gays and lesbians who refuse to deny their sexual identity do so at their own risk. In 1998, U.S. society finally expressed horror about the attack on gays' lives in the wake of Matthew Shepherd being killed by heterosexual men because he was gay. Given that gays are killed on a regular basis because they are gay, I found it interesting that this case finally pierced the American conscience. No doubt race and class made a huge difference. Two years later, little was said about the brutal killing of Arthur Warren, an African American gay man, in West Virginia. As indicated earlier, throughout history men and women of all races have been killed because they make love with the same sex. In much of this history, religious and civil law required the death of women and men for loving in this manner. These deaths did not occur because women and men raped or abused their sexual partners, but simply because heterosexual supremacist culture forbade same-sex sexual practice or lovemaking. In Gary David Comstock's *Violence against Lesbians and Gay Men*, he points out that gay men and lesbians, among others, who engage in same-sex sexual expression reap the wrath of men and women acculturated in a world — often a religious world — that teaches them that gay people deserve death.[1]

---

1. Gary David Comstock, *Violence against Lesbians and Gay Men* (New York: Columbia University Press, 1991), 130–31.

Lesbians and gay men both experience a history of ridicule, hostility, pain, suffering, and death. On the one hand, sexism in cultures throughout the world often ignores women's sexuality or leads those societies not to take women's sexuality or their lovemaking that seriously (the obsession with the phallus convinced Queen Victoria and even contemporary individuals that it was impossible for women to have sex with each other), while on the other, men are especially despised, maligned, and attacked for expressing themselves sexually with other men. Black gay men in the church have been the target of this derision and live with the reality of scriptures, perspectives, and actions being directed against them and their love relationships. Black heterosexual Christians use scripture in their emphasis of heterosexuality as God's intention for all people. In their minds, no righteous person can be gay and Christian.

This thinking prevents those in the church from considering the possibility that Sojourner Truth, Carter Woodson, Sallie Martin, or Daddy Grace could have been gay or lesbian. And black congregants still avoid confronting the fact that gospel great James Cleveland was gay. In spite of openly or perceived gay Christians living exemplary Christian lives around them, African American heterosexual Christians generally resist a reassessing of homosexuality as sin and viewing fellow lesbian and gay Christians as moral individuals. Given that the average black parishioner has come to believe that lovemaking between women or between men is wrong, it is not surprising that African American lesbians and gays are not received in black churches.

This does not mean that lesbians and gays are totally discriminated against or banned from black churches. Since few would identify themselves as gay, it would be presumptuous on the part of church leaders to do so. Even those who would refer to stereotypical behavior and identify the effeminate men in the choir as gay, the invisibility of sexual desire would allow any gay man, or lesbian for that matter, to deny his or her homosexuality, avoiding the possibility of punitive action or discrimination. Lesbians and gays in most black churches are subjected to being silent about their partners, vague or deceptive about marriage interests, or dishonest about their relationships for fear of repercussion. Gay relationships are not recognized publicly along with those of heterosexuals, and, in order to pastor or serve in the black church, gays and lesbians must learn to stay in their place and shut up about "it." In the name of God, black ministers denigrate gays and lesbians with little regard for their feelings, arguing that they are called to preach a gospel that may hurt others.

H. Beecher Hicks, a black minister who identifies himself as heterosexual, appears to boast of his castigation of gays by stating that "if they don't know [my position], it is because they can't read or can't hear."[2] Hicks, the pastor of Metropolitan Baptist Church in Washington, DC, does not mince his words about homosexuality to his congregation with a sizable lesbian/gay membership. Using the pat language of "abomination" that has become associated with homosexuality, Hicks states that "it is the sin, according to Paul, which God gave up.... Those who seek to find a way to legitimize this particular lifestyle will meet with no success."[3]

After interviewing Hicks, African American gay Christian Keith Boykin notes that Hicks fails to consider that what he uses against gays can also be applied to heterosexuals. According to Boykin, Hicks believes that "homosexuality...places the emphasis on the individual's satisfaction and exalts the self over God," citing an often thoughtless comment about procreation without realizing, or at least acknowledging, that most heterosexual intercourse occurs simply for pleasure, with the lovemaking of infertile and elderly heterosexuals, like that of gays, solely for pleasure.[4] I agree with Boykin's response to Hicks that "heterosexuality places the same emphasis on self," and that "if procreation is the only justification for sexual activity" then heterosexuals are just as guilty of "violating God's law" as homosexuals when such activity is engaged in simply for pleasure.

---

2. Boykin, *One More River to Cross*, 130.
3. Ibid., 129.
4. Ibid.

In the hostile climate of the black church and society toward homosexuals and well-adjusted lesbians and gays, it is patently clear why even black gay and lesbian Christians such as Barbara Jordan and James Cleveland who lived in the late twentieth century remained in the closet, shielded from their enemies. Today, little has changed. Black lesbian and gay Christians, like those in Metropolitan Baptist, are still faced with the dilemma: (1) live with integrity, challenging the oppression that destroys you as a gay or lesbian person and face attacks, ridicule, and opposition from a heterosexual majority; (2) avoid this hostility, remain closeted, and suffer the psychic, emotional, and perhaps sexual costs of denying one's freedom to be whole in relationships that are affirmed by family and community; or (3) "live a lie" with the opposite sex as a means for religious and social reward and damage the soul.

The invisibility of one's sexual orientation or sexual identity, as opposed to a visible skin color determining racial identity, makes it impossible for us to know not only how many lesbians and gays are presently within our families, communities, and society, but how many homosexuals (individuals with a primary sexual attraction toward the same sex) have existed in history.[5] While we cannot resolve this question, documentation about George Washington Carver and the cause of death for gospel legend James Cleveland confirmed the long-held, if not dreaded, assumption by many that they both were homosexual. Their lives as homosexual men, amid their extraordinary gifts and Christian witness, offer us the potential not only for a new appreciation of them, but for other gays of faith in our sanctuaries.

African American Gay Men in Black Churches: Carver and Cleveland

George Washington Carver gained notability as the famous Negro scientist of Tuskegee University — not just among African Ameri-

---

5. See Richard A. Isay, *Being Homosexual: Gay Men and Their Development* (New York: Farrar, Straus, Giroux, 1989).

cans, but as one of the few African Americans in the early twentieth century whom whites listened to and held in esteem — and mainstream society could not conceive that this wise and kind Christian servant of God was also homosexual. Unlike Bruce Nugent, Wallace Thurmond, Alain Locke, and Countee Cullen, black homosexual luminaries of the 1920s Harlem Renaissance, Carver lived a clandestine life as a homosexual. Without question, Carver achieved fame and recognition afforded few people in history, with a foundation established in his honor and museums displaying his works, writings, and other accomplishments. There is no doubt that as long as Carver refrained from identifying with what the culture considered perverse behavior, it could make his race an exception and consider him a great person.

Prior to the sexuality studies of the mid–twentieth century, religious and social thinking identified homosexual and Christian morality as incompatible. Carver's Christian life and church involvement removed him from the category preserved for the mentally ill and sexually degenerate homosexual. Perhaps Carver's frequent profession as a Christian countered some of the conflicting messages that he had internalized about himself from the church and culture. Regardless of the purpose, as a faithful Christian, scientist, and educator, Carver endeared himself to whites as much as any black man could in pre–World War II Alabama. He declared throughout his career that if he were special, it had all to do with having been made "as an agent for the divine."[6]

Since we have no record of how he felt about himself as a homosexual (although we could assume that he understood himself to be flawed and sexually immoral, as was the cultural thinking of his day), we cannot know about his self-perception or to what degree this reality affected his life. Whatever his views about his homosexuality, more than any gay person today, Carver understood that he had to be guarded in an early-twentieth-century Alabama culture steeped in racism and homophobia. Like other black educators

---

6. Linda O. McMurry, *George Washington Carver, Scientist and Symbol* (New York: Oxford University Press, 1981), 49.

working hard to gain respectability from upstanding whites, Carver "was also exceedingly sensitive about the impression that Tuskegee Institute made on outsiders. In his mind his own success and that of his school became a crucial test of the abilities of Afr[ican] Americans in an age of racism."[7] Along with a presentation of racial respectability, as a homosexual in an extremely antihomosexual culture, Carver had the additional burden of denying his sexuality and "quickly learned, as all Tuskegee teachers did, that he was expected to place the school's welfare above his own and refrain from any action that could jeopardize the crucial white support that it received."[8] Humiliated by racial injustice and the indignity of segregation, Carver lived his entire homosexual life without being able to speak its name. However, he recognized the limits to concealing his identity and the sexual yearnings and erotic desires that all humans experience.

Carver exhibited some of the characteristics commonly associated with many gay men: he never married; had a flair for knitting, style, drama, decoration and the arts, sought the female part in plays; possessed effeminate mannerisms and a high-pitched voice; and gave massages to football players at Iowa.[9] Certainly, there could be no determination of Carver's sexual orientation based on these facts alone; there are after all heterosexual masseurs, and some heterosexual men choose roles as female impersonators or women (Wesley Snipes, John Leguizamo, Patrick Swayze, and Robin Williams gave stellar and highly convincing performances as women in *To Wong Foo* and *Mrs. Doubtfire*), but the common reality of these traits in gay men and the following actions are compelling evidence about Dr. Carver's affection.

In the foreword to *Growing Up Gay in the South*, the respected historian and author of *The Spirit and the Flesh*, Walter Williams, included George Washington Carver along with gay playwright Tennessee Williams as a famous gay southerner. When I talked with

---

7. Ibid., 53.
8. Ibid., 49.
9. Ibid., 242.

him about Carver as homosexual — information overlooked by
most scholars — he informed me that Tuskegee administrators
recognized what others had only rumored. At a time when homosexuals were generally thought to be mentally ill, sinister and seedy
men preying on children, such a narrow and flawed association prevented blacks, whites, and others from thinking that homosexuals
could be good Christians or distinguished gentlemen like Carver.

The two most compelling examples of Carver's homosexuality
came from Tuskegee's administrators, who noted Carver's sexual
gestures directed toward male students and his love letters written
to males in Alabama. Tuskegee administrators often were embarrassed because Carver had a "bad habit" of placing his hands on the
buttocks of the male students. This evidence, along with his largely
young male following (known as Carver's boys) and the erotic letters to young Alabama males veiled in the flowery language of the
day, provide insight for us about Carver's sexual identity.[10]

Perhaps this also provides insight into the possibility that Carver
had strong yearnings to share his life with another man in an
intimate way but lived during a time when such relationships between men were virtually impossible, especially in rural Alabama.
Could Carver also have beaten the odds in this area as he had by
being a successful African American man in the strongly racist late
nineteenth and early twentieth centuries?

This is the question that would not leave me as I sat in the film
room at the Carver museum in Diamond, Missouri, and watched
a film about Carver and an attractive young man who would occasionally appear with Carver. At the time, I taught at the University
of Missouri, the flagship school of Carver's home state, and was
trying to find out more about one of the few famous African American homosexual men. I thought that this unidentified man may

---

10. Ibid., 203, 244, 245. Pre-1960s writings and film often used euphemistic
language and expressions in order to conceal same-sex sexual desire in a post-
Victorian, sexually prudish America. Scholars point out that given this historical
reality, one must read between the flowery language for an accurate representation
of what the writers and artists had in mind. See Carver's letters, Middle Tennessee
State Archives.

be Carver's housemate or possible companion and asked the park ranger for more information. The park ranger, up to this point, had been eager to share information about Carver's life, but became visibly uncomfortable with my questions about Carver's housemate. His facial expression, however, communicated that he was thinking what I was thinking, yet dreading any discussion about Carver's love life. The park ranger admitted that other visitors had raised questions about Carver's sexual orientation and living arrangement. In light of the fact that Carver, his housemate, and the people who may have known about a relationship would have taken that knowledge with them to the grave, we will never know the full story of this famous African American homosexual or that of the gospel legend James Cleveland.

As a writer of more than four hundred gospel compositions, a lead singer in widely acclaimed gospel groups, the music trainer of Aretha Franklin, three-time Grammy winner, and founder and pastor of the influential Gospel Music Workshop of America and Cornerstone Institutional Baptist Church, Cleveland is unquestionably a gospel legend and rightfully holds the title of the "King of Gospel."[11] His recordings of "Peace Be Still," "Stood on the Banks," and "The Love of God" remain some of the best gospel recordings of all time. Influenced by gospel greats Mahalia Jackson and Roberta Martin, Cleveland began composing gospel songs as a teenager and mastered the gospel style of piano playing while a youth. Cleveland grew up amidst the homophobia of black churches, and like most homosexuals of his generation, followed the social and religious conventions by getting married. Like so many mixed-sexual-orientation marriages, the marriage ended in divorce.

Cleveland's story is not an unfamiliar story in the black church. Men understood to be gay, like Cleveland, are allowed opportunity and success if they play by the rules of keeping silent about their "private life." This is not acceptance; it is merely tolerance, and it is tolerance because of the benefits heterosexuals are afforded by the

---

11. Robert Johns, in Smith, *Notable Black American Men*, 211–12.

spiritual and monetary contributions of gays.[12] Cleveland realized that heterosexuals would not respect and affirm him and his relationships but would rather attack his personhood and relationships, as experienced by Leonard Patterson and Tommie Watkins.

Heterosexuals do not experience such restrictions of having to hide their sexual orientation. Gospel artists Rev. Janice Brown and her husband, and Mom and Pop Winan are all public about their "private life," and there is no opposition to their openness. There is an unspoken agreement between black heterosexual Christians and gay Christian gospel artists, gospel radio and television show hosts, choir members and choir masters, that there will be tolerance as long as gays understand that their gayness is their sin and must be treated as other sins — and remain unspoken.

Baldwin and Bayard

Although Carver and Cleveland left many people guessing about their sexual orientation, noted African Americans James Baldwin and Bayard Rustin chose to take the unusually courageous step and live as openly gay men within black communities and white societies. Both sons of the church, Baldwin suffered oppressive homophobic and physical abuse by his Pentecostal father and the members of the black Pentecostal denomination, eventually ostracizing him, while Rustin escaped considerable abuse by being in the more accepting white Quaker tradition. Despite the hostility that they experienced from black Christians, neither man abandoned his belief in God and commitment to helping poor, disenfranchised black people in black churches and communities.

Baldwin acknowledged at an early age his same-sex sexual attraction in much the same way that adolescent heterosexual males identify and respond to their opposite-sex sexual attraction. His decision to turn from the sins of New York and to the Fireside Pentecostal Assembly Church resulted in his becoming "saved" and

---

12. Boykin, *One More River to Cross*, 131–32.

a Pentecostal minister at fourteen. Baldwin soon learned, however, that being homosexual and Christian were incompatible, at least in the Pentecostal denomination, leaving him "disillusioned with the church, and armed with an increasingly negative view of its people, its past and its current practices. . . . [Baldwin subsequently] abandoned the ministry, denounced the Christian church and began writing his first novel."[13]

Baldwin had exemplified characteristics common to many gay boys; he was good, kind, and caring with a strong sense of faith and devotion to God. He, like gay writer Brian McNaught, enjoyed the many days that allowed him opportunities "to commune with Jesus, [his] dearest friend, who would never fail [him], who knew all the secrets of [his] heart."[14] Also, like a number of gays and African Americans who remain in dire situations after praying for God to deliver them, Baldwin concluded that God did fail him.[15] He channeled his anger and frustration over the injustices of homophobia and racism into his novels, namely, *Go Tell It on the Mountain*, *Another Country*, *Giovanni's Room*, and *Nobody Knows My Name*.

Unlike Baldwin, Bayard Rustin used the teachings of his faith to live with integrity as an openly gay man. But even in a more progressive church and political venue, Rustin did not engage the ethics of homosexuality in his writing in the same way that he addressed nonviolence or economic and racial injustice. Coming of age as a homosexual in the early and mid-twentieth century did not allow for much written discussion and identification. For "even when he did move from the public to the personal, Rustin wrote in ways that were stilted and detached. But much of the silence can be attributed to the times. It was an era in which homosexual and heterosexual cooperated in an elaborately choreographed dance of discretion."[16]

---

13. Floyd Ferebee, in Smith, *Notable Black American Men*, 47.
14. Ibid.
15. Ibid.
16. John D'Emilio, *Lost Prophet: The Life and Times of Bayard Rustin* (Chicago: University of Chicago Press, 2003), 297.

Historians Taylor Branch and John D'Emilio note the major role that Rustin and Baldwin played in the civil rights movement of the 1950s and 1960s. While both men spoke out strongly against the racial injustices encountered by black people during this time, their participation received mixed reactions from a less than enthusiastic group of black ministers shrouded with the homophobia of this era. Although many tempered their misgivings about known homosexuals working in civil rights organizations, none expressed more disdain toward Rustin than the womanizing preacher/politician Adam Clayton Powell Jr., whose influence in civil rights circles caused Rustin to go underground.[17] Such opposition did not prevent Rustin's commitment to civil rights and the peace movements. King's primary advisor, Rustin was also a major influence in King's Gandhian nonviolence. Without the dedication and hard work of Rustin, the 1963 March on Washington would not have achieved its success as one of the greatest events in history.

Baldwin's presence at the March on Washington and other civil rights gatherings also reflected his commitment against white racism. In Baldwin's case, he protested such racism in his impassioned speeches and literary works. His 1961 essay, *Nobody Knows My Name,* emerged as a powerful work that "focuses on inequality of the races and especially the inhumane treatment of black people in the North as well as in the South."[18]

The protest and presence of these men contribute to younger gay Christian men's religious pursuit of wholeness. Growing up in the civil rights movement era of religious equality for blacks and gays, young black gays find inspiration from the theological convictions of other African Americans addressing racism in Christian churches and European American gays challenging homophobia and heterosexual supremacy within their Christian bodies. Such Christian actions provide witness to the first openly gay African American Christians challenging black church leaders on their discrimination against them.

---

17. Ibid., 108.
18. Floyd Ferebee, in Smith, *Notable Black American Men,* 48.

Tommie Watkins

On October 3, 2000, Tommie Watkins made history as the first black gay person to seek ordination in the oldest of the historically black denominations — the African Methodist Episcopal (AME) Church. Watkins, a lifelong member of the denomination, was rejected by the denomination that also became the first to deny a woman, African American Jarena Lee, ordination in spite of the fact that its founder, the Reverend Richard Allen, left the white Methodist denomination under racist church practices that relegated him and other blacks to segregated seating during worship. Although Allen received ordination in the white Methodist Church in 1799, neither he nor his successors were willing to ordain black women or gays until 1948. The denomination has never ordained an openly gay person.

Like Jarena Lee, Watkins demonstrated a number of ministerial gifts, including preaching gifts at his home church, the Greater Bethel African Methodist Episcopal Church, where he also led a lesbian/gay ministry called the Ministry of Reconciliation. He began this ministry after his parents cut off contact with him because he is gay. His parents, having been taught that homosexuality is sinful by their black church, represent a majority of black parents in anguish over their lesbian and gay daughters and sons. Since black lesbian and gay Christians generally experience this rejection, Watkins realized that there needed to be some ministry to help them heal from this devastation. In a recent interview, he argued that "if certain people can't come to God's house and serve, where are they going to go?"[19] This is an issue very dear to Tommie Watkins since the church is denying him the opportunity to serve in the capacity as minister, a calling by God that is really clear to him.

By all standards, Watkins was highly qualified for ordination to the Diaconate (the first of two stages toward full ordination as a minister in his denomination). In addition to his church service, preaching, and pastoral ministry, he had successfully completed

---

19. Juan Carlos Rodriguez, "All God's Children (Except Some)," *Miami New Times*, October 26, 2000.

two years of ecumenical study. Challenging the black church as it has never been challenged before, "Watkins made his disappointing discovery... in Melbourne [Florida, when] he traveled to the church in hopes that the 213-year-old religious institution's South Florida chapter would ordain him as a deacon at its annual conference."[20] The ordination service took place at a packed Greater Allen Chapel AME Church. It was the AME's Eleventh Episcopal District annual conference, a meeting where "hundreds of congregants, from Melbourne to Key West, would set policy, select new leaders, and chart a course for the coming year."[21] When the names of the 2000 Diaconates to the Ordained Ministry in the AME Church were called, Tommie Watkins's name was not on the list.

In contradiction to his own actions in the Watkins case, Bishop John Hurst Adams declared that "we're [church leaders and members of the AME Church] going to be sensitive to issues and calls of support before us.... Leadership is expanding the definition of what is possible where issues like justice, fairness and opportunity are concerned," a reference to the admirable, albeit rather late, church's actions earlier in the year when Bishop Vashti Murphy McKenzie became the first woman bishop in the denomination. Refusing to see this contradiction in the treatment of lesbian and gay AME parishioners, Bishop Adams defensively claims a clear AME Church position:

> if a person is openly practicing homosexuality, we are unlikely to ordain them, because [homosexuality] is not consistent with creation; it's not consistent with scripture and the church.... In my opinion the homosexual lifestyle is not the same type of issue as racial discrimination.... It is not the same, and I do not accept putting the two together.[22]

Although Adams's earlier grand statement served as justification for the actions that AME leaders had taken to ordain Bishop McKenzie

---

20. Ibid., 1.
21. Ibid., 2.
22. Ibid., 4.

as the first woman bishop of the AME Church and any black denomination, this action nonetheless went against AME Church tradition and Christian scripture that arguably prohibits and certainly does not sanction such ordination. It is this break with tradition and the selective use of scripture that baffles many lesbian, gay, and heterosexual clergy and laity within black denominations and the larger Christian church. While such an action should be supported, Watkins and others in the AME denomination question why that same change is not occurring related to matters of homosexuality.

Watkins is in a league by himself when it comes to challenging black church discrimination toward African American gay ordination. Black gay and lesbian ordained clergy or those seeking ordination remain in the closet in some form (either as a silent gay person or heterosexually married or divorced) or find acceptance as an openly gay minister in the more accepting white denominations, nonmainline church bodies, or gay denominations. Unlike some of their white gay counterparts in white denominations, black gays experience fellow black clergy and laity as more discriminatory and less willing to treat them on par with heterosexuals and allow them full participation as openly gay Christians in the church. Watkins (now an outreach AIDS minister at St. Stephen's Episcopal Church, Coconut Grove, Florida) battled the intransigent Bishop John Hurst Adams and church leaders in the African Methodist Episcopal Church, as did Leonard Patterson in the Baptist Church two decades earlier.

Leonard Patterson

In 1972, at the historic Ebenezer Baptist Church in Atlanta, where Martin Luther King Jr. and his father pastored, the Reverend Leonard Patterson, an African American gay man, "had many idealistic views of what Atlanta, Ebenezer Baptist Church, Martin Luther King Jr. and Morehouse College represented. For [him] these institutions symbolized honesty, integrity, tolerance, and compassion."[23]

---

23. Leonard Patterson, "At Ebenezer Baptist Church," in *Black Men/White Men*, ed. Michael J. Smith (San Francisco: Gay Sunshine Press, 1983), 164.

His experience as an openly gay minister in an interracial relationship would test the limits of integrity, tolerance and compassion of Ebenezer's black church leadership.

After leaving medical school and responding to God's call to ordained ministry, Patterson, like Jesus and King, felt compassion for the disenfranchised, the dispossessed, and those in captivity. He also felt called to "Ebenezer to help the image of 'the homosexual' in America since the church represents liberation and stands as an oasis for the downtrodden in a desert of persecution. After all [Patterson reasoned], the son of this church, Martin Luther King Jr. had given his life marching for the rights of garbage workers in Memphis who had been mistreated and oppressed by an insensitive society."[24] Patterson emerged as a very able minister, leading Bible study and providing a significant presence in the Children's Chapel Ministry and prison ministry while offering support to the sick and shut-in ministry and the Young Adult Fellowship. His partner, Jim, also a member of Ebenezer, joined him in revitalizing a faltering youth group. By organizing cookouts and swimming parties and listening to their problems, Jim and Leonard struck the right chord with the youth, enabling them to find that they had a part in the life of the church.

It is not clear how many parishioners at Ebenezer chose to accept Patterson's gay reality. I find that much of the black church insists on seeing the emperor as clothed when it is clear that he is naked. I know this from personal experience. Although I have been very clear about my being gay and often worshiped with my partner at the time, introducing him as my *companion*, there remained several women who ignored my reality, flirted with me anyway, and made comments about marriage to me *after* meeting him. I find this heterosexual behavior of entitlement, though common, disrespectful to gays. Heterosexuals, on the other hand, have not been shy in expressing their disapproval about gays expressing romantic interests in them. One person at Ebenezer understood all too well that Leonard Patterson and his partner Jim were a gay interracial

---

24. Ibid.

couple and expressed his displeasure with Patterson's white partner if not Patterson's homosexuality. The person was the pastor, the Reverend Joseph Roberts.[25]

In his essay "At Ebenezer Baptist Church," Patterson writes about the dishonest lives that heterosexual ministers and pastors encourage black gay men to lead, the same gay men who are later condemned for putting black women and their children at risk. Patterson's following account articulates a version of what many gay men have encountered from older ministers:

> I was told, in effect, that as long as I played the political game and went with a person who was more easily passed off as a 'cousin,' I would be able to go far in the ministry. Perhaps, I should even marry and have someone on the side. Apparently, these arrangements would make me more "respectable." Well, there are many black ministers in Atlanta who are gay. Most of them live double lives. I had decided not to do this; and for that, the . . . pastor decided to make my life miserable.[26]

Rather than be blatant about his discomfort with homosexuality and gays as H. Beecher Hicks has been at Metropolitan Baptist Church, Roberts was more subtle, though no less vicious. Refraining from diatribes against homosexuality, Roberts instead chose to attack Patterson, the homosexual, in his sermons from the pulpit. Roberts later prohibited Patterson from "entering the study for prayer with the other associate ministers, and had seeds of animosity planted against [him] in the minds so that in meetings the subject of homosexuality would inevitably be brought up."[27]

In attempt to "sabotage" Patterson's ministry, Roberts lied to the organist, telling him that worship had been canceled on the Sunday Patterson was scheduled to preach so that the organist and choir would be absent from worship. Roberts was out of town. These incidents eventually took their toll on Patterson (and his partner),

---

25. Ibid.
26. Ibid., 164–65.
27. Ibid., 165.

and they left the church that has gained an international reputation as an oasis of liberation and justice for all humankind. The irony is that some of Patterson's last memories of the church are of homophobic parishioners expressing to Patterson their disdain for homosexuality by stating that "if you lie down with dogs, you get up smelling like dirt." Contrary to the claim of the guest pastor at the seminary where I did my graduate work, these are common attitudes and practices of heterosexuals in black churches that continue to inform black gay ministers and members that it is not safe and welcoming if you come out of your place and request to be treated like fellow Christians.

The above examples of Watkins and Patterson stand alone; most gays in black churches live in silence or denial with an enormous amount of shame. Many convince themselves that their sexuality, unlike that of their heterosexual family members and fellow parishioners, is private and unworthy of church recognition. The more common story of gays in the church is leaving their gayness out of the church and treating their sexuality as a "lifestyle," something they do on Saturday night and pray on Sunday to be forgiven. This reality serves as a constant reminder that while black churches may allow gays to remain within their doors and experience emotional highs from worship, like Metropolitan Baptist in Washington, DC, these places of worship certainly cannot be considered communities that affirm gay Christians' loving sexual expressions as life-giving and sacred.

This is certainly not the case among Jehovah's Witnesses. The homosexual-negative teachings heard by Malcolm, a gay parishioner in this largely black denomination (the denomination of Michael Jackson), and his acquiescence to those teachings, is the common experience of gays in black churches. The Jehovah's Witnesses, known for their ministry of door-to door evangelism and the distribution of the denomination's (Kingdom Hall) publication, *The Watchtower*, also publishes *Your Youth: Getting the Best Out of It*. As a gay adolescent, Malcolm read what the church had to say about his homosexuality in a chapter on masturbation and homosexuality. These areas were taught as sinful practices, and "violation of these strict moral and doctrinal beliefs result in 'disfellowship' in which other Witnesses (parishioners), including family, are barred from any interaction with these 'eternally damned' persons."[28] When one considers the depth of sexual desire with everyone's bodily constitution and the importance of family and community for black people in a racist society, it is easy to understand the devastation and the dilemma experienced by gays in black churches.

Black heterosexual Christians' claim to religious and social justice and black liberation often ignores this reality. Given their experiences of homophobia and heterosexual supremacy in black churches, black gays recognize that black heterosexuals have been dishonest about the level of opposition and oppression they inflict on gays. Although black gay Christians acknowledge the racism of whites and the homosexual hatred of white heterosexuals, many, such as Jacob, a gay member of a black Southern Baptist church, still feel that on average "the white community is a little more open-minded, even in the South, about homosexuality. With the black community it's more strictly religious as far as our faith and up-bringing."[29] Perhaps there is validity to this claim when considering that in the 1990s, two white Southern Baptist churches in North Carolina, the Pullen Baptist Church and the Brinkley Memorial Baptist Church, ordained an openly gay man and held a wedding for a gay couple, respectively. No church of any black denomination has demonstrated the gospel message with this level of liberation and religious justice for black lesbian and gay Christians.

James Sears comments that

the life stories of African-American [gay] males ... illustrate how their family religious faith and its intersection with the black community, culture and history complicate their emerging homosexual identity. The experiences of Malcolm living under the watchtower supervision of his elders are an extreme

---

28. Sears, *Growing Up Black in the South*, 61.
29. Ibid., 65.

example of the more common difficulty that lesbian and gay persons of color confront.[30]

Openly gay African American writer Joseph Beam writes about gays' experience with black heterosexuals in even more poignant ways:

> Because of our homosexuality the Black community casts us as outsiders. We are the poor relations, the proverbial black sheep, without a history, a literature, a religion, or a community. Our already tenuous position as Black men in white America is exacerbated because we are gay. We are even more susceptible to the despair, alienation, and delusion that threaten the entire black community.[31]

As difficult as many heterosexual leaders make it for gay Christian men, many remain committed to the black church, enduring homophobia and hoping for its end.

Lesbians find themselves confronted with the same reality but, because they are women, sometimes with children, often feel compelled to respond in different ways. The lack of emphasis placed upon lesbian identity and female homosexuality may spare them in some ways but can lead them to feeling isolated and unclear in their search for other lesbians as romantic partners and support. And given its unfriendly history toward women (also upheld by some gay men), lesbians frequently bear the greatest burden in the black church.

African American Lesbians in Black Churches

Most of us grew up with some awareness that gay men existed, if not in our world, somewhere in the universe. Most of us heard whispers about a male teacher or florist who was "like that." Those of us thirty-five and over grew up during a time when body language, raised eyebrows, facial gestures, and hand movements said more about gays than our mouths. As difficult as it is for most people

---

30. Ibid.
31. Joseph Beam, ed., *In the Life* (Boston: Alyson Publications, 1986), 17.

still to talk about homosexuality, more people experienced difficulty discussing homosexuality three decades ago and found such a
discussion virtually impossible before then. Even though homosexual men remained esoteric, the effeminate man became the
association with gays. Those of us who grew up in black churches
probably associated the swishy pianist (or organist, if we came out
of a large urban parish) and effeminate male choir members with
homosexuality. Regardless of whether we emerged from a rural or
urban church; wealthy or poor; Baptist, Methodist, or Pentecostal;
large or small, practically every black congregant can conjure in
their minds, even at this very moment, a man in their home church
understood to be gay.

Our images of lesbians in churches are not as clear. Since gay men
fit the stereotype as choir members in the church, gay men were
known to be present. Although lesbians existed in black churches
and choirs as well, they were more difficult to identify, largely because the stereotypical lesbian did not have a church affiliation.
Historically, black lesbians became associated with hard women
on the streets or in prison and friendly to bars and nightclubs, as
was true with the legendary lesbian/bisexual blues singer, Bessie
Smith. The general association made by black church members that
lesbianism was a sinful "lifestyle" precluded them from conceptual-
izing bisexuals and lesbians also as good women of the community,
nurses, schoolteachers, and mothers serving in the church as choir
members, ushers, and church mothers. As a college student, I
adopted a different understanding of black lesbian women when I
discovered that my elementary school teacher, who had taught va-
cation Bible school during my childhood, and a schoolteacher who
sang in my church choir were also lesbian Christian women.

Though I have noted that there is very little history on black lesbians and gays, especially those in black churches, there appears to
be slightly more history and writing on black gay men. Literature
and films such as *Brother to Brother*, *In the Life*, *Stonewall*, *One
More River to Cross*, *Growing Up Gay in the South*, the E. Lynn
Harris series, *Gay Readers*, *One of the Children*, *Black, Gay and
Christian*, *Tongues Untied*, and *Black Is, Black Ain't*, to name a

few, are works produced largely by black gay men, highlighting black gay men's experience. There is indeed a solid body of literature on love between black women from the brilliance of African American lesbian and bisexual writers Barbara Smith, Cheryl Clark, Alice Walker, Ann Allen Shockley, Jewelle Gomez, and Audre Lourde. But with the exception of the Reverend Dr. Renee Hill, an African American lesbian scholar and Episcopal priest, and the Reverend Irene Monroe, a public intellectual and minister, the published stories of African American lesbian Christian women are virtually absent.

When we consider the shameful sexist history of black churches, it is not so surprising that black lesbians would have difficulty in giving voice to their presence. Since black churches have always allowed men opportunities to hold whatever position they desired in churches, the invisibility of gay men allowed them to "pass" as heterosexual and hold any office in the church. Thus, gay men can be found in all denominations and throughout black Christendom from the highest offices as bishops and ministers to the lay positions as trustees and deacons. Black men's exclusion of women from most positions throughout black church history has not allowed for lesbians, and heterosexual women for that matter, to excel and be granted power.

There is plausibility in the notion that the sexist history of black churches largely contributes to a void of visible lesbian church presence. In an institution that emphasizes families with children, gay men, like lesbians, endure the unfortunate pressures of adopting heterosexual identities. While gay men could at least find small consolation in the prestige of being a church leader, lesbians generally experienced exclusion from leadership positions. In his excellent study of black lesbians in the Harlem Jazz Age, Eric Garber points out that lesbians, like Mabel Hampton, experienced fewer professional opportunities than their gay male counterparts but found resolve in show business life. This profession allowed Hampton and others to earn a good income, limit their social contact with men, and move within a predominantly female social world. Many bisexual and black lesbian women, including Gladys Bentley, Jackie

"Moms" Mabley, Alberta Hunter, Gertrude "Ma" Rainey, Josephine Baker, and Ethel Waters are other examples.[32]

Lesbians also accounted for a number of schoolteachers in the church. In the tradition of spinsters, they devoted their lives to education, a profession that gave them respectability without requiring that they marry men. Of course, all lesbians in the church could not be or chose to be schoolteachers. Some may have left the sexist restrictions in mainline black churches to become church founders, evangelists, gospel singers, and writers. We can draw some fairly substantial conclusions about lesbian church leaders in history, but the present ministries of openly lesbian ministers, such as the Reverend Monique Ellison, Rev. Alma Faith Crawford and Rev. Karen Hutt (a clergy couple), Rev. Louise Rose, Bishop Yvette Flunder, Rev. Wanda Floyd, and Rev. Irene Monroe, offer us brilliant stories of lesbians finding ministries in the midst of black church oppression. One of the greatest African Americans in U.S. history was a lesbian congresswoman and lifelong member of the Baptist Church. Her name was Barbara Jordan.

Barbara Jordan

In March 1996, the *Advocate* featured an exclusive on Barbara Jordan, the black lesbian congresswoman from Texas, entitled "Barbara Jordan: The Other Life. How the Revered Congresswoman Kept Her Lesbianism a Secret for Almost Two Decades."[33] If one has adopted an attitude that homosexuality is sin or pathology, this title may be read as a scandal. This is certainly not the intent of the *Advocate*, a gay publication and newsmagazine that informed the public that one of the most respected congresspeople in history was also lesbian. Unfortunately, like many African American Christians, Barbara Jordan lived her life in hiding, battling suspicions, innuendo, rumors, and insults about her lesbianism, as she

---

32. Eric Garber, "Spectacle of Color: African Americans in the Harlem Renaissance," in *Hidden from History: Reclaiming the Gay and Lesbian Past*, ed. Martin Bauml Duberman et al. (New York: Meridian, 1989), 325–26.

33. Moss, "Barbara Jordan."

also fought the unavoidable battles surrounding her gender, race, and debilitating multiple sclerosis, a disease that ended her life at fifty-nine.[34]

Like Cleveland, Jordan remained publicly silent about her sexual orientation, even after much public speculation and having been with her "longtime companion" for over twenty years.[35] Having experienced many battles along racial and gender lines, and knowing the religious and social bigotry against lesbian and gay people, Jordan "was straightforward about her sexual orientation in private but did not think it should be fodder for public consumption. [Jordan] never denied who she was," but she knew that her political career would be over if she were outed as a lesbian congresswoman in the 1970s, as supporters of her opponent, Curtis Graves, tried to do in 1972.[36]

In the wake of her death, however, the media confirmed what had been known and discussed for years: Barbara Jordan was lesbian. Although such confirmation failed to shock the public, many people, including other gay civil rights activists in Texas, refused to discuss this fact. This avoidance, anguish, and distance remind us of the discomfort and shame that generations have internalized about homosexuality. Even her longtime companion Nancy Earl, who was singled out like a spouse in several tributes at Jordan's funeral, took a backseat during the services as if she understood her place not to be at the head of the funeral of the woman with whom she shared her life. This silence reflects a tradition of homosexuality at odds with southern and black religion.

Barbara Jordan grew up in a southern black church and community that adopted the church teachings and black social mores of respectability.[37] Her father, a Baptist minister, and mother, a devout member of the family's Good Hope Baptist Church in Houston, believed that black people could counter the prevalent 1930s white

---

34. Mary Beth Rogers, *Barbara Jordan: American Hero* (New York: Bantam Books, 1998), 354.
35. Moss, "Barbara Jordan," 39.
36. Rogers, *Barbara Jordan*, 164.
37. Ibid., 29.

racists' view that black people were immoral and sexually perverse by opting to portray themselves as faithful Christians with a tame sexuality within their marriages and family. Being deeply moved by her pastor's sermons, at the age of ten Jordan did what is familiar practice in black Baptist churches throughout the country: going to the front of the church, she extended her hand to the pastor and stated, "I want to join the church to be baptized and become a Christian."[38] She became a committed Christian, heavily involved in church activities, including a church quartet formed by a sister and two of the other girls in the church. Her commitment to church would remain throughout her life, even as she developed her gift of oratory and began her political career.

Early in her life following college, Jordan was under great pressure from her father to get married and live the kind of respectability that he and the church had emphasized throughout her life.[39] This strict teaching influenced both the private life and the public role for some black civil rights activists. Reflecting on Jordan's family and church teachings and how they influenced her response to the civil rights demonstrations around her, Mary Beth Rogers, Jordan's biographer, asserts that "her upbringing had been too conservative and her Baptist notion of respectability was too ingrained to violate the law deliberately — even if the law was unjust."[40]

Jordan resented the stern control that her father had on her life and the way that her mother acquiesced to his behavior, and found herself limited in how much she could openly be herself. Realizing that her unrelenting father, family, and church would never accept the truth about her homosexuality, Barbara, like gays throughout the world, was left with the difficult option of hiding things, keeping secrets, and sneaking off.[41] Though Jordan found some escape from this rigidity in her new political circle of friends, the extreme measures that she took to be perfectly "normal" to her people and the society by concealing her lesbianism and multiple sclerosis are

---

38. Ibid., 32.
39. Ibid., 91.
40. Ibid., 80.
41. Ibid., 143.

undoubtedly marks that Ben Jordan left on her that she could never escape. This is apparent in how she lived her life.

Most people can understand why she remained closeted in the conservative political milieu of Houston, Texas (a climate similar to what professional gay athletes encounter); fewer understand her remaining in the closet when she retired and taught at the arguably most liberal place in Texas, Austin's University of Texas. As African Americans generally frown on those African Americans who "pass," understanding the need for role models and proponents of self-pride in a racist society, gays share the need to have model gays dispel vicious stereotypes in a homophobic culture. Since Jordan would have been such a role model for gays, there are gays and lesbians disappointed and bothered by Jordan's silence, feeling, as one gay reporter put it, "if anybody had the luxury to say, 'by golly, I'm a lesbian, and this is the woman I love,' it was Barbara Jordan."[42] The woman who had spoken so eloquently, so passionately and compellingly about the integrity of the Constitution during the Watergate hearings, convincing the American public that Richard Nixon's concealment and dishonesty to the American public about the Watergate tapes made him unfit to remain as president, ironically said nothing about the religious and social injustice that she and the countless millions of gays faced within and outside church communities. Jordan's story regrettably is the rule and not the exception of lesbians and gays in black churches.

Yvette Flunder

Such oppression moved gospel artist and ordained lesbian minister Dr. Yvette Flunder in the founding of the City of Refuge Church in 1991. The San Francisco church is a "thriving inner-city congregation that celebrates the radically inclusive love of Jesus Christ" and functions as a ministry "to underserved people, including women

---

42. Moss, "Barbara Jordan," 39.

and men living with AIDS and HIV and disenfranchised members of the transgendered, gay and lesbian communities."[43] Flunder followed the path of her father and grandfather by becoming a Church of God in Christ preacher. Her ministry brings the rich black church worship tradition into a progressive faith community for those gay African American Christians estranged from mainline black churches. While a native of San Francisco, Flunder also spent much of her childhood in small towns of Mississippi and conservative black churches. Her church is a powerful and needed community for many black lesbians and gays wounded by black church castigation. In addition to this ministry, Flunder is also a gospel recording artist and author of *Where the Edge Gathers: Building a Community of Radical Inclusion.*

Irene Monroe

It is not just black churches that have been unwelcoming to black lesbians and gays; black religious institutions of theological education like Howard University Divinity School and the Interdenominational Theological Center have hardly been accepting of lesbian and gay students and faculty, often leaving the homophobic positions of its students to go unchallenged. Dr. Elias Farajaje-Jones did not only receive condemnation from black pulpits in Washington, DC, when he came out as bisexual at the Howard University Divinity School, but was also condemned by students.

Although a few seminary professors challenge homophobia at the Interdenominational Theological Center (ITC), namely, Drs. Randall Bailey and Jacquelyn Grant, as an institution ITC is less committed to combating institutionalized church homophobia than one that actively promotes and allows it. Situated in the black metropolis of Atlanta, ITC is a seminary comprising seven denominational seminaries: Gammon Theological Seminary (United Methodist), Turner Theological Seminary (African Methodist Episcopal), Phillips School of Theology (Christian Methodist Episcopal), C. H.

---

43. *www.sfrefuge.org/yf_bio.shtml.*

Mason Theological Seminary (Church of God in Christ), More-house School of Religion (National Baptist), Johnson C. Smith School of Religion (Presbyterian), and Richardson Fellowship at large (general seminary). Each seminary instructs its seminarians regarding its own particular denominational requirements and is governed by the administrative structure of the Center.

Such a rich ecumenical flavor and black church tradition at-tracted Irene Monroe, an African American lesbian Christian, to apply for admission to ITC after experiencing a call to ordained ministry. Monroe, like Patterson and Watkins, has chosen to live with integrity in black churches and stands as one of the leading black lesbian Christian ministers of our time. Throughout her doc-toral studies at Harvard, Monroe has devoted her amazing skill as a civil rights activist for the only group of U.S. citizens still denied their civil rights: lesbians and gay men. Like the civil rights min-isters of the 1950s and 1960s, Monroe remains active in church leadership, including Christian education for youth, and ministry as assistant pastor of United Baptist Church in Boston. Being selected in 1997 as one of "The 50 Most Intriguing Women in Bos-ton," the following year she served as Grand Marshall of Boston's Gay Pride Parade in recognition of her commitment to racial and sexual justice for lesbians and gays in the United States.[44] She is one of the few people chronicling the lives of African American gays and lesbians, African American sexuality, and anti-Semitic rhetoric in the black Christian and Muslim communities. Her award-winning essay, "Louis Farrakhan's Ministry of Misogyny and Homophobia," has received critical acclaim.

The fight for her life began early at approximately six months when "someone discarded her — that is the word she uses, quite sadly — in a trash can in a park in Brooklyn."[45] Not only did she begin her social existence on the lowest rungs of society, but her faith was nurtured in a dilapidated house of worship known

---

44. Gary David Comstock, *A Whosoever Church* (Louisville: Westminster John Knox Press, 2001), 59.

45. Ibid.

as a storefront church. Storefront black churches gained prominence in the urban North as blacks from the South migrated to
urban centers during the first few decades of the twentieth century.
These churches shared space with rundown or abandoned stores
and offered a grassroots quality in worship. Monroe describes this
experience as "Baptecostal," referring to the demonstrative worship
style strongly linked with urban poor black worship. After a difficult childhood of foster care, Monroe beat the odds and obtained a
degree from prestigious Wellesley College in Massachusetts.

After college, Monroe experienced a call to ministry and, like
most college-trained African Americans feeling this call, began dis-
cerning where she would attend seminary for theological education
and ministry training. Two black seminaries in particular appealed
to Monroe because she felt "who better to train me for ministry
in the black church than a black seminary?" "If I am going to be
a black Baptist minister, I'll go down to either D.C. or Atlanta
and learn from professors who are schooling folks for the black
church."[46] Both black seminaries, Howard Divinity School and the
Interdenominational Theological Center, told African American
Irene Monroe that they were denying her admission not because
of her academic ability (she was told by the admissions officer that
she was "academically strong, [more than] the rest of the applicant
pool"), but because she was lesbian. Monroe did not have to specu-
late about the institutions' homophobia, for both of them actually
informed her that they were denying her admission because of her
sexuality. Such actions parallel those of white seminaries that denied entry to black people like Howard Thurman solely on the basis
of race.

The admissions officer informed Monroe that her "faith statement as a born again black lesbian Christian" was "very problematic." Monroe wrote, "I honestly had written about having been
closeted and fearful of being Black and lesbian and also Christian,
about letting go of that fear, about how I felt I embraced the wonder

---

46. Ibid., 65.

of God."[47] Black committee members had such trouble with her words that they communicated to Monroe that she had two options: agree to be closeted in the program or remain identified as lesbian and experience rejection. At this time in the 1980s, Monroe was informed that she would have no support from faculty or students and that no church in the city of Atlanta would take her in for her student ministry, a requirement for all students in the M.Div. program. When she, like Patterson, felt that Martin Luther King's church, Ebenezer, must be a place that would stand against injustice anywhere, Monroe says that the admissions officer gave her "this response like, 'Girl, please!'"

Monroe pointed out that her treatment paralleled past discriminations toward black people and women. It would take another courageous act to correct this wrong against lesbians and gays. The admissions officer remained unmoved, insisting that Monroe must live as anything but a lesbian or else be denied admission. Unwilling to be subjected to treatment imposed on no heterosexual at ITC, Monroe told the admissions officer, "I really felt called to be who I really am. . . . This was one of those times when I didn't want to leave my identity at the threshold of the church. I wanted to bring it fully in." Monroe cried for months about being in an institution that claimed a theology of liberation and justice yet failed terribly with its application.

Even when she attended the progressive Union Theological Seminary where black liberation theology experienced its birth from the Charles Briggs Professor of Theology James Cone, she experienced ostracism from fellow black seminarians and black faculty simply because of her being lesbian. Monroe's case shows that there is much interest in black heterosexual Christians in keeping openly lesbian and gay Christians away from black churches. The ITC admissions officer told her that no black church in Atlanta would accept her because she is openly lesbian, yet in the more accepting New York environment a black professor at Union blocked her field placement at one of the leading black churches in Brooklyn because

47. Ibid.

she was lesbian. Monroe, as well as any other openly lesbian or gay person in a mainline black congregation, feels the pain of being cut off from her people. But rather than deny her very being in order to make heterosexual supremacists comfortable, Monroe has spoken out in black church settings as a prophetic voice against homophobia, believing that lesbians and gays are missing opportunities from God because they have not accepted themselves. She argues, "Lies will not live forever and lies left unchallenged get more power."[48]

The narratives of Watkins, Flunder, and Monroe are rare exceptions and reflect extraordinary acts of courage and sacrifice. With few exceptions, lesbians and gays in these religious communities enter into an unspoken covenant of silence and restriction about their sexual identity for the reward of worship, status, title, and fellowship with family and friends.

Knowing the loss gays would experience for speaking out, black pastors use gays' silence and lack of complaint to argue that homosexuals are not frustrated but happy. This was reflected in the comment made by the black pastor teaching the seminary class when I was a graduate student, "We (the black church) don't have the problem of homophobia." A more common attitude of black Christians is that homosexuals know that they are wrong and thus have no right to expect any other treatment. Most gays, like those at Metropolitan Baptist, accept this place to which they are relegated, and unfortunately many are not disturbed that this treatment is unjust.

Lesbians and gays in black churches are constantly weighing the odds, compromising their present reality, and working to convince themselves of the best decision with no good options. This game of Russian roulette has placed us in black churches in a no-win situation. The typology below is a common categorization in which closeted gays and lesbians in black churches find themselves.[49] These have become unfortunate survival strategies that usually cost

---

48. Ibid.
49. Here the term "closet" is used to describe lesbians and gays who refuse a public identification about their sexual orientation in ways that heterosexuals

lesbians and gays their soul, if not their integrity, family, and lives. This "predicament of the closet" manifests itself in various ways. Here are four closet categories present in black churches:

> Type 1, Guilty Passing: Homosexuals who feel that they are sinful and deserving of the rage and condemnation imposed on them by heterosexual church members; they may or may not participate in church actions that define homosexuality as immoral.
>
> Type 2, Angry Passing: Homosexuals who publicly deny or remain silent about their *own* homosexuality and live (pass) as heterosexual by expressing rage and condemnation of homosexuality and/or lesbians and gays.
>
> Type 3, Silent Passing: Homosexuals who publicly deny or remain silent about their sexual attraction and live (pass) as heterosexual.
>
> Type 4, Opportunistic Passing: Lesbians and gays who have accepted themselves but remain in the predicament of the closet, feeling that they cannot "come out" and may or may not speak against the homophobia and heterosexual supremacy in black churches.[50]

Teachings of deliverance from homosexuality, Christian change therapy, and exorcism create more denial and inner conflict for lesbians and gays. Historical black church practices of condemnation and the current rejection of lesbians and gays present an undue burden on lesbian and gay lives and cause black suffering.

---

comfortably and frequently inform the public of their opposite-sex sexual attraction. Considering that there are degrees to being "out," a closeted person is defined here as one who has not accepted her/his sexual attraction or disclosed her/his sexual orientation in heterosexual majority settings.

50. Type 4 is probably the group that experiences the greatest conflict because these lesbians and gays have reached a consciousness and maturity about their self-worth and ego strength that are missing with the other three groups, but they feel like they need to stay in anti-gay black churches for family and community reasons.

With these homophobic and heterosexual supremacist structures existing alongside a contemporary black cultural gay consciousness, internal church conflict, secret lives, and family turmoil often abound. In the following two chapters I examine this predicament of closetedness, which by its very nature leads to compromises with one's identity, integrity, courage, and self-esteem.

Chapter 5

Passing, Silence, Denial, and Gay Deceptions in Black Churches

> *We wear the mask that grins and lies,*
> *It hides our cheeks and shades our eyes, —*
> *This debt we pay to human guile;*
> *With torn and bleeding heart we smile...*
> — Paul Laurence Dunbar

IN THE CLASSIC 1959 FILM *Imitation of Life*, Hollywood exposed the psychic pain of light-skinned African Americans who "passed" for white and the widespread destruction that their family members endured as a result of their passing. In order to pass as white, light-skinned African Americans often had to sever all ties with black friends and family or run the risk of revealing their "true" racial identity.[1] The film, *Imitation of Life*, starring Hollywood legend Lana Turner as a wealthy movie star along with the lesser-known African American actress Juanita Moore, playing the role of Turner's maid, centers around Moore's many, albeit unsuccessful, attempts toward establishing a bond with her light-skinned daughter, Sarah Jane (Susan Kohner). Throughout the film, Kohner demonstrates unhappiness with her African bloodline and eventually disowns Moore due to her dark skin, a rejection that eventually leads to Moore's death and ignites an unresolved guilt in Kohner.

This powerful drama, which comes to a climax in Mahalia Jackson's stirring rendition of "Soon Ah Will Be Done," sheds light on an often ignored, yet major tragedy of racism: the complicated

---

1. Lawrence Graham, *Our Kind of People: Inside America's Black Upper Class* (New York: HarperCollins, 1999), 180.

shame and suffering of being African American in the United States. For a number of African Americans, passing was commonly viewed as justifiable behavior in order to avoid the unnecessary pain, discrimination, and exclusion encountered by dark-skinned or identifiable blacks. All too often, however, the practice of passing reflected a discomfort from being colored based on centuries of social and religious teachings that equated "whiteness" with goodness, beauty, and the sacred, and "blackness" with everything having to do with ugliness and evil. Moore's riveting words at the beginning of the film capture the common problem of living as other: "It's sad to be ashamed of what you are, it's even worse to pretend, to lie."

This line resonates with millions of black people across the country and speaks to their familiar struggle with racism in the United States. The subtle and the blatant messages heard about blackness as bad often caused African Americans a deep sense of shame. Even those blacks like Marcus Garvey who possessed a rare sense of black pride understood that life would be so much easier if they were white.

Susan Kohner's movie character, Sarah Jane, represents a tragic figure — one who has a deep sense of shame and low self-esteem for being African American. Unlike her mother, Sarah Jane possesses light skin which enables her to pass and avoid the denigration, discrimination, and exclusion faced by her mother and black people in the pre-1960s United States. The film poses moral questions about social systems and individual accountability and responsibility.

Sarah Jane represents victims of a racist system that devalues and punishes some members of the society solely on the basis of skin pigmentation. Although society is guilty of imposing such a system that fosters self-hatred in African Americans, *Imitation of Life* raises religious and social concerns. Did Sarah Jane have a moral obligation to combat racial injustice instead of buying into it for self-gain? As a member of an oppressed minority, is Sarah Jane justified in her decision to become a member of the dominant group in order to avoid oppression? Given her substantial white ancestry, did Sarah Jane not have a right to live as white?

These questions have plagued U.S. society since its beginning. Considering that racial classifications, like sexual categories, are social constructions of the post-Enlightenment, some have criticized any claim to a racial or sexual identity. These categories are artificial, they argue, pointing to the fact that individuals with more melanin and same-sex sexual desire exhibit the same moral and intellectual capacity and personality traits as the white and heterosexual majority. In *Who Is Black?* F. James Davis points out the arbitrariness of racial lines drawn in this country, lines largely after the 1896 *Plessy v. Ferguson* Supreme Court case. This Supreme Court ruling gave rise to the infamous one-drop rule, "defining [an African American] as anyone with a 'trace of black ancestry.'"[2] Davis points out that non-U.S. citizens frequently comment on the racism embedded in the U.S. race classification with "typical questions [such as] shouldn't Americans say that a person who is passing as white *is* white, or nearly all white, and has been previously passing as black? Or to be consistent, shouldn't you say that someone who is one-eighth white is passing as black?"[3] Yet racial construction is not logical but rather a social construct generally accepted by whites and blacks; even for those who resist the classification, other members of the society do not accept their rationale. Since I, like most African Americans, cannot pass as white, and live in a world that will respond to me as black, it is really preposterous to pretend that the world does not see the naked truth of my dark skin and does not respond to me as a black man.

Since "passing" is not unique to African Americans, but has been practiced by Jews and others, other minority group members, including gays, make similar arguments. At any time and any place, gays, like light-skinned blacks living as white and Jews who change or conceal their names, can simply avoid hostile oppression by trading their despised gay identity for a universally celebrated and idealized heterosexual identity. Jewish philosopher Hannah Arendt perhaps offers the best response against passing for any religiously

---

2. F. James Davis, *Who Is Black? One Nation's Definition* (University Park: Pennsylvania State University Press, 1991), 55.

3. Ibid., 13–14.

or socially oppressed group. She asserts, "When you are attacked as a Jew, you must fight back as a Jew." History supports Arendt's claim that progress toward religious and social acceptance of an oppressed group occurs in a significant way when identified oppressed members disprove negative stereotypes and oppose unjust systems and practices directed toward them.

Presently, African American lesbians and gays are in a similar situation of oppression. In black churches, they find that they are coerced to live as heterosexual. Everyone within black churches realizes that there is reward and acceptance for those presenting themselves as heterosexual, while gays and lesbians encounter ridicule and condemnation. Even in churches where it is "known" that the pastor is gay, black church Christians are content to remain in the church if the pastor is willing to present himself as heterosexual with a wife and children.

As chapter 4 points out, in black churches there is ridicule and punishment for those lesbians and gays who refuse to be silent like the docile gays at Metropolitan Baptist. Openly gay black Christians who speak out, requesting equal treatment with their heterosexual sisters and brothers, usually experience Tommie Watkins's and Irene Monroe's fate of punishment and rejection. While Arendt is correct, it is, however, much more difficult to "fight back" when your oppressors are also your community leaders, pastors, fellow parishioners, colleagues, friends, mothers, and fathers. This reality often leaves black gays with the sad option to remain aligned with oppressive African Americans. As the blacks in my hometown learned survival personas to enable them to handle white racism, many black gays, likewise, accept a similar place in a black heterosexual world that deems them sick and sinful. With this feeling of having nowhere to go in a white racist world, one may understand better why there is a large degree of silence, denial, rage, and condemnation of homosexuality and gay identity by black gays. Individuals already struggling with one oppression find it more difficult to confront another. Therefore, in a strange irony, black heterosexual and gay Christians generally agree on passing as heterosexual, even if for different reasons. Passing as heterosexual in black churches is not only common, *it is expected.*

Since African Americans generally did not accept passing of light-skinned African Americans, in spite of their ability to understand why African Americans passed, there is some irony in expecting gays to pass as heterosexual. African Americans generally felt that blacks should have racial pride and resist passing, avoiding any hint of being ashamed or denying their racial identity as colored people, even if it meant immense suffering. There is a curious inconsistency here. For while, on the one hand, African American heterosexuals constantly question openly black gays as to why they must be public or talk about their sexual identity as gay in a homophobic world, these same African Americans, like most of their ancestors, did not question why white-looking John Hope, Walter White, Lena Horne, or Adam Clayton Powell Jr. were public about being black in a hostile racist society. To the contrary, they adopted an enormous sense of pride that these African Americans were willing to endure hardship for the sake of standing with their people and fighting racism instead of escaping all hardships and passing for white. The sentiment of "coming out" as colored was so strong that some dark-skinned blacks resented light-skinned blacks who took advantage of whites' inability to distinguish them as black.

While a college student, I listened to my aunt tell a story about her days of living in segregated Atlanta. Aunt Ola shared the story of returning home from work on the city bus with light-skinned and dark-skinned colored people. One day a light-skinned colored woman from my aunt's neighborhood accepted the white bus driver's order for a colored man to give up his seat for her, "a white lady." This newly deemed "white lady" took the seat and exited the bus along with the other coloreds in her neighborhood. Many, including my aunt, were furious at her passing. The indoctrination into one's racial identity from birth and the need to follow the culture's expectation not to pass makes this example an atypical one. Boyd-Franklin's work notes that "for many light-skinned black people, the dilemma of not being identified as black can cause pain and discomfort," a striking contrast for gays generally feeling discomfort and pain from being identified as gay.[4] "Nella Lawson's 1929 novel *Passing* recounts the loneliness and emotional damage of the racially mixed Claire..., who...passed from poverty to wealth and social position by concealing her race and marrying white."[5] It is not altogether clear why African American heterosexuals, Christian and non-Christian alike, often encourage gays passing as heterosexual, when their passing for white, as Davis notes, was generally condemned.[6]

Heterosexuals often deny gay reality when gays display admirable qualities, desiring to view gays as heterosexual even when there is no indication. Perhaps there are two principal reasons that heterosexuals resist the parallel of racial and sexual passing: (1) skin color, they argue, is a given and cannot be changed, and (2) being black is not a sign of immorality as is the case with homosexuality. Since we have discussed that most heterosexuals, like gays, experience their sexual desire and arousal for sex as immutable, centered, and unchanging from day to day and that Paul's and the early Hebrew writers' descriptions of homosexual activity is not the same as love between men and love between women, there is reason for the parallel. The only consistency in the two responses is that many are unwilling to accept that the true sexual identity of lesbians and gays is toward the same sex and not the opposite.

The denial of their sexual identity is a battle that most gays have endured in black churches. When African American gay Christians are believed to be gay, however, they often live with messages that define them as problematic, immoral, and inferior to heterosexuals in black churches. At some point, every black lesbian and gay Christian contemplated what she or he would do about this incompatibility with black church teachings. Even taking a vow of silence about one's homosexuality carried its own risks. Christians

---

4. Nancy Boyd-Franklin, *Black Families in Therapy: A Multisystems Approach* (New York: Guilford Press, 1989), 37.

5. Grace Elizabeth Hale, *Making Whiteness: The Culture of Segregation in the South, 1890–1940* (New York: Pantheon Books, 1998), 38.

6. Davis, *Who Is Black?* 15.

silent about their homosexuality never know when a church visitor or parishioner making conversation or trouble will ask about their dating or marrying the opposite sex. The simple "no, I am not married" often leads to other questions that tempt lesbians and gays to pretend to be heterosexual for respect or an end to uncomfortable questioning. Single and divorced heterosexuals may experience similar uncomfortable discussions, but these discussions involve real and true options, regardless of how remote. Perhaps more black gay Christians assimilate by talking about an opposite-sex love interest. Every lesbian and gay person has been in the awkward company of a group of heterosexuals talking about dating and sexual activity with the opposite sex. Gays experience pressure to contribute to the conversation for fear of drawing suspicion by their silence.

Like Claire married into "whiteness" for a privileged life in the novel *Passing*, gays pass in heterosexual marriage for a number of reasons: denying their homosexuality; the relative ease, comfort, and social respectability of a conventional life; pleasing parents; desire for children; and the more recent fear of AIDS.[7] They live in marriage while carrying the burden of denying their erotic desire for intimacy and companionship with the same sex. A former gay friend described this feeling as a "monkey on his back." When I asked him why he married, he said because the church demands heterosexuality, regardless of whether or not a person is heterosexual. He commented that if the church and society were different, he would have remained with the man he loved.

African American gay activist and author Keith Boykin writes that black religion continues to be "the most frequently cited factor in black homophobia."[8] In his groundbreaking work *One More River to Cross*, Boykin offers a classic example of what the few openly gay African American Christians often encounter:

---

7. Richard Isay, *Becoming Gay: The Journey of Self-Acceptance* (New York: Pantheon Books, 1996), 88.

8. Boykin, *One More River to Cross*, 155.

Malik . . . considers himself a good Christian. Malik's parents, however, have been so influenced by their minister that they have challenged his faith. "You cannot be homosexual and be a Christian," they told him. A few weeks after I met Malik, he began moving out of his parents' suburban Maryland home and into an apartment of his own in Washington, DC. During the first of two trips to help him move his belongings, I met his mother, who greeted me graciously. By the time of the next trip, however, Malik had admitted to her that I, too, was gay. When I arrived the second time, I was banned from entering the house. I waited for thirty minutes outside in the car while Malik, inside, packed his belongings on his own and argued with his family. "God doesn't want homosexuals in his kingdom," Malik's mother insisted.

This black-church-sanctioned homophobia produces a lot of twisted black people. In a pilot study that I conducted in 1989 of African American Christian men's attitude about homosexuality, of the respondents between the ages of twenty-five and thirty all stated that their family members would view homosexuality as the worst thing for them, even worse than being a drug dealer or an alcoholic. With this heterosexual supremacist attitude and negative assessment of gays and their relationships as sinful by so many black church heterosexuals, African American lesbians and gays have reason to conceal their gay identity. Many gay Christians have also adopted these beliefs about themselves and harbor within themselves that they are inherently sinful because they are sexually attracted to the same sex. Unfortunately, this black church teaching that homosexuality is immoral fosters closetedness, a behavior that often leads to deception and dishonesty in the lives of black lesbians and gays. Although being closeted often involves passing, being homosexual in black churches does not necessarily mean passing as heterosexual.

There are four primary *types of closetedness* in black churches, with several involving passing as heterosexual:

1. Lesbians and gays who feel that they are sinful and deserving of the rage and condemnation of heterosexual church members;

2. Lesbians and gays who publicly deny their sexual orientation and pass as heterosexuals by expressing rage and condemnation of homosexuality;

3. Lesbians and gays who publicly deny or are silent about their same-sex sexual attraction and pass as heterosexual generally with silence about homosexuality but may participate in dismantling homophobia; and

4. Lesbians and gays who accept themselves but feel that they cannot come out or consistently speak against heterosexual supremacy in black churches.

Type 1: Guilty Passing

Every Sunday throughout the United States thousands of African American homosexual women and men attend black churches that define homosexuality and lesbian and gay relationships as sin. As in the case of Metropolitan Baptist in Washington, DC, or West Angeles Church of God in Christ in Los Angeles, many of the clergy and lay worship leaders at some of the largest black churches in the country are homosexuals, agreeing with the theology of these churches that their same-sex sexual attraction is a sin. In some cases these homosexuals live sexually repressed lives, denying themselves sexual relationships with the same sex because of their view that any sexual expression with the same sex would be sinful. This type of closeted homosexual may or may not participate in conversations that define homosexuality as immoral. She or he may be silent about the issue but will define homosexuality as sin when asked for a response.

Perhaps more common of this type of closeted homosexual is the one who has sex occasionally or even regularly with the same sex but feels guilt and shame about engaging in "sinful activity." Garrett, a sixty-seven-year-old black gay Baptist living in Florida, recently shared with me his ongoing struggle with homosexuality as sinful. Despite being around progressive lesbians and gays earlier in his life and hearing gay Christians expressing another Christian view that homosexuality is not sinful, he continues to idolize the normality of heterosexuality and feels that something is not quite right with his sexual attraction. With this thinking, he, like a battered wife, centers himself in churches that constantly rail against homosexuality and same-sex marriage, keeping him in a state of confusion and low self-regard.

In a conversation with David, a parishioner at Chicago's Church of the Open Door, he described the difficulty of not being able to attend church with his closeted partner. His partner engaged in sex but experienced an enormous amount of guilt from being in a relationship that he found sinful. Given the common cultural responses to homosexuality as immoral, it is not so uncommon to find African Americans in the church struggling with feelings of immorality because their true sexual identity has been taught to them as sinful, degrading, shameful, pathological, and unnatural. As a result of such teaching throughout their lives and the absence of a Christian view that loving sexual expressions are moral, even when they are with the same sex, these homosexuals often internalize feelings of shame, low self-esteem, and self-hatred. The sermons and actions by a condemning black church satisfy this person who feels deserving of such condemnation.

This self-hating behavior is not uncommon in oppressed populations. The self-hating black has existed throughout the history of this country and is pointed out in *Imitation of Life* when Sarah Jane's desire to be white leads her to the destructive behavior of denying her mother and passing as white. Also, "Jewish self-hatred or Jewish anti-semitism . . . appears to have been a Central/East European phenomenon, which stressed the failure of many Jews to liberate themselves from the anti-Semitic stereotyping deeply embedded in Gentile societies."[9] Oppressed individuals participate in a system that degrades them and can lead to rage against those like

9. Leonidas Donskis, *Forms of Hatred: The Troubled Imagination in Modern Philosophy and Literature* (New York: Rodopi, 2003), 12.

themselves. This self-hating behavior, also identified as reaction formation, leads to the second type of passing, in which they identify themselves as heterosexual and adopt rage against gays in order to secure their heterosexual identity.

Type 2: Angry Passing

When I arrived in Nashville to begin graduate study at Vanderbilt University, I was shocked to find out that "Marvin Gates," the pastor of a leading Baptist church, was known to be gay among heterosexuals and gays. My former partner had mentioned to me that this pastor was out to him as homosexual but had decided to present himself as heterosexual for the homophobic and heterosexual supremacist congregation; he obliged the congregation by showing up every Sunday with a wife and children and regularly preached sermons against homosexuality. With this façade, his congregation and other black church Christians could pretend that he was straight. In this respect, the congregation responded like the people in Hans Christian Andersen's classic children's tale *The Emperor's New Clothes.* In both cases, everyone pretended to see what they wanted, as opposed to what was really there. The people wanted to see an emperor dressed in fine clothes instead of a naked emperor, and the congregation wanted a heterosexual man happily married with children instead of a dynamic gay pastor with a male lover. Both cases point to the denial that people will endure when they are unwilling to accept a reality that makes them uncomfortable.

Many lesbians and gays in general struggle with this kind of homosexual. While there is recognition that a homophobic and heterosexual supremacist church and society create such persons, there remains the struggle that lesbians and gays are being hurt and in some cases destroyed by the actions of self-hating homosexual women and men. Understanding the eagerness of black church Christians to deny the homosexuality reality among them, these homosexual women and men maintain a status in the church by participating in homophobic preaching, teaching, and practices that cause more gay suffering in black churches.

Some recognize this behavior of condemning homosexuality as a way of squelching rumors or suspicions about their homosexuality. For those who live these double lives, such as the above case of pastor Marvin Gates, there is a general feeling that gays in black churches will keep their secret and not entertain outing themselves like the more politicized gays. These homosexuals living as heterosexuals take comfort in the fact that in the village there is a desire to see things as they have always been, to admire the emperor's new clothes and not face the naked truth of homosexuality. They may also take comfort from having played by the rules of the game and accepted the script of compulsory heterosexuality. They accept that they will be rewarded for not being rebels or radicals of the black church, accepting the heterosexual tradition and downplaying their feelings for the will of the black heterosexual majority. Above all, they know that their invisibility is their best protection. If anyone outs them, their sure line of defense is to say that they are not homosexual.

In *One More River to Cross,* Boykin is amazed that he had seen so many gays at the gay club who were also members of the homophobic Metropolitan Baptist Church. A statement from Boykin that he witnessed a church member being intimate with the same sex at a gay club can simply be denied by any of the homosexuals at Metropolitan or the hundreds of other homophobic black churches in the United Sates. Although the stereotypical effeminate gay men in church choirs and the like may have a more difficult time convincing others that they are not gay, there are a significant number of gay men and lesbians who blur this category by presenting stereotypical heterosexual butch and feminine mannerisms, respectively. Some present this behavior as a way of being accepted into the celebrated heterosexual majority. Other gays, like Rock Hudson and African American baseball player Glenn Burke, shock heterosexuals when they do not fit this stereotype and can live in the familiar "gay world" of Boykin's while passing as heterosexual and eluding a naïve and an unsuspecting heterosexual church majority. They receive acceptance in the heterosexual world in the same way as light-skinned blacks won privilege and favor from clueless whites in the days of segregation. Other than photographs of individuals expressing themselves in erotically intimate ways, there is little that can be done to prove one's sexual status, thus allowing an undetected homosexual status for thousands of homosexual women and men passing in heterosexual relationships.

Still others are not aware of their homosexuality as they participate in this attack. Homosexuals with strong desires to be heterosexual may feel qualified in delivering homosexuals from their "sin" after having internalized the fallacy of homosexual change therapy or exorcism. During college I lived as heterosexual and thought that such a change had occurred. My preoccupation with saving the world from homosexuality only heightened, rather than lessened, the suspicion of other lesbians and gays and informed heterosexuals that I was homosexual and manifesting signs of reaction formation. This pattern will be discussed in further detail in chapter 8.

Type 3: Silent Passing

Other homosexuals in black churches choose to deny publicly their homosexuality and live as heterosexual, avoiding the topic of homosexuality altogether. Rather than being enraged when openly gay Christians are around, many homosexuals prefer that homosexuality remain unmentioned. The comfort of their lives depends upon this silence. While some homosexuals discovered their homosexuality in a heterosexual marriage, what is more common among homosexuals is choosing to be married because they consider living as homosexual to be outside of the will of God.

Even those who have moved beyond the view that homosexuality is sin often feel that living as gay would be too difficult. During my graduate school days, a homosexual acquaintance in the Baptist Church told me that he was going to get married because he had a hard enough time making it in the society as a black man;

he concluded that being openly gay would be a tremendous burden for him. Marriage to a woman would provide him church and professional accolades as an attorney. He soon married a woman. Despite the sexual and integrity struggles inherent with this decision, this friend is correct: there are many social and church rewards for passing as heterosexual. Once again, this statement supports the general tendency for gay people in this heterosupremacist culture to choose the path of least resistance and live life as heterosexuals.

In addition to over a thousand benefits for being married as a heterosexual, including tax breaks, family privilege, and prestige, society embraces heterosexuals and their marriages with support, celebration, and comfort. There is the freedom to express one's heterosexuality in every corner of society, including black churches. In addition to prayers for the anniversaries of married couples in high liturgical settings, many black churches provide support groups for married couples. There is often recognition of the couple before marriage or encouragement for marriage by the church pastor. In this heterocentric climate, it is difficult for anyone, homosexual or heterosexual, to feel appreciated unless they are married. Though this may be daunting for heterosexuals, it does not violate their sexual space. Homosexuals, on the other hand, are coerced into taking on a relationship that does not provide sexual fulfillment and wholeness.

The expectation for gays to be in romantic relationships with the opposite sex is what many lesbians and gays rebuff. They rightfully point out that heterosexuals would find it unconscionable to be forced to be with a person of the same sex and expected to find lifelong happiness and sexual and emotional satisfaction. Again, the issue for this discussion has to do with primary sexual attraction and the motivation to be identified as heterosexual. Later we further explore the problems that can occur with this forced identity. Indeed, social and church sanctions afford homosexuals affirmation as heterosexuals, but as our earlier assessment states, these homosexuals go through life without reaching total sexual fulfillment or live with the shame of unfaithfulness and guilt for desiring or having sex with the same sex. With this as the price for heterosexual acceptance, still a number of gays endure black church homophobia without living as heterosexual.

Type 4: Opportunistic Passing

One of the major differences that distinguish the struggle of African American heterosexuals over racism from that of African American lesbians and gays and other gays over sexual orientation is where the struggle takes place. By and large, the struggle against racism has been one that has resisted white racist structures and institutions being maintained solely for the benefit of other whites. Although experiencing an inordinate amount of pain and suffering, black individuals rarely found themselves alone and almost always could come home to families, churches, and communities that could stand with them if not protect and support them. The battle over homosexuality has played itself out in different ways. While lesbians and gays can and do give birth to lesbian or gay children, in most cases, they do not produce lesbian and gay offspring. Unlike the visibility of African Americans who produce other African American offspring, lesbians and gays generally emerge from heterosexual parents and families strongly opposed to them. Lesbians and gays enter the world of invisibility, not knowing other lesbian and gay people, and most times find themselves battling not only the society, but the very communities that most oppressed groups have counted on to help them confront injustice: their own families, churches, and communities.

Because the greatest challenges one can encounter in life involve speaking against one's family, church, and social community, African American lesbians and gays, like other gays, are placed in a particularly difficult position, unlike that faced by most oppressed groups. Other than the struggles endured by women in families and churches, other historically oppressed groups have not had battles just as hostile and oppressive within the family as they experienced in the society. Already struggling with the never-ending racism of the society, this reality is primary as to why more African

Americans do not come out and confront the homophobia of identified African American heterosexuals. African American lesbians and gays rightly and faithfully speak against the racism of Anglo-American lesbians and gays, but they are typically reticent about African American heterosexuals' damaging homophobia.

African American family therapist Nancy Boyd-Franklin has written about the importance of the black church community in the lives of African Americans. African American lesbian and gay Christians in black churches who understand their sexual identity and expression to be equal to that of heterosexuals must confront harrowing questions about whether to endure continued denigration in those churches or to sever ties not only with a primary family unit, but also with a wider communal unit that serves important functions within a racially polarized society.[10] Many African Americans cannot conceive of life without the presence and support of the black church community offering worship, social interaction, encouragement, and catharsis for the day-to-day hardships facing African Americans. The need for the church does not change for African American lesbians and gays. Most have grown up in black churches and seek the support of the church, even when the institution's homophobia and refusal to affirm their relationships and support their struggles against discrimination and exclusion impede their health. Nonetheless, black church gay Christians, like other Christians in the church, confront the notion that their lives may get worse if they stop attending church.[11]

Fred, a gay Christian organist for several black churches, described the suffering of sitting at the organ through countless sermons as the pastors railed against homosexuality. Although he endured years of this abuse as he continued to play the organ for these churches, his reason for staying had much to do with his being connected to black families and black communities. In some ways, Type 4 lesbian and gay Christians experience the greatest conflict because they have reached a consciousness, a maturity, an

---

10. Boyd-Franklin, *Black Families in Therapy*, 81.
11. Ibid., 87.

acceptance about their sexual orientation that is missing in the first three group types. Like Fred and my graduate school acquaintance, they often find that they need to remain within black mainline churches due to family and community ties, while experiencing a great struggle in their subjection to hostile homophobia from the pulpit and pews. As the Reverends Leonard Patterson and Irene Monroe discovered, black church and seminary leaders often forbid black lesbians and gays being out, or if they choose not to hide their gay identity, they suffer the consequences of retaliation and rejection.

Patterson and Monroe refused to participate in sexual identity deception and went elsewhere. In spite of their disagreement with black church teachings that homosexuality is immoral, many African American gays find that it is too painful and costly to challenge or denounce black church teachings about homosexuality. They are in the precarious situation of enduring verbal assaults or severing church ties and leaving family and church friends. In addition to their spiritual nurture, a significant number of gays focus on the social aspect that black churches provide for them. In William Hawkeswood's black gay ethnography, *One of the Children*, he notes, "Church affiliation is still an important mark of identity for gay black men.... The majority agrees that the strong socialization into church particip[ation] when they were young explains their continued attendance, along with the kin pressure from mothers, grandmothers and siblings."[12]

Many, like the gay men at the West Angeles Church of God in Christ church, are motivated to stay based on the "friendships with other congregation members, especially other gay men; [this] is also an important motivating force for participation."[13] These aspects help to explain Boykin's query as to why lesbians and gays would remain at a homophobic church like Metropolitan Baptist, or the more intransigent St. James A.M.E. in Tampa, Florida. There are Type 4 lesbians and gays who will remain and even work to change

12. William G. Hawkeswood, *One of the Children: Gay Black Men in Harlem* (Berkeley: University of California Press, 1996), 108.
13. Ibid.

homophobia within black churches. In this group, "Even the anti-homosexual teachings of the Bible and the blatantly homophobic sermons of many preachers have not shaken their faith."[14] As stated by Wilbert, a Type 4 black church gay, "All the friends I have in New York are gay. They all come to church. My best friends sing in the choir, Leslie and Clayborn. They're the first two good friends I made here. And I met them at church. . . . All the choir boys are sissies. . . . There's a strong network of us in the church. . . ."[15] Even with this overstatement about male choir members (there are, of course, also heterosexual men in church choirs), Wilbert makes the point that there are a number of gay men in Types 1 and 4 who appreciate the church and gay support network of friendships and relationships despite the verbal attacks and ridicule that they have endured from many heterosexual church members.

With all these advantages of being in black churches, one might question whether too much is being made of the general view that homosexuality is sinful and lesbians and gays are sinners who must "change" to heterosexuality or else live without sexual intimacy and fulfillment. Perhaps, some would argue, lesbians and gays can be like Fred in the above example and simply ignore those comments and actions that demean or exclude them. Similar comments are frequently suggested to women encountering verbal abuse from men. Historically, women have been expected to remain in verbally abusive marriages that belittled their worth, neglected their needs, and subjected them to a barrage of insults. Many abused wives remain in these unhealthy relationships for the sake of family (children), social reputation, religious teachings, and economic advantages. Like abused lesbians and gays in churches receiving fellowship of other gays and spiritual uplift, abused wives receive some benefits from the relationship — for example, a home, car, and other material goods. However, the ultimate psychic costs are arguably too great to justify remaining in this unhealthy relationship, disrespecting the integrity and equality of the other.

---

14. Ibid., 110.
15. Ibid., 111.

Despite the absence of physical violence, lesbians and gays who remain in homophobic churches like Nashville's Mt. Zion Baptist and Washington, DC's Metropolitan Baptist, where pastors regularly castigate gays from the pulpit, do so at the expense of their emotional, mental, and spiritual well-being. The psychic costs can be much greater than lesbian and gay Christians understand. They are constantly reminded that their most basic self is flawed and unworthy before God. Unlike their heterosexual sisters and brothers, they do not form romantic relationships and families within God's intention. Such a message ultimately lowers one's self-esteem and self-worth and can lead to the depression and self-hatred that are explored in chapter 8.

There is another category of black men in the church and beyond engaging in sex with other men. Some of these men have regular anonymous encounters and others have long-lasting contact with primarily gay or bisexual men. It is more difficult to classify these men (or their female counterparts), more recently referred to as men on the Down Low. The Kinsey scale, discussed in the first chapter, may provide some help here.

Following the Kinsey reports in the 1950s, humans could no longer think of sexuality as they had in the past. The Kinsey studies exposed a lot of sexual activity and feelings that had previously been hidden. The Kinsey scale revealed to an uninformed world that homosexuality or same-sex sexual attraction was not as rare as previously thought. Homosexuality could no longer be relegated to hard women and skinny effeminate men. So while Marlon Brando could not be classified as gay or bisexual (his life supports his primary sexual attraction to women), he expressed that he was not ashamed of also having made love to men. A number of gay men married to women and lesbians married to men had already proven that the converse was also true, thus supporting the Kinsey finding that many people may have a few satisfying sexual experiences with individuals outside of their primary sexual attraction. As noted in the Kinsey research, African American men and women also experience this same range of sexual desire and expression.

As more heterosexuals and bisexuals, especially male hetero-sexuals, become more comfortable with their sexuality and can provide open and honest discussions about sexual attractions other than those toward the opposite sex, the fluidity in human sexuality will be realized. The growing trend to view all loving sexual relationships as good contributes to the record numbers of lesbians and gays, including black lesbians and gays, coming out. The present sea change about sexuality and the visibility of gays in all segments of society has evolved over the last few decades.

Gay liberation in the 1970s provided more visibility, and with the coming of AIDS in the 1980s, gay men like Rock Hudson who appeared to be heterosexual and passed without a problem became exposed and gave a new face to gay men. Thus, it became clear that one could not tell heterosexuals from gays. This blurring of the line caused many problems.

For reasons that have been stated, African Americans approach homosexuality with more guardedness and anxiety. With so many African American heterosexuals being closed in their acceptance, at least in attitude, of same-sex lovemaking, African Americans who are primarily heterosexual but also find some members of the same sex sexually attractive frequently find that they cannot share their feelings with family members. The closeness of the church, family, and community contribute to another category of closetedness among largely bisexual and heterosexual men called the "Down Low."

The Black Church and the Down Low

It is a fact that throughout time primarily heterosexual and bisexual women and men have engaged in satisfying sexual experiences with the same sex. Some of these experiences have been attributed to or blamed on discovering one's sexuality, too much alcohol at a fraternity party, college experience, military loneliness, and a host of other reasons. A condemning church and society have not allowed for people to be honest about most sexual experiences, especially those considered as taboo as homosexuality. Attempting to make sense of this not so uncommon reality, in the last decade black men started using the term "Down Low" (DL) to describe this sexual behavior. Coined in the 1990s by singers TLC and R. Kelly, it means "secret," and for many, Down Low "has a sexy ring to it, a hint that you are doing something wrong that feels right."[16] The term may be new, but the behavior is not. However, it may have emboldened others who have come to realize that they are not alone in their secret. And yet unfortunately, this has become another way in which black men may continue being dishonest about their sexuality.

The level of shame about their behavior is astounding. In a *New York Times* article about the Down Low, many men on the DL suggest that "sociological and financial considerations are beside the point: they say they wouldn't come out even if they could. They see black men who do come out as having chosen their sexuality over their skin color or as so effeminate that they wouldn't have fooled anyone anyway. . . . Many DL men take pride in not playing by society's rules of self-identification, in not having to explain yourself, or your sexuality, to anyone."[17] This is an interesting perspective but maybe not as progressive or liberating as it sounds. Indeed, there is a serious academic argument to be made about labels of any kind. Social constructionists have argued that categories of sexuality or racial identification are artificial categories socially constructed in the eighteenth and nineteenth centuries that say nothing about essential qualities of individuals. I do not find that the DL response is quite this virtuous.

As my gay friend Jim commented when we discussed this perspective, DL men are identifying themselves as heterosexual. They are not hiding the fact that they have girlfriends and wives. In their daily lives they are quite public about their heterosexuality. So it is not true that they have freed themselves from playing by modern society's rules of self-identification. DL men simply have not gained the courage to be public about their sexual attraction to men in the unaccepting black communities in which they find themselves. It

---

16. Benoit Denizet-Lewis, "Double Lives on the Down Low," *New York Times Magazine,* August 3, 2003.

17. Ibid.

is easier and more rewarding to identify as having sex with the opposite sex as a heterosexual than to admit that there is also an attraction to some men, as Marlon Brando courageously admitted. Everyone has a right to choose identification, but DL men who have not reached a level of comfort to be honest about themselves should not criticize openly gay African American men for their courage. The view that openly gay African American men have placed their sexuality over their race once again beats the drum that race and homosexuality cannot coexist like race and heterosexuality.

The DL phenomenon is the current attempt for a large number of black men and some women to cope with their reality of a sexuality that is so unaccepted by a majority of their own people. Their secretiveness about real sexual feelings is a seemingly safe, if unhealthy, way to address their sexual needs. The unwillingness of a majority to understand this sexual fluidity leads to some inappropriate responses. J. L. King, a former DL man of twenty-five years, now recognizes the problems with this sexual encounter. He considers the predicament facing black men: religious and social pressures to be a (heterosexual) man in a heterocentric and homophobic culture and subculture. He also realizes that by "denying [women] the truth, [he and others] denied them the respect, honor and freedom of choice they were rightfully due." J. L. King also argues that the "finger-pointing and judgment by the church and its leaders have not saved lives. They have turned people away from the very thing that may save their lives and their souls — God." J. L. King believes that, "the church leadership needs a new approach because the message of fire, brimstone and damnation is not working."[18] He understands that the Down Low continues because so many black men and women have nowhere to turn as they struggle with their God-given sexuality, whatever it may be. He further believes that "ministers have an excellent opportunity to provide education, compassion and understanding. The black church must preach the truth and become a place where all men can come and hear the

---

18. J. L. King, *On the Down Low: A Journey into the Lives of "Straight" Black Men Who Sleep with Men* (New York: Broadway Books, 2004), 80.

Word without feeling they will be judged or ostracized, regardless of their sexual orientation. It should be a place where sisters can depend on getting sound advice and be counseled to love and protect them first."[19]

Prior to the disclosure of these sexual secrets in the *New York Times* article, I was asked by a young African American woman my thoughts on the Down Low during a question/answer period following my presentation on the black church and sexuality. I made it clear that I did not condone this behavior; it is dishonest and violates the covenant established in a primary relationship. Secrets and lies eventually cause pain and suffering for the individual and his family members and friends. I also made it clear, however, that the black church can continue neither its hostility toward loving same-sex sexual relationships nor its coercion for gays to present themselves as heterosexual. I made it clear that no one wants to be ridiculed because of a sexual difference and have his or her sexual relationships demeaned. Heterosexuals would not accept this response to their relationships. Heterosexuals cannot expect men and women to be honest about their sexuality if they are going to be ostracized.

Boykin has written a masterful response to this issue in his book *Beyond the Down Low*. Boykin emphatically declares that it is time to move beyond the Down Low, and that black church leaders ought to lead in deconstructing deception, irresponsible sexual behavior, and homophobic structures. These systems and practices keep black people in a state of sexual bondage, preventing them from living in open liberating communities offered to us by Jesus in the Gospels.

Until black church leaders adopt different Christian approaches, Down Low practices will continue. Boykin summarizes this problem: "We may wonder where these men get off by endangering the lives of women, but we should also stop to think about the ways in which we contribute to our own oppression by participating in a culture that drives these men underground. Unfortunately, too

---

19. Ibid.

many black churches have become co-conspirators in the silencing of black men on the down low. More than almost any other institution in our community, our churches have perfected the policy of 'don't ask, don't tell.' "[20] The racial passing phenomenon provides a fitting backdrop for the sexuality issues we are now confronting. Racial passing teaches us that unjust systems create monsters for us. The liberation model compels us to dismantle those systems that favor one group of people over others. In those systems, individuals will identify with the favored group, even if it means living deceitful lives. If black churches are not communities that recognize all God's children as equal sisters and brothers, they will leave black people, heterosexuals and gays, constrained and unfulfilled.

In the 1980s with the onset of AIDS, the comfortable closet doors opened, exposing gay men who would never have come out. As gays in black churches confronted the dread of homosexuality, black church leaders and congregants also found themselves having to personalize a message that had up till then been directed at a particular group of people. This approach had allowed some distance. Before AIDS, black church pastors could preach their harsh message against homosexuality and homosexuals without having the more difficult task of specifically tying their message or the issue of homosexuality to their organist, choir member, or fellow clergy. Many longtime church mothers and deacons were hearing these messages about their sons. Ironically, black pastors, by and large, did not pause and reconsider their theological understanding of homosexuality as immoral when it was discovered that so many loving Christian gay men had AIDS, but concluded that God was punishing them for their sinful sexual behavior. As outlined in the next chapter, during this day of AIDS, black churches once again demonstrate that they typically have been places of condemnation instead of places of refuge, compassion, and kindness.

---

20. Keith Boykin, *Beyond the Down Low: Sex, Lies, and Denial in Black America* (New York: Carroll & Graf Publishing, 2005), 188.

Chapter 6

The Black Church and AIDS

Black lesbians and gays have often found themselves caught in the middle.... Black and gay was not wholly approved in either the black or gay communities. — James Tinney

Black Ministers and AIDS

IN 1988 AT ZION HILL BAPTIST CHURCH in Nashville, I gave a slide presentation to a group of black ministers on AIDS within black communities. I had tired of the typical responses to AIDS by black church leaders: either silence or the proclamation of God's punishment on homosexuals. After years of observing their failure to understand AIDS and act responsibly, I decided to do what was most needed: educate black church leaders. Despite the many reports that I had read about black ministers' negative attitudes toward AIDS sufferers, I rather naively felt that once the facts were presented about AIDS, black ministers, unlike white ministers Jerry Falwell and Pat Robertson, would resist further maligning gays (the group that was most affected) and offer a compassionate, responsible response. I was wrong.

After my presentation, it became clear to me that the ministers had one interest: moralizing that AIDS was God's punishment for the immorality of homosexuality. One of my goals in providing this slide presentation was to disprove AIDS as God's punishment of gays by explaining that people — including many heterosexuals — contracted AIDS from unprotected sex and drug use, not as a result of same-sex sexual expression. It has always been rather alarming to me that so many men and women of all cultures remained uninformed or chose to ignore the facts about AIDS in order to

166

satisfy their own desires for the demonization of homosexuals and homosexuality. Their quick judgments, met with more delight than sorrow, failed to consider that: (1) since the dawn of AIDS in the early 1980s, the overwhelming majority of AIDS sufferers in Africa have been black heterosexual men and women. And in Europe and South American countries, heterosexuals and homosexuals are equally affected. It is only in the United States that the majority of people with AIDS are gay men;[1] and (2) lesbians throughout the world have been least affected by AIDS, which led to the quip that if AIDS is God's punishment to homosexual men then lesbians must be God's chosen people. The conclusion that AIDS was God's punishment to homosexuals said more about the people eager to make the claims than about the nature of the disease.

Though I shared these basic facts about AIDS with the ministers, they would not take on board any of the factual information. Led by the pastor, Amos Jones, minister after minister took turns preaching to each other and me about the horrors of homosexuality. Unwilling to view AIDS as anything but a homosexual curse, Rev. Jones finally commented, "America has this thing with homosexuality. In Africa, you did not hear about homosexuality. African men were strong...warriors."

Ministers resented any perspective other than AIDS as retribution to homosexuals, especially a perspective such as mine that humanized a group of black men for whom they cared very little, if at all. I had hoped that this topic would challenge them to confront their discomfort and fears about sexuality and encourage them to rethink their notions about gender identity and black male difference. Yet, in an effort to shore up black male security, with his final comment Jones had once again simply provided the common black male defense: "black men (unlike 'weak sissy white men') evolved from a line of strong, black manly warriors." Hence, if black men remain true to what it means to be a black man, AIDS will not affect them. Jones offered the ministers a calming, albeit erroneous,

---

1. Earl Shelp and Ronald Sunderland, *AIDS and the Church* (Louisville: Westminster/John Knox Press, 1992), 48.

conclusion that hard, butch, macho behavior prevents a man from having sexual desire for or making love with another man. History supports the fact that one has nothing to do with the other. It is desire that determines sexual partners, not how one walks or talks. Both claims, that African males are strong warriors and that being an African warrior necessarily means being heterosexual, lack foundation.

At the onset of AIDS and in the years that followed, African American heterosexual ministers and pastors, like their white counterparts, espoused these condemnatory and scurrilous attacks on black gay lives, defining AIDS as God's punishment. Even after two decades of AIDS research identified AIDS as another tragic and burdensome illness not unlike past epidemics such as the Bubonic plague, yellow fever, and malaria, African American ministers for the most part display almost no change in their attitudes that AIDS is God's retribution on the "sinful."

Poised as leaders on this front, black ministers generally ignored the facts about AIDS, exacerbating the widespread ignorance and hysteria present within black faith and social communities. Contrary to the notion that all homosexuals would perish from AIDS — a modern-day version of Sodom and Gomorrah — research revealed that AIDS was not an airborne disease and could only be contracted in the most intimate of contact with infected blood and some bodily fluids.[2] The research also revealed that some people did not get infected despite sexual contact with HIV-positive people or sharing needles, indicating that AIDS was even more difficult to contract than the above diseases. Most important, the research indicated no correlation between one's sexual orientation in the way that correlations existed between polio and children or sickle-cell disease and African American populations.

Despite education efforts teaching that people contract AIDS based on how they have sex (engaging in unprotected sex), as opposed to the amount of sex they have or whether they have sex with the same gender, there continues to be a view that AIDS is

2. Ibid., 44.

God's punishment. In a recent conversation with a friend who had just completed three years of AIDS education for her church task force on AIDS, she mentioned that two decades of education have done little to quell the attitudes of black ministers that AIDS is just punishment for sinful homosexuals. Just as Susan Sontag defines AIDS — acquired immune deficiency syndrome — as not an illness at all but "a medical condition, whose consequences are a spectrum of illnesses" in her book *AIDS and Its Metaphors*, AIDS is a health issue, a health crisis for not only this country but the entire world. This realization has done precious little, however, in reversing the opinion that AIDS is a moral issue and an indictment on homosexuality.

In 1989, I became certified as an AIDS educator with the American Red Cross and made a slide presentation entitled "Couldn't Hear Nobody Pray: The Black Church and AIDS" for AIDS education with African American ministers and pastors. Although each meeting had its by-now accustomed share of homophobia and moralizing, at a meeting of black pastors at Jackson State University in Jackson, Mississippi, I was unprepared for the vitriol of a pastor and physician. Weaving passages about lesbianism in the Hebrew scriptures (a group that is not mentioned in Hebrew scriptures at all) and the wretchedness of gay men, the physician/pastor gave a jumble of homophobia and lies about AIDS. I sat in shock that a physician could travel so far to be so irresponsible and heartless when so many were dying in those early years.

As the mid- to late 1980s gave us data about AIDS, these facts flew in the face of the declarations of ministers that this was God's punishment — such as the Reverend Jerry Falwell's comments that the "sexual revolution" is being brought to an end by the "Almighty God."[3] This was frequently and boldly followed by claims that AIDS was God's punishment of homosexuals. Such comments could not have been more wrong.

Even though some conservative antihomosexual white church traditions, like the Southern Baptists, have softened their positions

---

3. Ibid., 23.

and participate in pastoral care ministry to persons with AIDS, black ministers trail as some of the most resistant in responding with care and compassion. News reporters offered numerous articles "on the established institutions of the black community, highlighting their discomfort with this disease and the 'immoral' behavior that leads to its transmission."[4] Confronting this reality of black ministers especially in the early days being least likely to offer compassionate pastoral care to persons with AIDS and their family members, "black gay men and lesbians, families — most often mothers, lovers, and friends — all stepped forward to [compensate pastoral] care and sometimes empower those with AIDS in black communities."[5]

Not only have black gay men found black ministers to be a problem, in his plea for help with the AIDS health crisis, C. Everett Koop, the former surgeon general, experienced black ministers as some of the most uncompassionate and moralizing people he had encountered.[6]

I further experienced Koop's assessment when I heard the inappropriate comments made by a pastor eulogizing, or in this case preaching, the funeral of Rev. Rodney Hampton, a black minister who had died from AIDS. Having been invited to the funeral by my graduate school colleague who had ministered to Rev. Hampton in his last days, I was horrified to hear the hostile words of Rev. Percy Clark: "Sometimes God will take your life to keep you from going to hell." In this sentence, Clark revealed several things about his understanding of God and Hampton. He understood Hampton as homosexual, homosexuality as sinful, and AIDS as God's vengeance on Hampton for his homosexual expression. At an AIDS conference, one of the panelists reported that at a funeral the pastor told the family, "Take a good look at your son because you will not see him again, because he is going to hell and you are going to heaven." At another funeral, the pastor imposed judgment on

---

4. Cohen, *Boundaries of Blackness*, 166.

5. Ibid., 98, 100.

6. "An Interview with the Surgeon General on AIDS in the Black Community," *Ebony*, September 1988, 154–60.

some of the attendees with this comment: "All you men with wigs on are going to hell." These attitudes and teachings by black ministers and their lack of pastoral ministry to suffering black people are a sad commentary on black church leaders and why so many African Americans have expressed an especially harsh judgment on gay men with AIDS.

Black Public Responses

African Americans have learned well from these ministers. Like other groups, they have taken on various responses to people with AIDS — from the sympathetic to the "I told you so, you got what you deserve" response — responses typically based on how persons with AIDS contracted the disease. Most of the sympathy was preserved for the "innocent victims" of AIDS, children and people like Arthur Ashe, who contracted AIDS through birth or blood transfusions, respectively. A hierarchy of tolerance and compassion emerged. Those contracting AIDS from parents or blood transfusions received the most compassion with drug users and heterosexual men coming behind them. Even in cases of promiscuity, there was hierarchy. Heterosexual men with AIDS or those identifying themselves as having contracted AIDS from opposite-sex sexual relationships received sympathy and support, as in the case of Magic Johnson, unlike the thousands of black gay men. Even though both groups of men typically exercised unfaithful promiscuous behavior, heterosexual men were given a nod of understanding and compassion. Underscoring this revulsion toward gay male love-making, George Bellinger Jr. of the Gay Men's Health Crisis in New York notes that drug users were received better than gay men:

> The horrible joke that used to go around [in black communities] when AIDS first started.... There's good news and bad news. The bad news is that I have AIDS, the good news is I'm an IV drug user; this joke indicates the degree to which IV drug use can serve as a shield against the implications of male homosexuality that are always associated with AIDS, and thus

hover as a threat over any discussion of sexual transmission of HIV.[7]

Often touted as a friend to gays based on his political views in predominantly white settings rather than his moral teaching and preaching in black churches, Jesse Jackson's emotional defense that Max Robinson did not contract AIDS from a man raises questions about how understanding and accepting Jackson really is with the issue of homosexuality and black gay men. His comments sent a clear message that it would have been a problem if Robinson were gay, an impossibility for such a together brother, a black male role model, so distinguished and fine, so much of a man. This response resurfaced black men's ongoing struggle with homosexuality, indoctrination with machoism, and need for respectability from the mainstream. This attitude, promoted by so many African American leaders, leaves others asking the question, why does sexual orientation have relevance when someone has AIDS or died from AIDS?

Clearly, it mattered to Jackson and others as they rushed to dispel any notion that Robinson could be gay or simply contracted AIDS from sexual relations with a man, the most common mode of transmission in the United States. As it was for anti-gay whites when the media reported the nonstereotypically gay Rock Hudson as gay and having AIDS, Harper notes that because Robinson

> was [also] cut from a different cloth, formed in the intersection of discursive contexts that do not allow for the expression of black male homosexuality in any recognizable form ... the silence regarding the topic that characterizes most of the notices of his death actually marks the degree to which the possibility of black male homosexuality is worried over and considered problematic.[8]

---

7. Philip Harper, *Are We Not Men?* (New York: Oxford University Press, 1996), 19.

8. Ibid., 14.

While Robinson requested that his death be used as an opportunity to educate black people about AIDS and AIDS prevention, it became clear that what was more important to Jackson and other African Americans was convincing everyone that Max Robinson was not gay. The initial silence about Robinson's sexuality (and possible homosexuality) or how he contracted the disease, and the attempts by Jackson and family members to characterize him as a "family man" more than Robinson demonstrated in his life "leaves open the possibility that Robinson engaged in unprotected sex with a man (or with men)" or that he was bisexual or homosexual.[9]

Criticized by black AIDS activists for missing an opportunity for AIDS education among blacks, Jackson chose this statement:

> Max shared with my family and men that he had the AIDS virus [*sic*] but that it did not come from homosexuality, it came from promiscuity. . . . And now we know that the number one transmission [factor] for AIDS is not sexual contact, it's drugs, and so the crises of drugs and needles and AIDS are connected, as well as AIDS and promiscuity are connected. And all we can do is keep urging people to not isolate this crisis by race, or by class, or by sexual preference, but in fact to observe the precautionary measures that have been advised. . . .[10]

Although Jackson is right to point out the ways of transmission and recognizing the pervasiveness of AIDS and the need for caution, the purpose and function of this statement seems to serve as a redemptive measure for Robinson's presumed heterosexuality. The statement's tone underscores the cultural attitude that being promiscuous with women and contracting AIDS as a (heterosexual) stud is better than contracting it with one man. However, as I mention above, it is simply false that there is a correlation with promiscuity and AIDS infection. AIDS is spread through irresponsible behavior of having sex without condoms and other preventive devices rather than the number of sex partners. Jackson later took

---

9. Ibid., 15.
10. Ibid.

advantage of another opportunity to set the record "straight" about Robinson's sexuality at his funeral.

Just in case people had not gotten the message that Robinson had been defined as heterosexual, Peter Boyer's article in *Vanity Fair* left no room for doubt, citing Robinson's three marriages; his attractiveness to women and his insistence that he was not gay, and reports that none of his friends believe that he was homosexual.[11] Responding to this "propaganda machine" in the wake of his death, Harper reminds us that "from early claims, then, that even Robinson's family had no idea how he contracted HIV, there developed an authoritative scenario in which Robinson's extensive heterosexual affairs were common knowledge and that posited his contraction of HIV from a female sex partner as a near-certainty."[12] While I am not saying that Max Robinson was gay — nor do I find Harper and other black gay men working to make such a case — I think that it is worth noting the level of defense, discomfort, and even disdain that people continue to express toward homosexuality and gay people.

A greater reaction in defining the appropriate way of contracting AIDS occurred after Earvin "Magic" Johnson announced in 1991 that he was HIV-positive. To a greater degree than the case with Max Robinson, "given the complex relation among sexual orientation, masculine gender identity and athletic competition, . . . it should not surprise us that it was the possibility that Magic Johnson contracted HIV through sex with a male partner, rather than the possibility that he injected drugs" or cheated on his wife that caused concern and feelings of disgust, in not only black people but the wider society.[13] As in the case of Robinson and the reports of the media, the United States was reminded once again in Johnson's case that female-to-male cases are rare and that it is more difficult to transmit the virus this way than male-to-female.

---

11. Ibid., 16.
12. Ibid., 17.
13. Ibid., 24.

Johnson, not surprisingly, wasted no time in taking advantage of his privileged access to the media, talk shows, and late night programming to end all rumors about his bisexual or homosexual status, knowing that a heterosexual claim would garner him sympathy and respect. In what can be considered a tad bit of protesting,

> Johnson made a widely remarked appearance on the popular late-night talk show hosted by Arsenio Hall, during which he countered the offensive insinuations by proclaiming, "I'm far from being homosexual" — an announcement that was greeted with wild cheers and applause from the studio audience. Four days later, *Sports Illustrated* published a sort of print-media . . . in which Johnson wrote, "I am certain that I was infected by having unprotected sex with a woman. . . . I have never had a homosexual encounter. Never." And, as to underscore what was really at stake in his detailing the extent of his heterosexual activity in this article, Johnson pointedly referenced his own putative bravery in publicizing his promiscuity: "I'm being a man about my past."[14]

In her carefully detailed and valuable study on AIDS and its effect on African Americans, *The Boundaries of Blackness: AIDS and the Breakdown of Black Politics*, Cathy Cohen describes this outpouring of support for Magic Johnson, and considerably more for tennis great Arthur Ashe, resulting from the fact that "the press not only had black celebrities who were highly regarded outside of black communities, Johnson and Ashe were respectable 'victims.' They were respectable not only because they professed to being infected by the more acceptable routes of heterosexual sex and blood transfusion, but also they conformed to normative ideas of manhood, in contrast to what had been represented for most men with AIDS."[15]

The deaths of Robinson and Ashe may have stymied black ministers' fervor of "AIDS as God's punishment to homosexuals,"

---

14. Ibid., 25.
15. Cohen, *Boundaries of Blackness*, 178.

but they still could avoid the pesky issue of the prevalence of homosexuality among African Americans by holding up the most prominent African American HIV-positive men as not having contracted HIV from sexual contact with men. Given that the AIDS deaths of black gay artists Sylvester, Alvin Ailey, Marlon Riggs, and James Cleveland had less national appeal for the media, black ministers could ignore these artists' contributions and influence in black communities and maintain their "AIDS as God's punishment" perspective. Those who thought that the fact of AIDS becoming public among such revered African American men would finally motivate African American ministers to play an active role in helping with the crisis were sorely disappointed.

From the beginning, the number of AIDS cases was disproportionately high among the black population. Of all women and children, African Americans made up the largest numbers, and a high percentage of black men, both heterosexual and gay, accounted for AIDS cases among men.[16] Black gay men experienced some of the greatest ostracism and discrimination, including no access to health care and banishment from their homes. The latter was the case, for example, with a black minister father of my college teacher. Black gay HIV-positive men found themselves subjected to the emotional toils of depression, anger, hurt, and shame as they battled the pain and wasting away of their physical health from diarrhea, pneumonia, meningitis, dementia, cancer, and a host of other opportunistic infections. In being treated as pariahs, "it is demonstrably true with few exceptions across the denominational spectrum, that the clerical leadership of the [African] American religious community increased significantly the final suffering of people with AIDS."[17]

Robinson's death and Johnson's announcement about his HIV infection did little to galvanize black churches, black communities, and the wider society in protecting African American women, children, and men from HIV infection. Since the epidemic, health-care

---

16. Ibid., 101.
17. Ibid., 4.

workers lament that AIDS advertising campaigns and community and funding efforts do not typically target black people. Though African Americans accounted for the largest percentages of new cases of HIV/AIDS, there is still little public care and concern for this population: black ministers remained woefully silent about prevention, black health-care professionals often dismiss its potential devastation, and many white gay AIDS activists involved with groups like ACT UP ceased their rhetoric that AIDS was a human problem when their incomes allowed them protease inhibitors, other HIV drugs, and longer life unavailable to less-well-off black people in this country and in Africa.

When I was on the board of Nashville Cares (an AIDS agency for the metropolitan Nashville area), I experienced firsthand the tension between African American leaders involved with AIDS and the white gay male leadership of the organization. As an intermediary, it was essential that suspicions and biases be put aside in order to save and support the hundreds of persons suffering and dying from AIDS.

As African American gays assumed leadership in black churches and communities, some breakthrough occurred in the early to mid-1990s. However, there remained a significant group of black Christian ministers who could not seem to move beyond their position of condemnation or silence. A major part of their dilemma involved encouraging African Americans to be sexually responsible and use a condom or to use clean needles when using drugs, whereas their theological teachings only supported sex in monogamous heterosexual marriages and drug-free lifestyles. Cohen notes that in an interview with one minister regarding his approach to AIDS, the minister "nodded and waved his hands in such a way as to indicate that this would be a short conversation because there just wasn't much to say here."[18] Appalled by the nonchalance, if not coldness, of these ministers, African American AIDS volunteers and educators frequently found themselves noting success if they could at least get the ministers' attention and commitment to AIDS

18. Ibid.

work. Cohen goes on to say that this minister, unlike many who felt justified in doing nothing for "sinners" contracting AIDS, told her "you have to understand . . . it goes against the general tenets of Christianity. How can you expect ministers to accept or acknowledge the behavior that causes AIDS? All we can do is take care of those who are sick — that is our Christian duty."[19]

Black Church AIDS Ministry

During this same period, African American heterosexual ministers organized some commendable AIDS ministries. In Nashville, the senior pastor of Metropolitan Community Church, Edwin Saunders, along with the director of AIDS ministry, Joanne Robinson, began the First Response Center, an AIDS support group and service that connects HIV-positive African Americans and their families with AIDS services and support. Trinity United Church of Christ, a leading black congregation in Chicago, pastored by Dr. Jeremiah Wright, a pioneer in AIDS ministry and a pastor who has befriended gay Christians and condemned the homophobia among black church leaders, has constructed an effective AIDS ministry program for the parishioners as well as other citizens in the surrounding community. Other pastors, like Cecil Murray of Los Angeles in the moving 1996 videocassette *All God's Children,* called for black church leaders to become more active in AIDS ministry.

Perhaps the best response of black ministers occurred in 1989 with the commencement of an annual weeklong project entitled the "Black Church Week of Prayer for the Healing of AIDS." It was begun by Pernissa C. Seele, CEO of the Balm in Gilead, who, in her role as director of this New York project, "acknowledges the extraordinary work that churches are doing in black communities everywhere to address the devastation of HIV/AIDS."[20] Responding in one of the areas hit hardest with HIV infection and disease,

---

19. Ibid.
20. *The Black Church Week of Prayer for the Healing of AIDS* 1 (Spring 2003): 5.

this annual week of prayer during the first week in March "is the largest AIDS awareness program targeting African American communities, with seventy-seven AIDS service organizations and health departments across the United States." These organizations have joined in partnership with The Balm in Gilead project to support churches in educating their communities and advocating for persons with HIV.[21] This recent work presents the best of the black church and places it once again in the rich tradition of being the center of black community and life.

Carl Bean, a black gay minister and founder of the black gay denomination Unity Fellowship Church, had a similar vision in the early 1980s when virtually no black church was reaching out to black people with HIV and AIDS. He recognized that a significant number of blacks felt alienated from AIDS prevention organizations because such organizations lacked cultural awareness in reaching black and Latino populations. Arriving in Los Angeles at the onset of AIDS, Bean emphasized that his church was a place where those who had contracted HIV would be treated with dignity, respect, and compassion. In 1982, he established the Minority AIDS Project as a ministry in his Unity Fellowship Church on Jefferson Street in the 'hood of Los Angeles. As Cohen rightfully notes, due to the "initiative and leadership of black gay men like the Reverend Carl Bean, Gil Gerald, Reggie Williams, A. Billy Jones, Lawrence Washington, David Naylor, the Reverend Charles Angel and Phil Wilson" in churches and communities, AIDS agencies — for example, the Black Coalition on AIDS and the Minority Task Force on AIDS — emerged.[22]

Although black churches are now beginning to respond in much more helpful ways as Christian institutions committed to the care of God's people, far too many churches are still immobilized by ignorance, fear, and tradition. Consequently, some of the people who need spiritual and medical help the most have no awareness about the process for obtaining medical treatment and behavior

---

21. Ibid., 9–10.
22. Cohen, *Boundaries of Blackness*, 98.

modification information for healthier lifestyles. So often gays do not respond to available resources because they have internalized the black church message that they have received due penalty for their homosexuality.

A Church Casualty

Throughout this chapter, we have seen that it was not just the terror from AIDS and its devastating affects that HIV-positive black gay men in particular faced during the height of the AIDS crisis; black church leaders contributed to their burdens by preaching harsh messages that death was their punishment for their sin of homosexuality. Such a message further contributed to their pain, disappointment, fears, low self-esteem, and general feelings of shame for the way they had engaged themselves sexually. Some responded to messages and repented for their perceived sins and bargained with God by choosing to be in romantic relationships with women if God would heal them from AIDS.

In her groundbreaking work *On Death and Dying*, Dr. Elisabeth Kübler-Ross identified bargaining with God as a common response of terminally ill patients.[23] It was a response that was especially prevalent in black churches, as black persons with AIDS received more distance and condemnation from the church community than compassion and care. Feeling abandoned and having internalized black church teachings that their sexual attraction was an abomination, many black gay Christian men made confessions that their gay lives were wrong, cried out for forgiveness, and offered testimonies of a new life with women, a desperate peace offering for a second chance on living. African American pastoral theologian Ed Wimberly points out that the act of "confessing shame or guilt is an attempt to acknowledge that shame has occurred and to relieve it by going to others and telling them about it."[24] These stories

---

23. Elisabeth Kübler-Ross, *On Death and Dying* (London: Macmillan, 1969),72.
24. Edward Wimberly, *Moving from Shame to Self-Worth* (Nashville: Abingdon Press, 1999), 75.

became sad narratives of false hope and misery during the last days of these men. The following is one such story.

In the winter of 1997, I received a full-page newspaper article from a small-town newspaper about "Reggie," a young black gay church musician with AIDS. I had known Reggie for a long time as an acquaintance. The article provided a detailed account of his life, including his church involvement and later street life. His homosexuality appeared in the story as one thread woven into his wayward life on the street. The year before I received this article, I had talked with Reggie about his having been diagnosed with AIDS. In what appeared to be an unusually long story for a small newspaper, it soon became clear that there was an unsubtle message about those who are homosexual ending up living destructive lives, and the only way to live in peace is to be heterosexual. The article appeared to be part confession and sermon by the musician and part apology to his family and the church for living a life of sin. His description that he "just went bad...determined to do [his] own thing and experience the world that he wanted to" resulted from a number of things; his comment, however, that this "was my choice" is conveniently read by a largely homophobic community that his "lifestyle" of street life, drugs, and so on was all part of a homosexual package. His own self-hatred as a homosexual man and lack of self-awareness are woven together as a decadent life on the fringe.

His early life is described as ideal: the son of an A.M.E. minister father and schoolteacher mother, reared in the church, loving music and worship and leading church choirs at a young age.[25] He describes this as one part of his life, shared with another life of parties, alcohol, and marijuana. As time went on, this activity escalated into drinking more heavily and getting involved with some really wild activities at parties. His behavior eventually led to more destructive and dangerous behaviors on the streets, resulting in prostitution after becoming homeless. He mentions that because

25. "The Rough Side of the Mountain," *Bradford County Telegraph*, 6B, January 23, 1997.

he did not have a relationship with God, he found that this behavior would "ease the pain of knowing it was all a lie." The writer of this article then describes that "pretense was characteristic" of his life, "pretending to live a life very different from the one he was actually living." It becomes clear that being rejected because of his "feminine characteristics" and because of his perception that people "hated my guts" was why he struggled so much to cope with a difficult life.

After describing a wretched life of homelessness, prostitution, and alcoholism, the musician explains that he hit rock bottom and turned to God for deliverance. He became a minister, very involved in church, and was engaged to a "wonderful, wonderful woman." The musician turned minister stated that it was very hard for him to share his testimony at first, particularly about the homosexual lifestyle that he lived for awhile. He doesn't believe that homosexuality is something people are born with. He said that, in his case at least, it was a choice. His words, "I chose to go into that lifestyle and now I've come out of it," are still the words that most heterosexuals love to hear, especially those in conservative church communities, as they resist the notion that same-sex lovemaking and relationships could be equally or more satisfying, healthy, and life-giving than many heterosexual relationships. It is stories like this one that many love to tell: a tragic homosexual hits rock bottom because of his homosexual lifestyle, finds God and the opposite sex, and lives happily ever after.

Unfortunately, his story does not end like so many wish that it had. Two years later, this man was dead. There are many tragedies to this story. First, Reggie's case is typical of many African American gay men who never accept their homosexuality as a good and normal sexual attraction and expression and later contract AIDS. Like Reggie, the coincidence that AIDS became prevalent among gay men in this country led them to make the false correlation — with much help from condemning black churches — that they were being punished for their sin of homosexuality. In addition, Reggie had no one to turn to for help in accepting his homosexuality. Not only did he struggle with the shunning and hatred that he experienced by others in his early life, but as a result of that experience, he internalized those feelings about himself and lived an obnoxious life, creating a self-fulfilling prophecy for others to hate him. Having spent his early life as a gay son of a preacher in black churches that condemned his perceived homosexuality, Reggie never overcame this teaching of being without value as a homosexual, and he therefore placed himself in situations that would destroy his life. According to "child development theorists, the experiences [that] we have as children, seeing our own 'naughty' behaviors reflected back to us in the scowling face of the parent, set the lifelong relationship with shame."[26]

Finally, Reggie needed to believe two things: that by having a woman he was no longer gay and that he would be cured of his AIDS. Of course, neither came true. There is no change for one's sexual orientation, and there is no need for such a change. Millions of dollars are wasted every year in campaigns and therapies that seek to end one's homosexuality. One of the most important messages for black churches is that one's sexual orientation does not define one's moral character. Just as Reggie described his messed-up life of substance and sexual abuse, there are countless heterosexuals abusing drugs, sex, and alcohol. By the same token, there are countless lesbians and gays, single and in relationships, living healthy, productive lives. One can no more use the minority of pathological lesbians and gays to generalize about the entire population of lesbian and gay men than one should use the sick, sinful, and criminally minded heterosexuals to generalize about heterosexuality. The negative messages of shame and guilt, religious and social condemnation, and the general lack of affirmation black gays receive in their black families are often the primary causes that lead to their misery, pathology, and even sinful behavior, not the homosexual attraction and expression itself.[27]

---

26. Karen McClintock, *Sexual Shame: An Urgent Call to Healing* (Minneapolis: Fortress Press, 2001), 22.

27. Isay, *Becoming Gay*, 163, 175.

This is one of many tragic stories that hide in the mosaic of black church life. As in Reggie's case, black church leaders and congregants often refuse to own their part in the death of their own people. With the continued battles that lead black pastors to the streets to enact legislation that damage black lesbian and gay lives, and their unsympathetic ears and condemning voices to those who suffer from AIDS, African American gays will continue experiencing mainline black churches as closed, hostile institutions. These common experiences of African American gays lead many to find refuge in those black communities that do not consider their sexual difference as a problem or antithetical to the inclusive gospel of Jesus.

Some black gay Christians are choosing the few predominantly heterosexual churches like Trinity UCC in Chicago or Metropolitan Interdenominational Church in Nashville that affirm lesbian and gay Christians and provide AIDS ministries. Some are choosing to be in open and affirming predominantly white heterosexual or gay churches or black gay churches that provide the black traditional worship style without the homophobia. In the next chapter, we examine this black church movement that has given black gay Christians hope and the message that their sexuality is a gift from God.

Chapter 7

The Emergence of African American Lesbian/Gay Christian Congregations in the United States

*When I dare to be powerful — to use my strength in the service
of my vision, then it becomes less and less important whether
I am afraid.* — Audre Lourde

THIRTY YEARS AGO, in Los Angeles, Troy Perry, a gay Pentecostal minister, founded the first Christian denomination
for lesbians and gay men, the Universal Fellowship of Metropolitan Community Churches, or Metropolitan Community Church
(MCC). Since that time, some lesbians and gay men prefer these
congregations in order to worship God without experiencing the
condemnation, discrimination, and exclusion that presently exist
in many mainline Christian churches. Black gays also are engaged
in the establishment of such churches and serve as leaders in the
gay Christian movement.

In his autobiography *The Lord Is My Shepherd and He Knows
I'm Gay*, Perry states, "the [Metropolitan Community] Church was
organized to serve the religious and spiritual and social needs of the
homosexual community of greater Los Angeles, but I expected it to
grow to reach homosexuals wherever they might be. I made it clear
that we were not a gay church; we were a Christian church, and
I said that in my first sermon."[1] Developing a new religious consciousness on the eve of the Stonewall Rebellion, Perry and other

---

1. Troy D. Perry, *The Lord Is My Shepherd and He Knows I'm Gay* (Los
Angeles: Nash Publications, 1972), 122.

185

lesbian and gay Christians began questioning the moral legitimacy of religious and social practices that granted merit to heterosexuals simply on the basis of their heterosexuality. They found no more justification in the church for heterosexual privilege and dominance than for white privilege and dominance.

When Perry began MCC on October 6, 1968, he joined a long tradition of Christian reformers, like Martin Luther, Richard Allen, and Jarena Lee.[2] The establishment of MCC distinguished Perry in history as the first openly gay founder of a Christian denomination. His unwillingness to accept the church's discriminatory practices toward its lesbian and gay parishioners parallels the righteous indignation displayed by African Methodist Episcopal church founder, Bishop Richard Allen. Allen and Perry both emerged from their parallel experiences with a theological view of God as just and liberating. They viewed themselves as children of God and equal members in the Christian family. Allen understood his racial identity to be distinct from his moral character and his ability to love and worship his God; Perry responded in a similar manner with respect to his sexuality. For both men, submission to church discrimination and exclusion violated a primary practice of the Jesus portrayed in the Gospels, that of allowing everyone an equal place within the religious community.

Although Allen left St. George's Methodist Church for its racial discrimination toward him, Allen later refused Jarena Lee's plea to be a minister in his church, Bethel AME. Once again, this example shows that recognition of religious discrimination on the basis of one characteristic, such as race, does not always translate into recognition of other discriminations, such as gender. Other examples are not hard to find. In her essay "Who Are We for Each Other? Sexism, Sexuality, and Womanist Theology," African American lesbian theologian Renee Hill argues that even in the academy, "Christian womanists have failed to recognize heterosexism and homophobia as points of oppression that need to be

---

2. Ronald Enroth and Gerald Jamison, *The Gay Church* (Grand Rapids: Eerdmans, 1974), 29.

resisted if all black women...are to have liberation and a sense of their own power"[3] Indeed, Hill and others point out the irony of the fact that heterosexual Christian womanists often use the term "womanist," a term coined by a nonheterosexual African American woman, Alice Walker, without being inclusive of lesbians involved in struggles for sexual justice within black churches, academic institutions, and society.[4] While fleeing the homophobia and heterosexual supremacy that has been identified in many black churches, some black lesbian and gay Christians have gone to the gay-affirming white Metropolitan Community churches only to be confronted with the racism of white lesbians and gays.

This sort of exclusion places black lesbians and gay men in a particularly difficult position. As noted in chapter 5, the heavy emphasis on church and family in African American culture makes it extremely difficult for African American lesbians and gays to leave black churches. This particular set of circumstances poses a greater difficulty in finding another faith community, even if it is one that affirms gay Christians.

There are African American lesbians and gays who were never involved in black churches, and others — as in the case of Rev. Leonard Patterson — who left black churches as a result of having received no affirmation of their romantic relationships and families. African American gay Christians who value the black worship experience, however, often feel that they must stay in black churches and encounter homophobic sermons and repeated instances of heterosexual supremacy, since most Christian churches that affirm same-sex relationships are predominantly white. Even the prospect of attending a Metropolitan Community Church can seem unappealing for black lesbians and gays who feel that same-sex attraction is the only characteristic that they share with white MCC parishioners. For many the risk of encountering racism by a group

---

3. Renee Hill, "Who Are We for Each Other? Sexism, Sexuality, and Womanist Theology," in *Black Theology: A Documentary History, vol. 2: 1980–1992*, ed. James Cone and Gayraud Wilmore (Maryknoll, NY: Orbis Books, 1993), 346.

4. Ibid., 349. In a wonderful response to Hill and others, womanists are some of the most affirming of lesbians and gays, opposing homophobia as oppression.

of strangers is not worth leaving the familiar, albeit homophobic, black church worship experience. An increasing number of African American lesbians and gays are responding to black church homophobia in a manner that parallels the moves of Allen and Perry. These gay and lesbian Christians are leaving congregations where they experience denigration and are forming or joining their own black gay churches. While such churches are still rare, their efforts provide a new song and spiritual hope for African American lesbians and gay men.

The majority of black Christians find the idea of a black gay church oxymoronic. As a young seminarian, I also shared this fallacious thinking with another seminarian as we left our Boston Baptist church by supporting her seemingly self-evident statement, "Why would someone be at a gay church? It's like if I were at a church for prostitutes." Her example was clear: homosexuals are sinful like other groups of sinners and those sinners — for example, prostitutes, liars, murderers — do not have a church, so why should gays?

The following is another example of opposition to gay and Christian as being compatible. While lecturing in my class on the black church at Fisk University, I mentioned that Dr. James Tinney, a black gay Pentecostal minister and leading scholar in Pentecostalism, had provided excellent research on the topic of black Pentecostalism. As I prepared my lecture, I felt that I could count on a reaction about Tinney from at least one student at this homophobic university. My suspicion proved true. Although I mentioned this tidbit in passing, one of the students was struck by the presumed contradiction. Nonplussed, the student raised her hand and asked me, "How could he be a minister and a homosexual?" I quickly responded that not all Christians understood being gay as sinful and an impediment to one's Christian identity. The student, clearly unaware that the Christian church could be divided in its view of homosexuality, retreated from the exchange with a rather blank and unconvinced look on her face.

This student is a good example of how so many African American Christians are responding to the openly lesbian and gay Christian body that is slowly emerging within African American communities. The majority of my African American Christian students resist affirming being gay and Christian as compatible but recognize that at least in white Christian minds a similar paradox existed for centuries regarding being black and Christian. The story of the late Dr. James Tinney and his founding of Faith Temple, a black gay church, serves to challenge the widely held assumption that blacks cannot be both gay and Christian and provides us with another interesting and compelling case as to why there is a present need for places of worship not just for gay Christians, but for black gay Christians.

A Black Gay Church

Tinney's church has continued to grow since his death from AIDS in 1988, and provides the space within the black church tradition for African American lesbians and gays. In his popular book *In Search of Gay America*, Neil Miller recounts the humiliation and ostracism Tinney experienced in the 1970s at his black church. Subsequently, his decision to live with integrity in his church as a gay Christian cost Tinney his membership and ministry, and an excommunication from his black Pentecostal denomination, the Church of God in Christ.

> At the Sunday evening service, with 500 people in attendance, the minister called Tinney to the front of the church. Speaking through a microphone, the pastor ordered the "demons of lust, homosexuality and perversion" to leave his body. Nothing happened. . . . The minister told him that he thought the demons had departed but he should be careful not to have any other sexual experiences lest they return. . . . On his way home, Tinney saw a man standing at a bus stop and was immediately attracted to him. He realized that whatever his problem, it was not one of demonic possession. Nothing had taken place in the church to change the way he was.[5]

5. Neil Miller, *In Search of Gay America: Women and Men in a Time of Change* (New York: Harper and Row Publishers, 1989), 247.

A decade later, Tinney organized a gay revival; "on the eve of the revival, however, the bishop of the Washington, DC, diocese of the Church of God in Christ, publicly excommunicated him."[6]

Tinney's story is a familiar one. He, like Perry, understood the dynamic of being gay in a hostile Pentecostal Christian church. Thus, in 1982, Tinney established the first black gay communion, Faith Temple, for the growing number of African American lesbians and gays in Washington, DC (the other black gay church that existed had affiliations with the white Metropolitan Community Church).[7] For Tinney, it was not enough for gays to form a separate church as a sanctuary for gay Christians. He recognized the added burden and unique dilemma of black gay Christians. His own experience in the historical black church informed him that the black church, like white racist churches, was not "fluid and dynamic enough to be comfortable with pluralism."[8] His church, like any church defining one's difference and loving expressions as sinful, had been a source of pain to his "sense of worth and well-being."[9] Neither homophobic black churches nor white racist gay churches exist as healthy places for the spiritual life of black gay Christians. Therefore, Tinney argues for black gay churches because "black lesbians and gays have often found themselves 'caught in the middle' (so to speak) since the 'twoness' of identity (to use a term of W. E. B. DuBois) reflected in being both black and gay was not wholly approved in either the black heterosexual or white gay communities."[10] Black gay Christians have been part of both but a part of neither. Under no illusion about the black church as offering true black liberation, Tinney recognized that while black gays find liberation from homophobia and heterosexual supremacy in white gay churches, white gay Christians have not completely shed racist attitudes and practices that are typically absent from black

---

6. Ibid., 248.
7. James Tinney, "Why a Gay Black Church?" in *In the Life*, ed. Joseph Beam (Boston: Alyson Publications, 1986), 78.
8. Ibid., 71.
9. Michael J. Smith, *Black Men/White Men*, 170.
10. Tinney, "Why a Gay Black Church?" 73.

mainline churches. In an article that appears in Joseph Beam's black gay anthology, *In the Life*, Tinney argues that "white gay churches have...come into existence under circumstances related to the oppression of sexual identity that parallel the circumstances related to oppression of black identity. Unfortunately, however, many black lesbians and gays experience the same racial oppression in these white gay churches that blacks generally experience in predominantly white churches of whatever label."[11]

In the wake of religious and social movements of the 1960s and 1970s that rejoined spirituality and sexuality, advocated gay equality, and affirmed black power and black liberation, many black gays emerged in the historical black church with a new social and spiritual consciousness. Such movements allowed black gay Christians the critical tools for assessing the failures of predominantly white gay churches and predominantly black heterosexual churches "to deliver the oppressed." Even without these categories that sought to lock in black as heterosexual and gay as white, Tinney asserts that "an identifiable black gay community would undoubtedly still come into existence, simply because of the uniqueness of talents, gifts, sensitivity, experience, dress and behavior that is inherently a part of being both black and gay — both as a manifestation of God's creation and our own creation."[12] These gay Christian communions and their ministers are not unlike the religious communities that emerged in the early and mid-twentieth century, often led by evangelists whose messages differed rather radically from the mainline position. Bishop Ida Robinson and Elder Lucy Smith found that they could have ministries in the newly formed Pentecostal and Holiness churches that recognized women ministers when most of the black denominations were closed to such leadership. The new black gay churches also share with these earlier communions a grassroots appeal and large working-class membership.

The emergence of black gay churches in urban centers like Washington, DC, Chicago, New York, Los Angeles, and Detroit respond

---

11. Ibid., 72.
12. Ibid., 73.

to the spiritual and community needs of black gay Christians in a way that neither the black church nor the white gay church has been willing to do. Many black lesbian and gay Christians are no longer willing to "check their sexuality at the door of the church, and come bearing gifts of talent" as African American lesbian pastor Renee McCoy argues gays must do in black churches.[13] It is because of this kind of black gay oppression that Tinney felt called by God to establish Faith Temple. A man of great faith, Tinney, like Perry before him, trusted that God's grace and strength would sustain him in the undertaking of something that had not occurred: the establishment of an independent church for African American lesbian and gay Christians.

Tinney believed that black gay churches should be supported by "nongay black Christians . . . because they are reaching out with the message of Christ to a gay community that has been alienated from Christ and from 'straight' churches [and] white gay Christians."[14] Tinney emphasized that the black gay church is not just a spiritual, sacred space for outcast gays, but it is strictly Christian. In describing Faith Temple, Tinney wrote, "We were saying not just that we were Christians. . . . We said then, a church holds to certain beliefs and practices that distinguish it from a sect or cult. . . . [Our church held] the essential, fundamental, orthodox beliefs that have identified most Christians throughout the ages."[15] Thus, the black gay church provides an affirming community for black gays in the treasured rich black church worship style that formed them.

He also recognized that, apart from certain MCC churches with largely black congregations, African American gays find that only in predominantly black heterosexual churches will they be able to experience "the freedom to worship using Afro-American traditions in liturgy."[16] The development of black gay churches makes it possible for black gay Christians for the first time to hear the gospel in their own ways and reinterpret the gospel in their own context —

---

13. Cited in ibid.
14. Ibid., 74.
15. Ibid., 81.
16. Ibid., 72.

taking into account both race and sexual orientation at every step in the process.[17]

The organization of black gay churches is "a necessary step before there can be mutuality, equality and reciprocal relationships between gay and nongay black Christians, and between black and white gay Christians."[18] I would extend Tinney's arguments for black gay churches by asserting that such churches are also places where one is more likely to find creeds and sermons inclusive of black liberation theology and blacks in leadership positions. The issue of sexism, however, may still be a challenge for some pastors and congregations. However, despite their sexist and heterosupremacist shortcomings, black churches still provide richness in worship and song that many African Americans feel will not be replicated elsewhere. Black church drama, largely created by black gay men, is the attraction that keeps many African American lesbians and gays locked in homophobic black churches.[19]

With this witness and vision, Tinney struggled in establishing a visible black gay congregation from largely closeted gay Christians. He felt compelled in providing this ministry to lesbians and gays living with shame, guilt, and destructive behaviors resulting from negative black church preaching on homosexuality. He believed that "a black gay Church has the unique opportunity and privilege and duty to 'reprove, rebuke and exhort' and bring healing and power to each person within its reach."[20] Presently pastored by Rainey Cheeks, Faith Temple, like many of the white Metropolitan Community Churches, is an evangelical charismatic congregation with the Pentecostal flair left by Tinney.[21] The worship experience focuses on the gospel and all the elements one would find in a typical black Baptist or Pentecostal church, most notably the demonstrative worship and the call-and-response style.

---

17. Ibid., 76.
18. Ibid., 74.
19. Boykin, *One More River to Cross*, 127.
20. Tinney, "Why a Gay Black Church?" 86.
21. Miller, *In Search of Gay America*, 241.

As Tinney formed the first black gay church in Washington, DC, on the other coast in Los Angeles, Bishop Carl Bean began the Unity Fellowship Church. Bean placed even more emphasis on the power of racism, arguing that much of the present homophobia in black churches is related to the effects of racism. In his view, black homophobia results in part from the fact that "all oppressed people try hard in that whole idea of assimilation to prove to the oppressor that they are okay."[22] After experiencing a turbulent period before accepting his gayness, Bean moved to Los Angeles in 1982 and began his church for black gay worshipers. The previous year, shock waves had run through gay communities with the threat of an epidemic referred to as "gay cancer"; Los Angeles was one of the hardest-hit areas. Bean responded early by developing an active AIDS ministry and "constructed a new AIDS care center in South Central Los Angeles."[23]

Carl Bean and Unity Fellowship

In a 2003 interview, Bishop Bean shared with me his life as a gay Christian in the church. His own experience as a young gay man growing up in a black Baptist church in Baltimore without affirmation of his gayness prompted him to found Unity Fellowship. He articulates an experience common to many, perhaps most, gay men. In his animated style, Bean said, "As a young boy in Baltimore, there was never a time I didn't know I was gay . . . there was never a time I didn't know I was attracted to men." He remembers being "mesmerized" and "fixated" on a neighborhood male as a child. His "puppy love" desires and experiences with other males reached a comfort level that is commonly associated with adolescent heterosexual boys and their initial contacts with girls. Unlike many gays, during his late middle and high school years, Bean had a number of positive sexual experiences with other males who recognized his sexual difference. He attributes the respect that he received from

---

22. Boykin, *One More River to Cross,* 132.
23. Ibid., 136.

these males (probably not exclusively homosexual) as having to do with his family's revered standing in the community.

As he grew older and began to understand the unpleasant neighborhood responses to gay males, he found these experiences informative: he did not exist in the world as a lone gay male. Later, he gained positive references from the gay males at the all-male high school which he attended after his tenth-grade year. And while his church, Providence Baptist Church, of Baltimore's black elite could not be identified as a gay-bashing church, like other congregations of its time, it did not play a role in affirming Bean's gayness as it did in nurturing spiritual and racial pride in him. To this end, Providence required all of its youth to become involved with the Jackie Robinson Church Youth Council of the NAACP. Civil rights activism became understood as a religious practice of Bean's formation. Encouraged by his activist pastor and friend of Martin Luther King, Rev. Wood, he participated in the 1957 Civil Rights Prayer Pilgrimage. During the same time the positive sexual experiences occurred, Bean experienced more pressure from his parents and church leaders to be a good example for black people. And as in the case of Barbara Jordan and other African Americans living in the early to mid-twentieth century, there could not be a display of anything that would give legitimacy to white racists' theory of blacks as morally inferior. For Bean, the pressure to be a "credit to his race" and the burden of a sexual "secret" proved to be dreadful.

Bean's budding homosexuality began to be noticed by his parents as a major concern and problem. In high school, his parents expressed strong opposition to him, even to the point of not eating from the same plate. Concluding that Bean was a homosexual and "God does not like you," they went to their pastor, who asked Bean to write his problem on a piece of paper. Bean wrote the word "homosexual" and expressed that he "could not handle this switch from complete familial support to this lack of connection and support within the home . . . " After a turbulent fight with his father about his homosexuality, Bean cried and went into the bathroom. He said to himself, "I do not know what to do. . . . Jesus, you do not love me anymore, and Mom and Dad don't love me anymore."

After saying that, Bean took every pill in the medicine cabinet and wrote a note to his parents, "I love them but I am sorry that they did not love me as if God did not love me." After pushing the dresser against the door, Bean was called by his parents but could not respond because of the overdose. When his father discovered what had happened, he broke down the door and Bean was taken to the hospital where his stomach was pumped of the medication.

Initially Bean experienced torture at the hospital when psychiatrists imposed "shock therapy" to "cure" his homosexuality, a familiar practice in the 1950s. He later experienced God moving in this situation when a German psychiatrist disagreed with her colleagues that homosexuality was a mental illness. She emphasized that though it was a sexual difference, it was no less appropriate than a heterosexual one. This began helpful counseling that eventually moved Bean toward emotional health. In this environment, he gained a positive sense of self and high self-esteem. With high school being such a negative experience in Bean's formation, at age sixteen, Bean left the homophobia that he experienced in Baltimore for the more accepting New York City. As a Christian interested in church music and the life of the church, Bean joined others in a gospel group and made contact with some renowned gospel artists like Alex Bradford and Calvin White of the Gospel Wonders ("Long As I Got King Jesus").

In the early 1970s, Bean felt called to Los Angeles, and began a music ministry. In the same city where Perry began the first gay denomination — MCC — Bean was contacted by Berry Gordy and the number-one black label Motown Records to do a song, "I Was Born This Way." Bean recalls this experience as a religious one:

> I get this package from Motown. I open it up. I take it out. I read it, 'I'm walking through life and in it disguise, you laugh at me, criticize because I'm happy, carefree and gay, I was born this way. . . . And no fault, it's a fact, I was born this way.' I don't believe I am reading what I am reading. . . . This is the song? The number-one black label . . . The Temptations all want me to sing about being a homosexual. I ain't buying

that.... It's in my hand, but something ain't right here. I take it home. I look at the lyric. I play the little demo and I begin to cry. Clear as day, it's like I heard, 'But you told me to show you what I wanted you to do and now I've shown you.' And I started to cry. And the path was set. I did not have to ask who this is...why this came. I didn't write the song, had no dealings at Motown and the song came to me. I go into the studio...and I have the contract with Motown. "I was Born this Way" hits in '77. I did it in '77 at Motown.... [It] climbs up the Billboard charts in Disco, *straight* up the charts. I won it with this amazing audience. I know now I am set on a path; I don't know for what. People started calling Motown, Motown says, "We need you to come in." People are calling in saying that they were going to commit suicide, but they heard your record at a disco, they don't want to commit suicide anymore. They want to talk to you. They want to meet you. They want to know....[24]

Thus began Bean's ministry. As he interviews, he begins to talk about Christ and stresses that Christ needs people to live truthful lives, lives of integrity.

During this time, he receives calls from friends in New York, those in show business, about people getting sick. There is a newspaper article that he receives about this disease, Gay Related Immune Deficiency Syndrome. Although he had plans to go to Europe, he feels called to minister at this time in Los Angeles. Bean has another spiritual experience, feeling the presence of God as he never felt it before. His praying and reading of scripture lead him to the conclusion that he is being sent. He writes the experience, "God is Love and Love is for everyone." Bean's ministry moves in another direction from the fundamentalism widespread in black churches. He starts a Bible study in his home and introduces his small following to the new liberation theology that stresses opposition to social oppression and advocacy for religious and social justice.

---

24. Interview with Carl Bean.

After ordination and significant press about his ministry with a focus on liberation theology and care for persons with AIDS in South Central Los Angeles, Bean emerged as one of the first ministers in the country showing compassion to persons with AIDS by touching them. Bean modeled this ministry after Jesus' command to love your neighbor as yourself, and Jesus' proclamation in Matthew 25 that "as much as you do it to the least of these, you do it to me." As a pastor primarily for African American lesbians and gays, Bean's dynamism inspires others to live full lives as people of faith. His influential ministry over the past two decades has inspired other ministers to organize other Unity Fellowship Churches in Seattle, Riverside (California), Baltimore, Atlanta, and New York.

In 1982, the Unity Fellowship received its charter as a Christian congregation. The church is a vibrant congregation, largely comprising working-class African American lesbians, gays, bisexuals, and transgendered individuals. Like Faith Temple, Unity Fellowship's mission statement is clear that it is a Christian church with an emphasis on love in the New Testament scripture and the teachings of Jesus. Unlike Faith Temple, however, Unity Fellowship goes on to state, "We do not dismiss all other faiths and beliefs as wrong or second to our way of believing."[25] The mission statement continues:

> God is spirit, alive and at work in the Moslem Mosque, the Jewish Synagogue, the Christian Church and the Tribal Ritual. God is everywhere present. We believe the Bible and all the great spiritual writings or guides must be read, taking into consideration the time of their writing, the traditions practiced at that time and the fact that we have the right to question and examine all interpretation. A person's belief system: must be supportive of healthy self-acceptance; must support spiritual growth; must encourage physical, psychic and mental health.[26]

---

25. Unity Fellowship 20th Anniversary Program/Informational Booklet.
26. Ibid.

Mike, a longtime member of Unity, felt compelled to become a part of Unity after hearing this refreshing message, having experienced black church communities with messages of "[Gays] are going to Hell" and "If you are a homosexual, we do not want you here." Unity changed his mind about the church and Christian ministry. He found that Unity lived up to its mission as a place where worshipers know that God is love and they are loved.

Pamela, a member of Unity for ten years, describes the church as allowing her to connect more deeply with God. Pamela admits that she had to work through a lot of homophobia that she had internalized from her previous black church, the Baptized Holiness Church. She argues that black mainline churches place emphasis on sexual orientation when it is irrelevant to one's relationship with God through Jesus Christ. Not having to worry about condemnation of her sexual difference in the worship experience, Pamela enjoys the church and says that Unity allows her to be "a vessel coming to . . . God, thanking God for all that [God] has done and all that God is going to do . . . openly and freely prais[ing] God, [without] worry[ing] about . . . sexuality."

Another vibrant example of a predominantly African American lesbian and gay congregation is the Church of the Open Door on Chicago's South Side with dual affiliation in the United Church of Christ and Unitarian Universalist denominations. The Church of the Open Door is co-pastored by an African American lesbian couple, the Reverends Alma Faith Crawford and Karen Hutt. They, like Tinney and Bean, recognize that their challenge is great: denouncing the moral claim of a black Christian majority that homosexuality is immoral.

When Crawford and Hutt met in 1993, they discovered that they shared a similar vision and call: to begin a church for African American lesbian, gay, bisexual, and transgendered people. In April 1996, they gave twenty-five hundred dollars — all of their personal savings — to begin the only black church in Chicago where out lesbians and gays can have weddings, receive spiritual guidance and affirmation, and be ordained into the Christian ministry. The mission statement of the Church of the Open Door defines the congregation as "A sacred assembly of black lesbian, gay, bisexual, transgendered and heterosexual sisters, brothers, lovers, friends and allies gathering at the invitation of Christ to seek justice, to extend hospitality, to deepen understanding and wisdom, to affirm our identities, to receive healing and power, and to celebrate the transforming presence of the living God."

Crawford finds Richard Allen's dedication and experience in the African Methodist Episcopal Church influential in her design of the church's liturgy. The granddaughter of an AME pastor, Crawford draws from the AME's Call to Worship, taken from Psalm 122: "I was glad when they said unto me, let us go into the House of the Lord, our feet shall stand within thy gates O Jerusalem." Crawford and Hutt chose the name, Church of the Open Door, to communicate the message of welcome for lesbians and gays as well as the message that lesbians and gays are a part of the church tradition. Church of the Open Door, like Faith Temple, Unity Fellowship, and the MCC congregations, appeals to a cross-section of socioeconomic classes. While there are professional members in this community, its working-class sector is a strong presence within the church.

There are several factors that may account for this reality: (1) the evangelistic and charismatic style that is present in these congregations has historically been associated with lower socioeconomic groups; (2) working-class gays and lesbians, like their heterosexual counterparts, typically have fewer resources other than the church to address their concerns and challenges; thus, they often turn to the church to meet their needs; and (3) the lack of financial resources of Tinney and others often places them in low-income neighborhoods. Residents of these communities and surrounding areas tend to make up the congregation. Crawford and Hutt's church fits within this tradition in several ways. The South Side of Chicago is commonly associated with high crime and poverty levels among African Americans residents. There is some truth to these associations, but many whites who have this perception of the South Side have not actually experienced the area firsthand. Such attitudes contribute to Chicago's infamous record as one of the most segregated cities in the United States, and this segregation manifests itself within Chicago's lesbian and gay social and faith communities.

Crawford argues that she and Hutt chose the location for the Church of the Open Door for that very reason: to make sure those affluent whites could not ignore the economic straits of many blacks if they decided to fellowship with black lesbians and gays. The church is located in Marquette Park, a community that is now largely black and Latino as a result of white flight in the 1970s. Like Tinney, Crawford makes it clear that the Church of the Open Door is a black church in its makeup and worship style. Although the church has an impressive day care program, holds classes for its large Latino community, and recently held a conference for Latino, black, and Arab women, it does not appear to have any immediate plans for outreach to openly gay white Christians, most of whom live on Chicago's North Side.

Just as there are stereotypes held by whites about blacks living on Chicago's South Side, so also blacks hold stereotypes about the gay community centered in the Lakeview area on Chicago's North Side. For many black gays and lesbians, the Lakeview community (or "Boystown," as it is often called) consists primarily of wealthy white gay men whose racism will not allow them to venture further south than Chicago's downtown area. Once again, while there is some truth to this characterization, such a perspective fails to acknowledge the existence of white gays who do not hold such attitudes.

Yet while I was doing research on this project a few summers ago, it became quite clear that there were strong misgivings on the part of both white gays and black gays about one another. Karl, one of the members of the Church of the Open Door, expressed a strong discomfort with the gay community on Chicago's North Side, which, in his view, showed no interest either in him or the issues important to him. Such perspectives show that Tinney's observation about the alienation many black gays and lesbians feel from white gays is still largely accurate. By the same token, some white gays express a feeling of alienation as a result of comments or attitudes that they associated with the Church of the Open Door. In spite of the fact that there are white attendees at the Church of the Open Door, some white gays have raised questions about just how open the door really is for them at Crawford and Hutt's church. A white lesbian shared with me that she did not feel welcome when she visited the church. It appears, then, that both white lesbians and gay men who worship on the North Side and black lesbians and gay men who worship on the South Side have invested more energy in building up mistrust toward the other than in entering a constructive dialogue or working together in coalitions around common issues of concern.

Nevertheless, Crawford and Hutt exercise an enormous amount of courage in their repudiation of the common black Christian claim that homosexuality is immoral. Because they both come out of conservative black denominations, there is a keen understanding of this claim and the adverse consequences that such teaching has not only in the lives of lesbians and gays, but in the lives of their heterosexual family members and friends. Crawford, Hutt, and Bean face a comparable challenge in convincing African American gay Christians that black gay churches are real Christian churches, with church leaders who provide spiritual nurture and show an abiding concern for the parishioners' faith and the issues that affect them and their families.

Crawford points out that one of the major tasks is dealing with a common question from lesbian and gay parishioners, "Am I going to hell?" Crawford finds that most of her congregants, having come from fundamentalist black churches, still hold a church view supported by the use of the Bible that homosexuals will go to hell. Thus, Crawford sits with them and, using the story of Jacob in the book of Genesis as metaphor, invites the parishioners to wrestle with the text. Crawford makes use of the Bible in what she calls a "proactive way," focusing on texts like Genesis 1 in order to drive home the point that her congregants are made in the image of God. By focusing on texts that she can use to communicate life-giving and liberating messages, Crawford hopes to ensure that a text such as Leviticus 18:22 or 20:13 "does not form the parameters of the conversation." Her goal is to use the Bible in order to convince African American lesbians and gays of the possibility that God loves them.

Crawford and Hutt discover that gay members of mainline black churches feeling the need to remain in those churches often come to them for such specific purposes as wedding ceremonies. They point out that a somewhat gay-affirmative Chicago black church still refuses to perform weddings for lesbian and gay couples. Hutt raises critical questions about the tendency for lesbian and gay members of such churches to come to the Church of the Open Door in search of specific services like weddings while remaining in the churches that refuse to honor their relationships.

In her view, such requests are comparable to "a secret affair in a marriage." Black gays and lesbians from other congregations are, in Hutt's words, "using them," receiving benefits from the Church of the Open Door while maintaining the security and social sanction of a "legitimate relationship" at a predominantly heterosexual black church. She sees this as evidence that lesbians and gays still find it difficult to view predominantly lesbian/gay churches as "real churches." They continue to seek approval from a heterosexual Christian majority and fear the repercussions of leaving a church that continues to treat them as "second class." Many lesbians and gays tied to these churches continue to believe that heterosexuality, in its worst form, is still superior to homosexuality and the most loving, caring same-sex relationship. Although several reasons have been mentioned for their ties to heterosupremacist churches, a refusal to leave is often an attempt to find moral legitimacy in these quarters.

Despite these negative experiences, mainline black churches understandably still hold a place of significance. The institution offers community and often is one of few constants in the lesbian or gay person's life. Hence, the church is a place that brings together many important components of an individual's history, family, and community. It is also the place where most people assume that their wedding will be held. Unfortunately, black lesbians and gays do not have options. Since only the state of Massachusetts has legalized marriage for lesbians and gays, gays living outside of the New England states of Massachusetts, Vermont, and Connecticut (a civil union law in Vermont and Connecticut provides most benefits of a marriage) must remain unmarried. and with very few exceptions, black lesbians and gays cannot have their relationships honored in a church wedding ceremony. With the recent attacks on gay relationships and marriage by T. D. Jakes, Eddie Long, Joe Watkins, Bishop Gilbert Patterson, and countless other black heterosexual ministers and churchgoers, it is clear that the acceptance of lesbian and gay weddings in black churches will not happen without a long and caustic battle.

Given the history of African Americans and the value placed on the church for blessing relationships, the present position not to perform weddings in black churches of faithful and committed black gay Christians is a travesty. In his discussion of African American slave weddings, religious historian Albert Raboteau notes that William Wells Brown commented, "Blacks always preferred being married by a clergyman."[27] This sense of sanctity that is associated with marriage continues to function in the lives of many, perhaps most, black lesbians and gays. African American lesbians and gay men who join the Church of the Open Door affirm in interviews that the church is ministering to this need in spite of mainline black churches' failings. Laura, one of the church members, names the importance of having a wedding ceremony for her relationship as one of the main reasons that she is at the church. She asserts, "Receiving affirmation of my relationship in front of my clergy and Christian congregation is a value that I hold. It has made my relationship feel special."

Given the bleak state of affairs for many black lesbians and gays, the Church of the Open Door serves as a support system, a family, healing broken lives and helping estranged black people find meaning in their spiritual and professional lives. Karl is a member of this congregation and learning to live with an absent biological family.

---

27. Raboteau, *Slave Religion*, 229.

He acknowledges that he would not have anywhere to go for support if it were not for this church. He still feels the pain of ridicule, taunts, and denigrating comments from his former church because he is gay. A committed Christian and a person living with AIDS, Karl finds that having a faith community is important at this point in his life. Since Karl has also been estranged from his family, the Church of the Open Door has become a family for him. Living in Chicago, Karl is afforded one of the few gay-affirming church communities in the country. Since most gays do not have a church of this sort in their city or community, there is a present need for the transformation of homophobic black churches.

Elias Farajaje-Jones, an African American bisexual religion professor, highlights this problem in terms of the silence and denial in black churches:

> In this particular case, this silence is a particularly dangerous one because it is now taking people's lives. When the Black Church does speak out about those who are in the life [slang for black lesbian, gay, bisexual, and transgendered people], it is never in a positive way. As long as people keep quiet about what they are doing, then there is no issue as such. As long as people don't fight for their rights as lesbian/gay/bisexual/transgender people within the Church, then there is no struggle and the church is not obliged to confront its reality.[28]

The emergence of black gay congregations — while needed for the present — should not prevent lesbians, gays, and heterosexuals from confronting the ongoing black church homophobia and heterosupremacy. Black church congregations must become affirming communities for African American lesbians and gays, whether they are predominantly heterosexual or predominantly lesbian/gay, as I have outlined in this chapter.

From Tinney's tent revival for African American lesbians and gays over twenty years ago to the day care center at the Church of

---

28. Elias Farajaje-Jones, "Breaking Silence: Toward an In-the-Life Theology," in *Black Theology: A Documentary History*, vol. 2: *1980–1992*, ed. James Cone and Gayraud Wilmore (Maryknoll, NY: Orbis Books, 1993), 152.

the Open Door, African American lesbians and gay men are seeking ways to embrace their sexual gifts together with their religious faith. And considering that African American lesbians and gays are being ministered to and empowered in unprecedented ways, these lesbian and gay religious leaders are to be commended for their impressive and prophetic ministries. They, like Richard Allen, refuse to be denigrated in a church community due to their difference. They represent a message of hope that black church Christians can find redemption in this time of transition and transformation.

What does this new presence of openly gay African American lesbian and gay Christians offer the larger black Christian church? How can mainline black church leaders learn from the ministry of openly gay and lesbian black Christians? These are challenging questions for the black church. Without a doubt, black gay churches provide a wonderful ministry for many lesbian and gay Christians ostracized from their home churches. For most lesbians and gays remaining in mainline black churches, however, few things have changed. The recent religious and civil discussions on the merits of gay marriage have caused fury among black church leaders as most cry out in defense of an exclusive heterosexual marriage. What are the merits of the black church and black theology in black churches that advocate lesbian and gay discrimination and exclusion?

In the final chapter, I consider the pastoral theological issues that surround the present moral discussion on homosexuality and African American gays in black churches. While many grieving black families remain convinced that their gay male relatives contracted AIDS as God's punishment for their homosexuality, others pray that their gay family member will become heterosexual. Numerous gays remain silent in their black families, living in a silent agony about their life and relationships unknown to their heterosexual family members. In this landscape, some prophetic heterosexual black church leaders are beginning to lead their congregations in becoming open and affirming houses of worship for gay congregants. It is here that black churches have the greatest potential for being true to their claim as well as being faithful to the gospel message of love, liberation, and inclusion.

Chapter 8

Toward a True Liberation Theology
for Pastoral Caregivers

I was empowered to minister the sacrament of One in whom there is no north or south, no black or white, no male or female, only the spirit of love and reconciliation drawing us all toward the goal of human wholeness.

— The Reverend Dr. Pauli Murray

The Need for Black Pastoral Care

A MAJORITY OF BLACK CHURCH FAMILIES live in conflict about the homosexuality of their loved ones. African American gays and heterosexuals typically either disagree about the morality of homosexuality or agree that homosexuality is an illness, a sinful behavior that must be removed from the family member's life. Few African American families in the church accept their lesbian or gay family members in the same way as they receive their heterosexual family members. Unfortunately, Malik, the young openly gay Christian man in chapter 5, rejected by his family, is the rule and not the exception.

Lesbian and gay family members bear the brunt of homophobia in families. Even though many families can truthfully claim that they are not battling like Malik and his mother, the false sense of peace is largely the result of many lesbians and gays remaining closeted in their families in order to avoid ridicule, ostracism, and psychic pain and fights such as Malik experienced. In this climate, it is understandable, although regrettable, that so many black gays remain closeted in their families. Rather than making it known

207

that all loving relationships of their children, siblings, or parents are celebrated, heterosexual family members typically deny a homosexual reality and work tirelessly and foolishly to pair their family members with the opposite sex, even at the expense of their family member's emotional and physical health and that of the used mate.

As a pastoral counselor, I encounter many black gay men who marry heterosexual women as a result of coercion from family members or to avoid the condemnation they would experience as a gay person in black families, churches, communities, and the wider society. When gays in these marriages are discovered to be unfaithful by having extramarital affairs with the same sex, they often experience the harshest criticism for "living a lie" from their heterosexual family or church members who ironically coerced them to get married. Many black Christians are led to this behavior by black church teachings that homosexuality is wrong and must be corrected at all costs. Such behavior is often justified based on the view that homosexuality will fade in time through prayer and being in a relationship or marriage with the opposite sex. Often these situations are approached without considering the tremendous burdens placed on their parishioners and clergy, as in the following tragedy.

Fifteen years ago, "Kevin," a young pastor, shared with me his pain, shame, and guilt for marrying a woman simply because of family and church pressures. Much of this internal conflict revolved around the pressure to marry a woman for the sake of church and family rather than the man he loved. Kevin met this man in an African country almost ten years prior to our discussion. The African man, "Ajen," had much affection for Kevin and they shared a deep love. Their relationship evolved over time until they realized that they could not endure a separation by the Atlantic Ocean. Ajen decided to leave his country and move to the United States to be with Kevin.

Kevin told me that they shared a passion for each other, often spending hours together talking, laughing, holding each other, and giving thanks to God for blessing them with their relationship. At the same time, Kevin's family objected to him spending so much time with Ajen rather than with a woman. They began questioning why he did not have a girlfriend and telling him that people were talking about the absence of a woman in his life. Kevin reported that such harassment caused him a great deal of stress, leaving him depressed and confused. He admitted that he began to break under the pressure. At the end of what seemed like months of torture, Kevin concluded that if he were going to pastor a church in his Baptist denomination, he would have to get married. Reluctantly, Kevin began to put distance between Ajen and himself and began a relationship with a woman, "Sheila," whom he eventually married. Ajen told Kevin he was extremely hurt. Ajen said to Kevin that he loved him so much that he left his country for him and that it was hard to think about Kevin leaving him for Sheila because of others' intolerance. Kevin told me that he lived with great sadness and that if only the church and society were different, he would have shared the rest of his life with Ajen. He said due to this forced separation, there would always be a void in his life.

This poignant story reflects the story of so many gays who fear retaliation and rejection from an unaccepting heterosexual majority. For African Americans, the life of the black church and family are integral parts of our being, and so in order to remain in the church, black gay Christians often sacrifice their feelings, their health, and a great deal of happiness that can be found in relationships. They feel that the alternative — a rejection of their black church home, family ties, and the homophobia that comes with them — may be an even greater burden.

The life of Kevin is but one of many examples of how the black church is failing its lesbian and gay sisters and brothers. Black church attitudes about homosexuality also promote unhealthy mixed-sexual-orientation relationships and marriages that create low self-esteem, low self-worth, depression, and shame for gays. They also place a burden on heterosexuals, especially heterosexual women, who find themselves unfulfilled and longing for adequate sexual companionship after marrying gay men. This is also true for lesbians marrying heterosexual men. Ultimately, institutions that restrict gays' sexual fulfillment through encouraging celibacy or mixed-sexual-orientation marriage inflict harm on God's people.

Teachings against homosexuality are destructive to black families, leaving family members emotionally distraught and believing that their loved ones are sick and sinful individuals to be pitied. They often fear embarrassment should family members ever be exposed as lesbian or gay.[1]

Church Ostracism

It is rare to find a black church that affirms black gays and their love relationships. If black heterosexuals are "less homophobic than whites," as some suggest, it is indeed curious as to why a significantly lower percentage of black gays come out in black settings and churches than their white counterparts. Although only "29 percent of blacks surveyed said that homosexuals should remain in the closet, while 65 percent disagreed," many blacks continue to argue that they "do not object to homosexuality [but] object to *open* expressions of it [emphasis added]."[2] Such a position points to mere toleration of gays or may even appear contradictory, in contrast with full acceptance afforded to heterosexuals. This attitude is strikingly similar to that of white racists who feigned acceptance of blacks as long as blacks stayed in their place and exhibited behaviors that did not reflect black cultural expressions. The expectation that gays refrain from a visibility of their love relationships is a reflection of the shame, discomfort, and embarrassment that African Americans still harbor about same-sex affection. Given that no heterosexual is saying that heterosexuals should not be open about their heterosexuality, this reaction is more than cultural modesty about sexual relationships. Rather, this kind of silencing is a means of control over gays and, like all silencing, works toward the death of a people.

The reported tolerance that many black church Christians and even gays claim about black churches is perhaps self-serving. Since it is generally known and accepted that gay men typically provide music ministry for black churches, an argument could be made that

---

1. Karen McClintock, *Sexual Shame: An Urgent Call to Healing* (Minneapolis: Augsburg Fortress, 2001), 80.
2. Boykin, *One More River to Cross*, 188.

heterosexuals largely benefit from this gay-led ministry. Like other majority cultures reap benefits from a subordinate minority class, black heterosexuals perhaps realize that banishing gays from black churches would significantly diminish their church experience and the quality of black church worship.

One of my former students, Q, challenged the claim that gays experience oppression in black churches. Q felt that since gays do not experience "Jim Crow" discrimination, restricted to separate water fountains and segregated seating, they do not experience oppression or discrimination. But such a position ignores the ways in which gays do experience discrimination. Once again, Iris Marion Young's discussion on various discriminations helps us understand that African American lesbians and gays do experience unjust discrimination in their own churches. While it is generally true that presumed gays are not banned from black churches, lesbians and gays always have had to stay in their place. Q is right that heterosexuals allow stereotypical gays some levels of power in their liturgical leadership as musicians and even as clergy; heterosexuals in these same churches, however, make clear in their sermons or comments that they still find their sexual expression sinful or even evil.

The Reverend Joseph Walker, an African American pastor of Mt. Zion Baptist Church, the largest church in Nashville, said that very thing as he led his mid-week Bible study. In a deliberate diatribe depicting gays as akin to Satan, Walker identified gays as sinister agents in the church. Their very effeminate and dramatic mannerisms in choirs, he claims, stem from their brush with Lucifer (the angel turned devil doomed to hell) and serve as a distraction to heterosexuals.

This message keeps gays informed that they are not viewed equally with fellow heterosexuals, and if they are out will receive neither affirmation of their relationships nor support in their struggles as gay people. Essentially, black gay Christians seeking a home in most black churches deny their sexuality or acquiesce for survival. Those lesbians and gays confronting black church oppression pay a price. Irene Monroe, Tommie Watkins, James Tinney, and Leonard Patterson bear witness to this fact.

Shame

The denigrating and sometimes angry messages that black lesbians and gays consistently receive from their family members also contribute to low self-esteem, shame, and depression. As I talked with Kevin, he emphasized that his family's shame that he would be considered homosexual if he did not find a woman contributed greatly to his decision to date and eventually marry Sheila. This also happened in the case of my graduate student friend who would not live as a gay man because of the hostility and suffering he would endure. This friend also recognized that his Baptist family in the South would be embarrassed to be around him if he were with a man. He, like so many black gays and lesbians, struggles against racist odds in the climb as a professional and refuses to take on a life that would alienate him from his black family. As in the church, African American gays who study, work, and play by society's rules for success make their family members proud. In the minds of many, coming out is too risky and will bring shame on their families. In a context that provides few resources for overcoming the shame, the "shame eats away at the core sense of well-being."[3]

Black church pastors create this sense of shame for lesbians and gays and their heterosexual family members through sermons that depict homosexuality as perverse, sick, wicked, and vile. Rev. Edwin Saunders of Nashville's affirming black Metropolitan Interdenominational Church reports that he has found that "African Americans more often than white gay people emphasize the importance of religion in their family, community, and history and say that most of the pain and sadness in their lives center around the church."[4] African American parents, like Malik's and Kevin's, often hold extremely negative views of homosexuality and abhor the thought

---

3. Ibid., 22.

4. Gary David Comstock, *A Whosoever Church* (Louisville: Westminster John Knox Press, 2001), 149.

that a son or daughter may be gay or lesbian. Parents often attack their children with harsh words as a way of compelling them to deny their sexuality. This verbal and emotional abuse is especially damaging to an African American person already enduring racism and perhaps sexism and other struggles in her or his life. In their unwillingness to accept that a son or daughter could be other than heterosexual, these parents may coerce them to marry the opposite sex, hoping that homosexuality will go away or at least be concealed.

Black parents of gays desiring another way of looking at homosexuality in their children typically find no alternative perspective expressed by black pastoral persons. In this climate, many feel like there is no other way of understanding their homosexual daughter or son but as sinful, regardless of how morally upright she or he might be. Many parents struggle alone, asking themselves the perennial question, "Where did we go wrong?" Generally, our society agrees that heterosexuality becomes a fixed state after individuals are fully developed. Many African Americans still consider homosexuality to be arrested development, a sexual malady resulting from a certain trauma at a young age, or from sexual abuse or some other sin. This thinking is encouraged not only by black pastors, but some heterosexual supremacist scholars and social scientists.

The American Psychological Association no longer considers homosexuality an illness. The APA does not support so-called change therapies. It argues that gays must not view their sexual orientation as a problem and should respond to religious and social prejudice as other oppressed groups do. Black pastors who assist parishioners to accept traditional theories of homosexuality as the result of negative influences — for example, bad parenting or child abuse — have had their theories disproved. Despite the work and purported claims of "homosexual change," there is no evidence indicating that such treatments are effective.[5] Even if one could change their sexual orientation, there is no need for it.

---

5. David Myers, "Accepting What Cannot Be Changed," in *Homosexuality and the Christian Faith: Questions of Conscience for the Churches,* ed. Walter Wink (Minneapolis: Fortress Press, 1999), 69.

Homosexuality continues to be thought of as a phase, choice, or sexual state that can be changed. One of the problems with the term "lifestyle" — aside from its incorrect usage — is that it connotes that one can choose to be gay in much the same way that one chooses to become a motorcycle gang member, a vegetarian, or a drug user. And since homosexuality is commonly perceived as bad, it is more often associated with bad choices like drug abuse or crime, rather than the choice for healthy eating or a noble profession. For many African Americans, there is nothing worse than a homosexual, especially a homosexual man. Family members are hopeful that their loved one will go "straight," as they might through a drug treatment program or criminal rehabilitation.

Silence and Anger

Many black gays exist in their families with the dread or even fear that family members, at any time, may express offensive comments or fits of anger because of their homosexuality. Black pastoral persons are in a position to help heterosexual church members look at their behavior toward gays as unnecessary and inconsistent with the gospel message to treat others as they desire to be treated. Considering the problem of anger and violent emotion over homosexuality often expressed by black family members and congregants, Christian theologian and ethicist Lewis Smedes raises some questions that pastors may use in helping heterosexual Christians reform such behavior. He asserts that it remains a curious phenomenon as to why

> heterosexual people get as fevered as they do about homosexuality. . . . What danger to [heterosexuals] is posed by homosexuals? Some say that they are a threat to the [black] family, but none tell us how. Some fear that they might abuse our children, but no facts have ever been adduced to show that they are any more likely to do so than heterosexuals. Do homosexuals threaten to invade our homes, steal our property, rape our daughters? What we know is that homosexual men are

murdered by heterosexual people just for being gay; what we also know is that there is no record of a heterosexual being murdered for not being gay. Why, then, I wonder, in a world of violence, starving children, cruel tyrannies and natural disasters, are Christian people so steamed up about the harmless and often beneficent presence of gays and lesbians among us?[6]

Since a majority of African Americans cannot work through these problems or find sanction about their lives without their pastor's approval, developing healthy perspectives about homosexuality is difficult. Black families usually live in silence about their family member's homosexuality, accepting that there are family secrets that are not discussed. As in the cases of family sexual abuse and adultery, homosexuality becomes another shameful family secret. Black pastors must begin talking about homosexuality in different ways in order to shift the conversation from simple condemnation to a thoughtful dialogue about the complexities of human sexuality and expressing gay sexuality in faithful and responsible ways. This action is the first step in moving black families from rage and silence about homosexuality to a creative space for constructive dialogue.

Ed Wimberly, an African American pastoral theologian, defines this shame as "feeling unlovable, that one's life has a basic flaw in it."[7] Black churches and families constantly send messages through their speech and behavior that lesbians and gays are not as valued as heterosexuals. A number of lesbians and gays have abandoned the idea that they could have a relationship. As "Philip," a gay black Pentecostal, told me about the thought of having a romantic partner, "I would not want to put him through this." Having to repress or live in a way that is not true to one's identity takes a toll on lesbians and gays. After years of being alone and considering that his small town and black neighborhood would ridicule him terribly if he were honest about being gay, "Barry," a Baptist, decided to get

---

6. Lewis Smedes, "Exploring the Morality of Homosexuality," in *Homosexuality and the Christian Faith* (Minneapolis: Fortress Press, 1999), 77.

7. Wimberly, *Moving from Shame to Self-Worth*, 11.

married to a woman. Although many raised questions about the integrity of his wedding, Barry decided to go through with it because of his family's homophobia.

Pastoral theologian Archie Smith has identified the denigrating black pastoral attitude toward lesbian and gay people as false consciousness, the unwillingness to critique the oppressive treatment of lesbians and gays in the same way African Americans have critiqued racist oppression. Black liberation theology has the potential of assisting black pastoral caregivers in a way that helps gay and heterosexual family members.

Black Liberation Theology and Black Gay Christians

According to its progenitor, James Cone, black liberation theology "must take seriously the reality of black people — their life of suffering and humiliation. . . . When black people affirm their freedom in God, they know that they cannot obey laws of oppression. [And in light of] the biblical emphasis on the freedom of [humans], one cannot allow another to define his [or her] existence."[8] If liberation is at the heart of the historical black church as Cone and others claim and if it is to be consistent with Jesus' gospel mandate "to liberate the oppressed" (see Luke 4:18–19), then black heterosexual Christians must work to end legal discrimination against gays in marriage, employment, and the military; legal discrimination that permits the government to remove children against their will from the homes of their lesbian and gay parents and denies lesbians and gays the right to adopt regardless of the quality of their parenting; and church teachings and practices that are demeaning to black gays and which contribute to their suffering and death. The continued opposition by black clergy toward marriage of African American lesbians and gays is the latest of many actions that seriously challenge the validity of the claim that the black church is on the side of liberation of black people and others.

---

8. James Cone, *Black Theology and Black Power* (New York: Seabury Press, 1969), 117, 137–38.

African American heterosexuals, for the most part, remain unconvinced that their present resistance toward lesbian and gay equality in the church and society is at odds with the gospel and black liberationist thought. Unlike European American denominations that are engaged in major battles over lesbians and gays in the church, freeing gays from church oppression is hardly an issue in the historically black denominations. In the largest black denomination, the National Baptist Convention USA, Inc., the governing body did not even discuss lesbian and gay issues or develop a theological position on homosexuality at its September 2004 meeting in New Orleans, Louisiana.

Those unaware of black church responses on this issue would be tempted to find that the absence of battles over homosexuality is a sign that African American Christians are more compassionate and accepting of their lesbian and gay Christians. An honest report, however, would reveal that the lack of tension centers around a generally agreed-upon perspective that homosexuality is sin and that lesbians and gays are sinners insofar as they honor their sexual longings by having sexual relationships with the same sex.

Dwight Hopkins, an African American heterosexual theology professor specializing in black liberation theology at the University of Chicago, has argued that any teaching or practice that does not support the full equality of lesbians and gays is inconsistent with Christian black liberation theology. He suggests that "the Bible is brought into conversation as a justification to oppress lesbians and gays . . . as condemning homosexuals to hell without salvation unless they become heterosexuals."[9] He further asserts that these Christians call for this theological response to gays while at the same time stating that "the [biblical] stories are wrong when they call on slaves to obey your masters, and black heterosexual women argue that the passages proclaiming women should obey men are sinful."[10]

---

9. Dwight Hopkins, *Heart and Head: Black Theology Past, Present, and Future* (New York: Palgrave, 2002), 187.

10. Ibid.

Since the black church has been a place attentive to the spiritual, political, social, and emotional needs of black people, it should also be a space for black families in crisis over their lesbian or gay family member. As womanist scholars have already pointed out, just as black theology consistently identifies whites' oppressive actions against black people, it "must also unmask oppression or domination within its own tradition as well."[11] Church leaders should continue to embrace scriptures that offer life, love, and liberation.

Reconciling and Healing for Lesbians and Gays

There is no need to impose a theological view that unfairly and significantly harms gay Christians. African Americans eventually spoke out and resisted the injustice, pain, and suffering that racist whites in the church and society inflicted on them. Black gays and lesbians must also resist oppression directed toward them by coming out and telling their stories of pain that heterosexuals constantly inflict on gays through heterosexuals' "theological constructions of the imago Dei, that pervasively insist that lesbian and gay people are inferior and evil."[12] Gay Christians must do this for their own survival and health. I agree with gay therapist Richard Isay that "any gay man or lesbian who does not oppose the prejudice and discrimination of organizations to which he or she may belong, remains enslaved by the self-hatred such institutions engender."[13]

The coming out and sharing of black gay Christian narratives — stories that reflect a Christian witness comparable to that of God's people within scripture — will demonstrate that "all human beings are capable of reflecting the imago Dei when their concrete and everyday lives and relationships are truthful, loving, creative,

---

11. Dale Andrews, *Practical Theology for Black Churches* (Louisville: Westminster John Knox Press, 2002), 109.

12. Larry Kent Graham, *Discovering Images of God: Narratives of Care among Lesbians and Gays* (Louisville: Westminster John Knox Press, 1997), 169.

13. Isay, *Becoming Gay*, 159.

just, and diverse," and consequently will transform others to recognize that black gays and their loving sexual relationships are also
moral.[14]

Black Liberation Theology and Pastoral Care and Counseling for Lesbian and Gay Christians

In light of black Christian liberation and black Christian resistance
to oppressive scripture, there is no reason that black heterosexual
church leaders cannot move toward a true black liberation theology that affirms all loving sexual relationships and commitments
as reflecting God's purpose in creation. In his book *Using Scripture in Pastoral Counseling*, Wimberly points out that he has found
scripture "a particularly helpful resource."[15] I would be interested in
knowing how many gay clients he has had. Black lesbians and gays
have an ambivalent relationship with the Bible because so many
black pastors have used the Bible against them. Still, their black
inculturation perhaps gives them an appreciation of the Bible that
is not as easily dismissed by them as it is by members of other cultures. They may find their response to the Bible similar to Nancy
Ambrose's response to the slavery passages, rejecting antihomosexual activity passages and appreciating others. Their response is
similar to Fred's ignoring of the pastor who castigates gays with
the Bible.

Wimberly finds that scripture can draw "readers and hearers into
the story based on the story's own narrative power. Biblical stories
often contain an invitation to the reader to adopt the perspective,
feelings and attitudes of the character."[16] I agree that such a use of
scripture can inspire a person to take control of life and find God
present in the midst of daily struggles. In addition to the powerful
example that Jesus provides as an estranged member of his commu-

---

14. Graham, *Discovering Images of God*, 172.
15. Edward P. Wimberly, *Using Scripture in Pastoral Counseling* (Nashville:
Abingdon Press, 1994), 12.
16. Ibid., 75.

nity overcoming suffering, the need to be as one as expressed by the
prophet Jeremiah or the bold witness of Esther may resonate with
black gay Christians as they find voice in an intimidating black
community. It is important that such passages are raised for gays
while others need to be avoided.

The way black pastors have often used the Bible regarding
homosexuality is problematic for gays in black churches. In his
helpful book *Pastoral Care of Gays, Lesbians, and Their Families*, pastoral theologian David Switzer notes that when counseling
gays, pastors often provide an authentic and perhaps well-meaning
response about homosexuality without recognizing its harmful effects. Having been indoctrinated in a homophobic church culture,
many pastors generally believe that all homosexual expression is
forbidden by God and that anything short of condemning such
expressions will lead the parishioners deeper into a sinful spi-
ral. Thus, it is the pastor's job to straighten this homosexual's
life out. In this respect, black pastoral homophobia can be understood. What might occur if the pastor allows himself or herself
to think that homosexual relations are another loving expression
but, like heterosexual practice, can be sinful acts if expressed in
uncaring and hostile ways? This perspective could allow for the
pastor to discuss the homosexual parishioner coming out and living within a committed sexual relationship of nurture, care, and
devotion that can be celebrated by the black Christian church.
Switzer recognizes that while such an awareness and approval may
take time, "if a pastor can be a trusted friend...relate to [gays]
in such a way that [will] facilitate their exploration and talking
about the advantages and disadvantages of coming out and assessing possible values to be gained over the risks of loss, then
[such a pastor has] performed an act of mercy in the name of
Christ."[17]

In the pastoral relationship, black pastoral persons can offer healing to lives that are broken by homophobia and can help reconcile

---

17. David Switzer, *Pastoral Care of Gays, Lesbians, and Their Families* (Minneapolis: Fortress Press, 1999), 77, 106.

those lives with family members, gay and heterosexual alike. The visibility of gays and their relationships in black church settings expands our capacity to see God's love and presence in community in a variety of ways. In the pastoral ministry of saving black families, black pastoral caregivers and leaders must move toward celebrating all loving sexual relationships in church communities. This bold act of leadership assists black people and all people in finding intimacy, health, and wholeness. This embrace allows us not only to appreciate our sexuality, whether with persons of the same or the opposite sex, but also to experience God's goodness within that sexual expression. This connection makes us whole beings so that we can become better stewards, providing care in our communities and opposing the violence and injustice that seek to abuse and destroy us.

Some African American pastors are reassessing their stance against lesbian and gay Christians. They are beginning to see that homophobia and heterosexual supremacy are oppressive and violate black liberation theology and the Christian gospel. At the heart of this transformation is learning a different response to passages that have been used for the condemnation of homosexuality. In his book *A Whosoever Church*, Gary David Comstock shares a glimpse of what the black church can be for gays and their families. Numerous accounts show the prophetic Christian witness of black heterosexuals in particular as they take on the sinful homophobic tradition of black churches. This is an important resource for black church leaders as they begin the important work of dismantling homophobic and heterosexual supremacy in black faith communities.

The title, *A Whosoever Church*, comes out of the cultural vernacular, and while this phrase and the congregational song at the beginning of this book are often expressed by those in black churches, full participation of gays has yet to be realized. Rev. Edwin Sanders is one black pastor living the prophetic Christian witness of inclusion for his parishioners. Referring to his church as a "whosoever church," Sanders asserts that his church tries "to be inclusive of all and alienating to none."[18] Sanders and other pastors offer hope for those committed to black church reform for liberation. As black pastoral persons engage family members and parishioners in other ways of understanding homosexuality, they also recognize the importance of responding to biblical passages used in the continuation of homophobia.

Rev. Dr. Arnold Thomas, an African American heterosexual conference UCC minister, states, "We read what we have been directed to read in scripture, and we don't look at the complicated nature of scripture." He believes that "all you have to do is direct [congregants] to those passages and to the context in which they were given. And when that happens ... another important journey in their faith journey has been accomplished."[19] As scriptures perpetuating slavery were eventually replaced with liberationist passages emphasizing freedom and oneness in Christ (see Luke 4:18–19; Gal. 3), pastors can respond with scriptures reflecting loving neighbor as self, treating all people in the same way as we desire to be treated and loving one another (Matt. 7:12; 1 John 4:7, 16)."

In a prophetic voice within the second-oldest black denomination, the African Methodist Episcopal Zion Church, Dr. Mozella Mitchell "speaks against those in the black community and black church who try to deny gay rights or discriminate against gay people."[20] Reflecting the animus that black pastors have toward treating gays as equal members of the community, her bishop tried to subpoena her, but did not have the authority to do so. The gospel calls us to a response like Mitchell's, an action celebrating all people in loving and nurturing relationships.

As we begin the twenty-first century, I suggest we are called to bring the spirit and flesh together in healthy ways rather than seeing them in dualistic ways and in a never-ending tension. History allows us to learn better ways of being and relating in the world. Kelly Brown Douglas argues that, for black people, many of our

---

18. Ibid., 120.
19. Comstock
20. Ibid., 51.

present negative attitudes toward our bodies and sex stem from this country's Puritan and Victorian past and "the way black sexuality has been impugned by white culture."[21] However, I hasten to add Douglas's view that

> there is an individual and communal responsibility for violating the humanity of another and precluding her or him from fully experiencing what it means to be created in the image of God. . . . A black sexual discourse of resistance is also constrained to make clear that homophobia and concomitant heterosexist structures and systems (those structures and systems that privilege heterosexuals while discriminating against non-heterosexuals) are sin . . . [Black and womanist theologies] should reveal the basic contradiction between homophobia and the church's belief in a God of justice.[22]

My challenge to African Americans is to critically engage the relationship between Christianity and homosexuality in the same faithful way that a critical engagement of Christianity and race is offered. In the inheritance of the black church as the center of black people's lives, black pastors as heirs and keepers of this sacred canopy can lead others in dismantling its sin of homophobia and heterosexual supremacy.

African American Christians now have an opportunity to reject the sex-negative messages and instead love our bodies and sexuality as God's gift to us. These gifts of sexuality must be appreciated and honored within mutual spiritual relationships for the community. Like heterosexuals, lesbians and gays do not need to deny their God-given capacity for sexual sharing and wholeness, but rather should embrace this gift as life-giving.

The black pastoral response recognizes the struggle of those with a traditional use of scripture and invites them to look at the historical context of the writings. This response considers a variety of

---

21. Douglas, *Sexuality and the Black Church*, 7.
22. Ibid., 126–27.

ways to educate and engage lesbians and gays and their heterosexual family members, fellow congregants, and leaders and members of communities. This movement that is occurring in black churches and communities is consistent with other Christian movements of change, including change that occurred after the 1950s in white churches regarding traditional racist attitudes and practices toward black people. A significant part of that change happened when whites observed other whites speaking out against racial injustice and dying for the cause of justice.

Many black heterosexuals have not heard the stories of the pain and discrimination that their own fellow black lesbians and gays experience because of black homophobia in churches and families. If there is any possibility for change to occur, that change must begin with the voices of black gays and their heterosexual allies. When this is realized in black houses of worship — whether in the urban sanctuaries or storefronts of the North, the suburban megachurches or rural one-room churches of the South — perhaps black heterosexual Christians will also hear the pain of gays and begin to claim the gospel in new and profound ways. In such a movement, black Christians will recognize that the mire of homosexuality debates threaten our measure to be faithful Christians for the poor, the infirm, the imprisoned, and those suffering from violence.

The black church has stood as a model of the gospel, opposing slavery and emphasizing black liberation. If Christians today in the black church ever plan to live into this historical witness as a Christian body committed to black people's liberation and the liberation of all oppressed people, they must ultimately stand with lesbians and gays as equal members in God's church and world. Homosexuality is part of human sexuality, just as African Americans are part of the human race. Thus, there will always be African American lesbians, gays, bisexuals, and transgendered persons within and outside of our faith communities. The question then becomes whether African American heterosexuals are going to do justice toward their sons and daughters, sisters and brothers, mothers and fathers, and other relatives, friends, colleagues, and fellow Christians who are lesbian and gay.

Our acceptance and celebration of lesbians and gays and their relationships with those of heterosexuals will allow us to appreciate the beauty of God's diverse creation. In doing this, in affirming the erotic in all of us, we will proclaim a true black liberation theology, and in so doing, we will honor God.

Bibliography

Andrews, William L., ed. *Sisters of the Spirit: Three Black Women's Autobiographies of the Nineteenth Century*. Bloomington: Indiana University Press, 1986.

Bailey, Derrick. *Homosexuality and the Western Christian Tradition*. New York: Longmans Green, 1986.

Baum, Robert. "The Traditional Religions of the Americas and Africa." In *Homosexuality and World Religions*, ed. Arlene Swidler. Valley Forge, PA: Trinity Press International, 1993.

Beam, Joseph, ed. *In the Life*. Boston: Alyson Publications, 1986.

Bennett, Lerone. *Before the Mayflower: A History of Black America*. 6th ed. New York: Penguin Books, 1993.

Boswell, John. *Christianity, Social Tolerance, and Homosexuality: Gay People in Western Europe from the Beginning of the Christian Era to the Fourteenth Century*. Chicago: University of Chicago Press, 1980.

Boyd-Franklin, Nancy. *Black Families in Therapy: A Multisystems Approach*. New York: Guilford Press, 1989.

Boykin, Keith. *Beyond the Down Low: Sex, Lies, and Denial in Black America*. New York: Carroll & Graf Publishing, 2005.

———. *One More River to Cross: Black and Gay in America*. New York: Anchor Books/Doubleday, 1996.

Browning, Don S. *Religious Ethics and Pastoral Care*. Philadelphia: Fortress Press, 1983.

Buckmaster, Henrietta. *Let My People Go: The Story of the Underground Railroad and the Growth of the Abolition Movement*. Columbia: University of South Carolina Press, 1993.

Cohen, Cathy. *The Boundaries of Blackness: AIDS and the Breakdown of Black Politics*. Chicago: University of Chicago Press, 1999.

Comstock, Gary David. *Violence against Lesbians and Gay Men*. New York: Columbia University Press, 1991.

———. *A Whosoever Church: Welcoming Lesbians and Gay Men into African American Congregations*. Louisville: Westminster John Knox Press, 2001.

Cone, James H. *God of the Oppressed*. New York: Seabury Press, 1975.

Corbett, Julia Mitchell. *Religion in America*. 4th ed. Upper Saddle, NJ: Prentice Hall, 2000.

Cornelius, Janet Duitsman. *"I Can Read My Title Clear": Literacy, Slavery, and Religion in the Antebellum South*. Columbia: University of South Carolina Press, 1991.

Davis, F. James. *Who Is Black? One Nation's Definition*. University Park: Pennsylvania State University Press, 1991.

D'Emilio, John. *Lost Prophet: The Life and Times of Bayard Rustin*. Chicago: University of Chicago Press, 2003.

Donskis, Leonidas. *Forms of Hatred: The Troubled Imagination in Modern Philosophy and Literature*. New York: Rodopi, 2003.

Douglas, Kelly Brown. *Sexuality and the Black Church: A Womanist Perspective*. Maryknoll, NY: Orbis Books, 1999.

DuBois, W. E. B. *The Souls of Black Folk*. New York: Signet Classics, 1969.

Elliott, E. N. *Cotton Is King, and Pro-Slavery Arguments*. Augusta, GA: Abbott & Loomis, 1860.

Elliott, Neil. *Liberating Paul: The Justice of God and the Politics of the Apostle*. Maryknoll, NY: Orbis Books, 1994.

Ellison, Marvin M. *Same-Sex Marriage: A Christian Ethical Analysis*. Cleveland: Pilgrim Press, 2004.

Enroth, Ronald, and Gerald Jamison. *The Gay Church*. Grand Rapids: Eerdmans, 1974.

Eprecht, Mark. " 'Good God Almighty, What's This!': Homosexual 'Crime' in Early Colonial Zimbabwe" In *Boy Wives and Female Husbands: Studies of African Homosexualities*, ed. Stephen O. Murray and Will Roscoe. New York: St. Martin's Press, 1998.

Eugene, Toinette M., and James N. Poling. *Balm for Gilead: Pastoral Care for African American Families Experiencing Abuse*. Nashville: Abingdon Press, 1998.

Falk, Kurt. "Homosexuality among the Natives of Southwest Africa (1925–26)." In *Boy Wives and Female Husbands: Studies of African Homosexualities*, ed. Stephen O. Murray and Will Roscoe. New York: St. Martin's Press, 1998.

Farajaje-Jones, Elias. "Breaking Silence: Toward an In-the-Life Theology." In *Black Theology: A Documentary History, Vol. 2: 1980–1992*, ed. James Cone and Gayraud Wilmore. Maryknoll, NY: Orbis Books, 1993.

Felder, Cain Hope. *Troubling Biblical Waters: Race, Class, and Family*. Maryknoll, NY: Orbis Books, 1989.

Franklin, Robert M. *Another Day's Journey: Black Churches Confronting the American Crisis*. Minneapolis: Fortress Press, 1997.

Frazier, E. Franklin. *Black Bourgeoisie: The Rise of a New Middle Class in the United States.* New York: Collier Books, 1957.

Garber, Eric. "Spectacle of Color: African Americans in the Harlem Renaissance." In *Hidden from History: Reclaiming the Gay and Lesbian Past*, ed. Martin Bauml Duberman et al. New York: Meridian, 1989.

Genovese, Eugene D. *Roll, Jordan, Roll: The World the Slaves Made.* New York: Pantheon Books, 1974.

Giddings, Paula. Interview on Frontline documentary "Clarence Thomas and Anita Hill: Public Hearing Private Pain," narrated by Ofra Bikel, 1992.

Gilman, Sander L. *Difference and Pathology: Stereotypes of Sexuality, Race, and Madness.* Ithaca, NY: Cornell University Press, 1985.

Graham, Larry Kent. *Discovering Images of God: Narratives of Care among Lesbians and Gays.* Louisville: Westminster John Knox Press, 1997.

Graham, Lawrence. *Our Kind of People: Inside America's Black Upper Class.* New York: HarperCollins, 1999.

Greenburg, David F. *The Construction of Homosexuality.* Chicago: University of Chicago Press, 1988.

Gudorf, Christine E. *Body, Sex, and Pleasure: Reconstructing Christian Sexual Ethics.* Cleveland: Pilgrim Press, 1994.

Hale, Grace Elizabeth. *Making Whiteness: The Culture of Segregation in the South, 1890–1940.* New York: Pantheon Books, 1998.

Harper, Phillip Brian. *Are We Not Men?* New York: Oxford University Press, 1996.

Hawkeswood, William G. *One of the Children: Gay Black Men in Harlem.* Berkeley: University of California Press, 1996.

Hill, Renee. "Who Are We for Each Other? Sexism, Sexuality, and Womanist Theology." In *Black Theology: A Documentary History, Vol. 2: 1980–1992*, ed. James Cone and Gayraud Wilmore. Maryknoll, NY: Orbis Books, 1993.

Hodes, Martha. *White Women, Black Men: Illicit Sex in the Nineteenth-Century South.* New Haven, CT: Yale University Press, 1997.

Isay, Richard A. *Becoming Gay: The Journey of Self-Acceptance.* New York: Pantheon Books, 1996.

———. *Being Homosexual: Gay Men and Their Development.* New York: Farrar, Straus, Giroux, 1989.

Jakobsen, Janet R., and Ann Pellegrini. *Love the Sin: Sexual Regulation and the Limits of Religious Tolerance.* New York: New York University Press, 2003.

Jung, Patricia Beattie, and Ralph F. Smith. *Heterosexism: An Ethical Challenge.* Albany: State University of New York Press, 1993.

Katchadourian, Helmet. *Fundamentals of Human Sexuality.* Orlando: Holt, Rinehart and Winston, 1989.

Katz, Jonathan. *Gay American History: Lesbians and Gay Men in the U.S.A.: A Documentary History.* Rev. ed. New York: Meridian, 1992.

Kendall. "When a Woman Loves a Woman in Lesothu: Love, Sex and the (Western) Construction of Homophobia." In *Boy Wives and Female Husbands: Studies of African Homosexualities,* ed. Stephen O. Murray and Will Roscoe. New York: St. Martin's Press, 1998.

King, J. L. *On the Down Low: A Journey into the Lives of "Straight" Black Men Who Sleep with Men.* New York: Broadway Books, 2004.

Kinsey, Alfred, et al. *Sexual Behavior in the Human Male.* Philadelphia: W. B. Saunders, 1948.

Kübler-Ross, Elisabeth. *On Death and Dying.* London: Macmillan, 1969.

Lewis, David Levering. *W. E. B. DuBois: The Fight for Equality and the American Century, 1919–1963.* New York: Henry Holt, 2000.

Lincoln, C. Eric, and Lawrence Mamiya. *The Black Church in the African-American Experience.* Durham, NC: Duke University Press, 1990.

Martin, Dale B. *Slavery as Salvation: The Metaphor of Slavery in Pauline Christianity.* New Haven, CT: Yale University Press, 1990.

McMurry, Linda O. *George Washington Carver, Scientist and Symbol.* New York: Oxford University Press, 1981.

Miller, Neil. *In Search of Gay America: Women and Men in a Time of Change.* New York: Harper and Row Publishers, 1989.

Mohr, Richard. *Gays/Justice: A Study of Ethics, Society, and Law.* New York: Columbia University Press, 1988.

Moss, J. Jennings. "Barbara Jordan: The Other Life." *The Advocate* (March 5, 1996), 38–45.

Murray, Stephen O., and Will Roscoe, eds. *Boy Wives and Female Husbands: Studies of African Homosexualities.* New York: St. Martin's Press, 1998.

Myers, David. "Accepting What Cannot Be Changed." In *Homosexuality and Christian Faith: Questions of Conscience for the Churches,* ed. Walter Wink. Minneapolis: Fortress Press, 1999.

Nelson, James B. *Body Theology.* Louisville: Westminster/John Knox Press, 1992.

———. *Embodiment: An Approach to Sexuality and Christian Theology.* Minneapolis: Augsburg Publishing, 1978.

Paris, Peter J. *The Spirituality of African Peoples: The Search for a Common Moral Discourse.* Minneapolis: Fortress Press, 1995.

Patterson, Gilbert E. *Marriage: A Proclamation to the Church of God in Christ Worldwide. www.cogic.org/marriageproclamation.htm* (October 12, 2004).

Patterson, Leonard. "At Ebenezer Baptist Church." In *Black Men/White Men,* ed. Michael J. Smith. San Francisco: Gay Sunshine Press, 1983.

Perry, Troy D. *The Lord Is My Shepherd and He Knows I'm Gay.* Los Angeles: Nash Publications, 1972.

Pinn, Anne H., and Anthony B. Pinn. *Fortress Introduction to Black Church History.* Minneapolis: Fortress Press, 2002.

Public Hearing, Private Pain: The Anita Hill–Clarence Thomas Hearings. Produced and directed by *Frontline.* Narrated by Ofra Bikel, 1992. Videocassette.

Quarles, Benjamin. *The Negro in the Making of America.* New York: Collier Macmillan, 1987.

Raboteau, Albert J. *A Fire in the Bones: Reflections on African-American Religious History.* Boston: Beacon Press, 1995.

———. *Slave Religion: The Invisible Institution in the Antebellum South.* New York: Oxford University Press, 1978.

Roberts, Samuel K. *African American Church Ethics.* Cleveland: Pilgrim Press, 2001.

Rogers, Mary Beth. *Barbara Jordan: American Hero.* New York: Bantam Books, 1998.

Scroggs, Robin. *The New Testament and Homosexuality: Contextual Background for Contemporary Debate.* Philadelphia: Fortress Press, 1983.

Sears, James. *Growing Up Black in the South: Race, Gender, and Journeys of the Spirit.* New York: Harrington Park Press, 1991.

Sernett, Milton C., ed. *Afro-American Religious History: A Documentary Witness.* Durham, NC: Duke University Press, 1985.

Shattuck, Gardiner H. *Episcopalians and Race: Civil War to Civil Rights.* Lexington: University Press of Kentucky, 2000.

Shelp, Earl, and Ronald Sunderland. *AIDS and the Church.* Louisville: Westminster/John Knox Press, 1992.

Simmons, Ron. "Some Thoughts on the Challenges Facing Black Gay Intellectuals." In *Brother to Brother: New Writings by Black Gay Men.* Boston: Alyson Publications, 1991.

Smith, Jessie Carney, ed. *Notable Black American Men.* Detroit: Gale Publications, 1999.

Smith, Michael J., ed. *Black Men/White Men: A Gay Anthology.* San Francisco: Gay Sunshine Press, 1983.

Sontag, Susan. *AIDS and Its Metaphors.* New York: Farrar, Straus and Giroux, 1989.

Staples, Robert. *Black Masculinity: The Black Male's Role in American Society.* San Francisco: Black Scholar Press, 1982.

Styron, William. *The Confessions of Nat Turner.* New York: Random House, 1967.

Swidler, Arlene. *Homosexuality and World Religions.* Valley Forge, PA: Trinity Press International, 1993.

Switzer, David. *Pastoral Care of Gays, Lesbians, and Their Families.* Minneapolis: Fortress Press, 1999.

Thomas, Hugh. *The Slave Trade.* New York: Simon and Schuster, 1997.

Thurman, Howard. *Jesus and the Disinherited.* New York: Abingdon-Cokesbury Press, 1949.

Tinney, James. "Why a Gay Black Church?" In *In the Life*, ed. Joseph Beam. Boston: Alyson Publications, 1986.

Vaughan, Megan. *Curing Their Ills: Colonial Power and African Illness.* Stanford, CA: Stanford University Press, 1991.

Walker, Alice. *Warrior Marks: Female Genital Mutilation and the Sexual Blinding of Women.* New York: Harcourt Brace, 1993.

Weeks, Jeffrey. *Sexuality and Its Discontents.* New York: Routledge Kegan Paul, 1985.

Weems, Renita J. *Just a Sister Away: A Womanist Vision of Women's Relationships in the Bible.* San Diego: LuraMedia, 1988.

Williams, Walter. *The Spirit and the Flesh: Sexual Diversity in American Indian Culture.* Boston: Beacon Press, 1986.

Wimberly, Edward P. *Moving from Shame to Self-Worth: Preaching and Pastoral Care.* Nashville: Abingdon Press, 1999.

———. *Using Scripture in Pastoral Counseling.* Nashville: Abingdon Press, 1994.

Wimbush, Vincent L., ed. *African Americans and the Bible: Sacred Texts and Social Textures.* New York: Continuum, 2000.

Wirth, Thomas, ed. *Gay Rebel of the Harlem Renaissance: Selections from the Work of Richard Bruce Nugent.* Durham, NC: Duke University Press, 2002.

Young, Iris Marion. *Justice and the Politics of Difference.* Princeton, NJ: Princeton University Press, 1990.

Index